A Philosophical Dictionary

by Voltaire

NATAL PUBLISHING LLC
ARS LONGA, VITA BREVIS

COUNTRY.

SECTION I.

According to our custom, we confine ourselves on this subject to the statement of a few queries which we cannot resolve. Has a Jew a country? If he is born at Coimbra, it is in the midst of a crowd of ignorant and absurd persons, who will dispute with him, and to whom he makes foolish answers, if he dare reply at all. He is surrounded by inquisitors, who would burn him if they knew that he declined to eat bacon, and all his wealth would belong to them. Is Coimbra *his* country? Can he exclaim, like the Horatii in Corneille:

Mourir pour la patrie est un si digne sort
Qu'on briguerait en foule, une si belle mort.

So high his meed who for his country dies,
Men should contend to gain the glorious prize.

He might as well exclaim, "fiddlestick!" Again! is Jerusalem his country? He has probably heard of his ancestors of old; that they had formerly inhabited a sterile and stony country, which is bordered by a horrible desert, of which little country the Turks are at present masters, but derive little or nothing from it. Jerusalem is, therefore, not his country. In short, he has no country: there is not a square foot of land on the globe which belongs to him.

The Gueber, more ancient, and a hundred times more respectable than the Jew, a slave of the Turks, the Persians, or the Great Mogul, can he regard as his country the fire-altars which he raises in secret among the mountains? The Banian, the Armenian, who pass their lives in wandering through all the east, in the capacity of money-brokers, can they exclaim, "My dear country, my dear country"—who have no other country than their purses and their account-books?

Among the nations of Europe, all those cut-throats who let out their services to hire, and sell their blood to the first king who will purchase it—have they a country? Not so much so as a bird of prey, who returns every evening to the hollow of the rock where its mother built its nest! The monks—will they venture to say that they have a country? It is in heaven, they say. All in good time; but in this world I know nothing about one.

This expression, "my country," how sounds it from the mouth of a Greek, who, altogether ignorant of the previous existence of a Miltiades, an Agesilaus, only knows that he is the slave of a janissary, who is the slave of an aga, who is the slave of a pasha, who is the slave of a vizier, who is the slave of an individual whom we call, in Paris, the Grand Turk?

What, then, is country?—Is it not, probably, a good piece of ground, in the midst of which the owner, residing in a well-built and commodious house, may say: "This field which I cultivate, this house which I have built, is my own; I live under the protection of laws which no tyrant can infringe.

When those who, like me, possess fields and houses assemble for their common interests, I have a voice in such assembly. I am a part of the whole, one of the community, a portion of the sovereignty: behold my country!" What cannot be included in this description too often amounts to little beyond studs of horses under the command of a groom, who employs the whip at his pleasure. People may have a country under a good king, but never under a bad one.

SECTION II.

A young pastry-cook who had been to college, and who had mustered some phrases from Cicero, gave himself airs one day about loving his country. "What dost thou mean by country?" said a neighbor to him. "Is it thy oven? Is it the village where thou wast born, which thou hast never seen, and to which thou wilt never return? Is it the street in which thy father and mother reside? Is it the town hall, where thou wilt never become so much as a clerk or an alderman? Is it the church of Notre Dame, in which thou hast not been able to obtain a place among the boys of the choir, although a very silly person, who is archbishop and duke, obtains from it an annual income of twenty-four thousand louis d'or?"

The young pastry-cook knew not how to reply; and a person of reflection, who overheard the conversation, was led to infer that a country of moderate extent may contain many millions of men who have no country at all. And thou, voluptuous Parisian, who hast never made a longer voyage than to Dieppe, to feed upon fresh sea-fish—who art acquainted only with thy splendid town-house, thy pretty villa in the country, thy box at that opera which all the world makes it a point to feel tiresome but thyself—who speakest thy own language agreeably enough, because thou art ignorant of every other; thou lovest all this, no doubt, as well as thy brilliant champagne from Rheims, and thy rents, payable every six months; and loving these, thou dwellest upon thy love for thy country.

Speaking conscientiously, can a financier cordially love his country? Where was the country of the duke of Guise, surnamed Balafré—at Nancy, at Paris, at Madrid, or at Rome? What country had your cardinals Balue, Duprat, Lorraine, and Mazarin? Where was the country of Attila situated, or that of a hundred other heroes of the same kind, who, although eternally travelling, make themselves always at home? I should be much obliged to any one who would acquaint me with the country of Abraham.

The first who observed that every land is our country in which we "do well," was, I believe, Euripides, in his "*Phœdo*":

"Ὡς παντακῶς γε πατρὶς βοσκοῦσα γῆ."

The first man, however, who left the place of his birth to seek a greater share of welfare in another, said it before him.

SECTION III.

A country is a composition of many families; and as a family is commonly supported on the principle of self-love, when, by an opposing interest, the same self-love extends to our town, our province, or our nation, it is called love of country. The greater a country becomes, the less we love it; for love is weakened by diffusion. It is impossible to love a family so numerous that all the members can scarcely be known.

He who is burning with ambition to be edile, tribune, prætor, consul, or dictator, exclaims that he loves his country, while he loves only himself. Every man wishes to possess the power of sleeping quietly at home, and of preventing any other man from possessing the power of sending him to sleep elsewhere. Every one would be certain of his property and his life. Thus, all forming the same wishes, the particular becomes the general interest. The welfare of the republic is spoken of, while all that is signified is love of self.

It is impossible that a state was ever formed on earth, which was not governed in the first instance as a republic: it is the natural march of human nature. On the discovery of America, all the people were found divided into republics; there were but two kingdoms in all that part of the world. Of a thousand nations, but two were found subjugated.

It was the same in the ancient world; all was republican in Europe before the little kinglings of Etruria and of Rome. There are yet republics in Africa: the Hottentots, towards the south, still live as people are said to have lived in the first ages of the world—free, equal, without masters, without subjects, without money, and almost without wants.

The flesh of their sheep feeds them; they are clothed with their skins; huts of wood and clay form their habitations. They are the most dirty of all men, but they feel it not, but live and die more easily than we do. There remain eight republics in Europe without monarchs—Venice, Holland, Switzerland, Genoa, Lucca, Ragusa, Geneva, and San Marino. Poland, Sweden, and England may be regarded as republics under a king, but Poland is the only one of them which takes the name.

But which of the two is to be preferred for a country—a monarchy or a republic? The question has been agitated for four thousand years. Ask the rich, and they will tell you an aristocracy; ask the people, and they will reply a democracy; kings alone prefer royalty. Why, then, is almost all the earth governed by monarchs? Put that question to the rats who proposed to hang a bell around the cat's neck. In truth, the genuine reason is, because men are rarely worthy of governing themselves.

It is lamentable, that to be a good patriot we must become the enemy of the rest of mankind. That good citizen, the ancient Cato, always gave it as his opinion, that Carthage must be destroyed: "*Delenda est Carthago.*" To be a good patriot is to wish our own country enriched by commerce, and powerful by arms; but such is the condition of mankind, that to wish the greatness of our own country is often to wish evil to our neighbors. He who could bring himself to wish that his country should always remain as it is, would be a citizen of the universe.

CRIMES OR OFFENCES.

Of Time and Place.

A Roman in Egypt very unfortunately killed a consecrated cat, and the infuriated people punished this sacrilege by tearing him to pieces. If this Roman had been carried before the tribunal, and the judges had possessed common sense, he would have been condemned to ask pardon of the Egyptians and the cats, and to pay a heavy fine, either in money or mice. They would have told him that he ought to respect the follies of the people, since he was not strong enough to correct them.

The venerable chief justice should have spoken to him in this manner: "Every country has its legal impertinences, and its offences of time and place. If in your Rome, which has become the sovereign of Europe, Africa, and Asia Minor, you were to kill a sacred fowl, at the precise time that you give it grain in order to ascertain the just will of the gods, you would be severely punished. We believe that you have only killed our cat accidentally. The court admonishes you. Go in peace, and be more circumspect in future."

It seems a very indifferent thing to have a statue in our hall; but if, when Octavius, surnamed Augustus, was absolute master, a Roman had placed in his house the statue of Brutus, he would have been punished as seditious. If a citizen, under a reigning emperor, had the statue of the competitor to the empire, it is said that it was accounted a crime of high treason.

An Englishman, having nothing to do, went to Rome, where he met Prince Charles Edward at the house of a cardinal. Pleased at the incident, on his return he drank in a tavern to the health of Prince Charles Edward, and was immediately accused of high treason. But whom did he highly betray in wishing the prince well? If he had conspired to place him on the throne, then he would have been guilty towards the nation; but I do not see that the most rigid justice of parliament could require more from him than to drink four cups to the health of the house of Hanover, supposing he had drunk two to the house of Stuart.

Of Crimes of Time and Place, which Ought to Be Concealed.

It is well known how much our Lady of Loretto ought to be respected in the March of Ancona. Three young people happened to be joking on the house of our lady, which has travelled through the air to Dalmatia; which has two or three times changed its situation, and has only found itself comfortable at Loretto. Our three scatterbrains sang a song at supper, formerly made by a Huguenot, in ridicule of the translation of the *santa casa* of Jerusalem to the end of the Adriatic Gulf. A fanatic, having heard by chance what passed at their supper, made strict inquiries, sought witnesses, and engaged a magistrate to issue a summons. This proceeding alarmed all consciences. Every one trembled in speaking of it. Chambermaids, vergers, inn-keepers, lackeys, servants, all heard what was never said, and saw what was never done: there was an uproar, a horrible scandal throughout the whole March of Ancona. It was said, half a league from Loretto, that these youths had killed our lady; and a league farther, that they had thrown the *santa casa* into the sea. In short, they were condemned. The sentence was, that their hands should be cut off, and their tongues be torn out; after which they were to be put to the torture, to learn—at least by signs—how many couplets there were in the song. Finally, they were to be burnt to death by a slow fire.

An advocate of Milan, who happened to be at Loretto at this time, asked the principal judge to what he would have condemned these boys if they had violated their mother, and afterwards killed and eaten her? "Oh!" replied the judge, "there is a great deal of difference; to assassinate and devour their father and mother is only a crime against men." "Have you an express law," said the Milanese, "which obliges you to put young people scarcely out of their nurseries to such a horrible death, for having indiscreetly made game of the *santa casa,* which is contemptuously laughed at all over the world, except in the March of Ancona?" "No," said the judge, "the wisdom of our jurisprudence leaves all to our discretion." "Very well, you ought to have discretion enough to remember that one of these children is the grandson of a general who has shed his blood for his country, and the nephew of an amiable and respectable abbess; the youth and his companions are giddy boys, who deserve paternal correction. You tear citizens from the state, who might one day serve it; you imbrue yourself in innocent blood, and are more cruel than cannibals. You will render yourselves execrable to posterity. What motive has been powerful enough, thus to extinguish reason, justice, and humanity in your minds, and to change you into ferocious beasts?" The unhappy judge at last replied: "We have been quarrelling with the clergy of Ancona; they accuse us of being too zealous for the liberties of the Lombard Church, and consequently of having no religion." "I understand, then," said the Milanese, "that you have made yourselves assassins to appear Christians." At these words the judge fell to the ground, as if struck by a thunderbolt; and his brother judges having been since deprived of office, they cry out that injustice is done them. They forget what they have done, and perceive not that the hand of God is upon them.

For seven persons legally to amuse themselves by making an eighth perish on a public scaffold by blows from iron bars; take a secret and malignant pleasure in witnessing his torments; speak of it afterwards at table with their wives and neighbors; for the executioners to perform this office gaily, and joyously anticipate their reward; for the public to run to this spectacle as to a fair—all this requires that a crime merit this horrid punishment in the opinion of all well-governed nations, and, as we here treat of universal humanity, that it is necessary to the well-being of society. Above all, the actual perpetration should be demonstrated beyond contradiction. If against a hundred thousand probabilities that the accused be guilty there is a single one that he is innocent, that alone should balance all the rest.

Query: Are Two Witnesses Enough to Condemn a Man to be Hanged?

It has been for a long time imagined, and the proverb assures us, that two witnesses are enough to hang a man, with a safe conscience. Another ambiguity! The world, then, is to be governed by equivoques. It is said in St. Matthew that two or three witnesses will suffice to reconcile two divided friends; and after this text has criminal jurisprudence been regulated, so far as to decree that by divine law a citizen may be condemned to die on the uniform deposition of two witnesses who may be villains? It has been already said that a crowd of according witnesses cannot prove an improbable thing when denied by the accused. What, then, must be done in such a case? Put off the judgment for a hundred years, like the Athenians!

We shall here relate a striking example of what passed under our eyes at Lyons. A woman suddenly missed her daughter; she ran everywhere in search of her in vain, and at length suspected a neighbor of having secreted the girl, and of having caused her violation. Some weeks after some fishermen found a female drowned, and in a state of putrefaction, in the Rhône at Condmeux. The woman of whom we have spoken immediately believed that it was her daughter. She was persuaded by the enemies of her neighbor that the latter had caused the deceased to be dishonored, strangled, and thrown into the Rhône.

She made this accusation publicly, and the populace repeated it; persons were found who knew the minutest circumstances of the crime. The rumor ran through all the town, and all mouths cried out for vengeance. There is nothing more common than this in a populace without judgment; but here follows the most prodigious part of the affair. This neighbor's own son, a child of five years and a half old, accused his mother of having caused the unhappy girl who was found in the Rhône to be violated before his eyes, and to be held by five men, while the sixth committed the crime. He had heard the words which pronounced her violated; he painted her attitudes; he saw his mother and these villains strangle this unfortunate girl after the consummation of the act. He also saw his mother and the assassins throw her into a well, draw her out of it, wrap her up in a cloth, carry her about in triumph, dance round the corpse, and, at last, throw her into the Rhône. The judges were obliged to put all the pretended accomplices deposed against in chains. The child is again heard, and still maintains, with the simplicity of his age, all that he had said of them and of his mother. How could it be imagined that this child had not spoken the pure truth? The crime was not probable, but it was still less so that a child of the age of five years and a half should thus calumniate his mother, and repeat with exactness all the circumstances of an abominable and unheard-of crime; if he had not been the eye-witness of it, and been overcome with the force of the truth, such things would not have been wrung from him.

Every one expected to feast his eyes on the torment of the accused; but what was the end of this strange criminal process? There was not a word of truth in the accusation. There was no girl violated, no young men assembled at the house of the accused, no murder, not the least transaction of the sort, nor the least noise. The child had been suborned; and by whom? Strange, but true, by two other children, who were the sons of the accused. He had been on the point of burning his mother to get some sweetmeats.

The heads of the accusation were clearly incompatible. The sage and enlightened court of judicature, after having yielded to the public fury so far as to seek every possible testimony for and against the accused, fully and unanimously acquitted them. Formerly, perhaps, this innocent prisoner would have been broken on the wheel, or judicially burned, for the pleasure of supplying an execution— the tragedy of the mob.

CRIMINAL.

Criminal Prosecution.

Very innocent actions have been frequently punished with death. Thus in England, Richard III., and Edward IV., effected by the judges the condemnation of those whom they suspected of disaffection. Such are not criminal processes; they are assassinations committed by privileged murderers. It is the last degree of abuse to make the laws the instruments of injustice.

It is said that the Athenians punished with death every stranger who entered their areopagus or sovereign tribunal. But if this stranger was actuated by mere curiosity, nothing was more cruel than to take away his life. It is observed, in "The Spirit of Laws," that this vigor was exercised, "because he usurped the rights of a citizen."

But a Frenchman in London who goes to the House of Commons to hear the debates, does not aspire to the rights of a citizen. He is received with politeness. If any splenetic member calls for the clearing of the house, the traveller clears it by withdrawing; he is not hanged. It is probable that, if the Athenians passed this temporary law, it was at a time when it was suspected that every stranger might be a spy, and not from the fear that he would arrogate to himself the rights of citizenship. Every Athenian voted in his tribe; all the individuals in the tribe knew each other; no stranger could have put in his bean.

We speak here only of a real criminal prosecution, and among the Romans every criminal prosecution was public. The citizen accused of the most enormous crimes had an advocate who pleaded in his presence; who even interrogated the adverse party; who investigated everything before his judges. All the witnesses, for and against, were produced in open court; nothing was secret. Cicero pleaded for Milo, who had assassinated Clodius, in the presence of a thousand citizens. The same Cicero undertook the defence of Roscius Amerinus, accused of parricide. A single judge did not in secret examine witnesses, generally consisting of the dregs of the people, who may be influenced at pleasure.

A Roman citizen was not put to the torture at the arbitrary order of another Roman citizen, invested with this cruel authority by purchase. That horrible outrage against humanity was not perpetrated on the persons of those who were regarded as the first of men, but only on those of their slaves, scarcely regarded as men. It would have been better not to have employed torture, even against slaves.

The method of conducting a criminal prosecution at Rome accorded with the magnanimity and liberality of the nation. It is nearly the same in London. The assistance of an advocate is never in any case refused. Every one is judged by his peers. Every citizen has the power, out of thirty-six jurymen sworn, to challenge twelve without reasons, twelve with reasons, and, consequently, of choosing his judges in the remaining twelve. The judges cannot deviate from or go beyond the law. No punishment is arbitrary. No judgment can be executed before it has been reported to the king, who may, and who ought to bestow pardon on those who are deserving of it, and to whom the law cannot extend it. This case frequently occurs. A man outrageously wronged kills the offender under the impulse of venial passion; he is condemned by the rigor of the law, and saved by that mercy which ought to be the prerogative of the sovereign.

It deserves particular remark that in the same country where the laws are as favorable to the accused as they are terrible for the guilty, not only is false imprisonment in ordinary cases punished by heavy damages and severe penalties, but if an illegal imprisonment has been ordered by a minister of state, under color of royal authority, that minister may be condemned to pay damages corresponding to the imprisonment.

Proceedings in Criminal Cases Among Particular Nations.

There are countries in which criminal jurisprudence has been founded on the canon law, and even on the practice of the Inquisition, although that tribunal has long since been held in detestation there. The people in such countries still remain in a species of slavery. A citizen prosecuted by the king's officer is at once immured in a dungeon, which is in itself a real punishment of perhaps an innocent man. A single judge, with his clerk, hears secretly and in succession, every witness summoned.

Let us here merely compare, in a few points, the criminal procedure of the Romans with that of a country of the west, which was once a Roman province. Among the Romans, witnesses were heard publicly in the presence of the accused, who might reply to them, and examine them himself, or through an advocate. This practice was noble and frank; it breathed of Roman magnanimity. In France, in many parts of Germany, everything is done in secret. This practice, established under Francis I., was authorized by the commissioners, who, in 1670, drew up the ordinance of Louis XIV. A mere mistake was the cause of it.

It was imagined, on reading the code "*De Testibus*" that the words, *Testes intrare judicii secretum,* signified that witnesses were examined in secret. But *secretum* here signifies the chambers of the judge. *Intrare secretum* to express speaking in secret, would not be Latin. This part of our jurisprudence was occasioned by a solecism. Witnesses were usually persons of the lowest class, and whom the judge, when closeted with them, might induce to say whatever he wished. These witnesses are examined a second time, always in secret, which is called, re-examination; and if, after re-examination, they retract their depositions, or vary them in essential circumstances, they are punished as false witnesses. Thus, when an upright man of weak understanding, and unused to express his ideas, is conscious that he has stated either too much or too little—that he has misunderstood the judge, or that the judge has misunderstood him—and revokes, in the spirit of justice, what he has advanced through incaution, he is punished as a felon. He is in this manner often compelled to persevere in false testimony, from the actual dread of being treated as a false witness.

The person accused exposes himself by flight to condemnation, whether the crime has been proved or not. Some jurisconsults, indeed, have wisely held that the contumacious person ought not to be condemned unless the crime were clearly established; but other lawyers have been of a contrary opinion: they have boldly affirmed that the flight of the accused was a proof of the crime; that the contempt which he showed for justice, by refusing to appear, merited the same chastisement as would have followed his conviction. Thus, according to the sect of lawyers which the judge may have embraced, an innocent man may be acquitted or condemned.

It is a great abuse in jurisprudence that people often assume as law the reveries and errors— sometimes cruel ones—of men destitute of all authority, who have laid down their own opinions as laws. In the reign of Louis XIV., two edicts were published in France, which apply equally to the whole kingdom. In the first, which refers to civil causes, the judges are forbidden to condemn in any suit, on default, when the demand is not proved; but in the second, which regulates criminal proceedings, it is not laid down that, in the absence of proof, the accused shall be acquitted. Singular circumstance! The law declares that a man proceeded against for a sum of money shall not be condemned, on default, unless the debt be proved; but, in cases affecting life, the profession is divided with respect to condemning a person for contumacy when the crime is not proved; and the law does not solve the difficulty.

Example Taken from the Condemnation of a Whole Family.

The following is an account of what happened to an unfortunate family, at the time when the mad fraternities of pretended penitents, in white robes and masks, had erected, in one of the principal churches of Toulouse, a superb monument to a young Protestant, who had destroyed himself, but who they pretended had been murdered by his father and mother for having abjured the reformed religion; at the time when the whole family of this Protestant, then revered as a martyr, were in irons, and a whole population, intoxicated by a superstition equally senseless and cruel, awaited with devout impatience the delight of seeing five or six persons of unblemished integrity expire on the rack or at the stake. At this dreadful period there resided near Castres a respectable man, also of the Protestant religion, of the name of Sirven, who exercised in that province the profession of a feudist. This man had three daughters. A woman who superintended the household of the bishop of Castres, proposed to bring to him Sirven's second daughter, called Elizabeth, in order to make her a Catholic, apostolical and Roman. She is, in fact, brought. She is by him secluded with the female Jesuits, denominated the "lady teachers," or the "black ladies." They instruct her in what they know; they find her capacity weak, and impose upon her penances in order to inculcate doctrines which, with gentleness, she might have been taught. She becomes imbecile; the "black ladies" expel her; she returns to her parents; her mother, on making her change her linen, perceives that her person is covered with contusions; her imbecility increases; she becomes melancholy mad; she escapes one day from the house, while her father is some miles distant, publicly occupied in his business, at the seat of a neighboring nobleman. In short, twenty days after the flight of Elizabeth, some children find her drowned in a well, on January 4, 1761.

This was precisely the time when they were preparing to break Calas on the wheel at Toulouse. The word "parricide," and what is worse, "Huguenot," flies from mouth to mouth throughout the province. It was not doubted that Sirven, his wife, and his two daughters, had drowned the third, on a principle of religion.

It was the universal opinion that the Protestant religion positively required fathers and mothers to destroy such of their children as might wish to become Catholics. This opinion had taken such deep root in the minds even of magistrates themselves, hurried on unfortunately by the public clamor, that the Council and Church of Geneva were obliged to contradict the fatal error, and to send to the parliament of Toulouse an attestation upon oath that not only did Protestants not destroy their children, but that they were left masters of their whole property when they quitted their sect for another. It is known that, notwithstanding this attestation, Calas was broken on the wheel.

A country magistrate of the name of Londes, assisted by graduates as sagacious as himself, became eager to make every preparation for following up the example which had been furnished at Toulouse. A village doctor, equally enlightened with the magistrate, boldly affirmed, on inspecting the body after the expiration of eighteen days, that the young woman had been strangled, and afterwards thrown into the well. On this deposition the magistrate issued a warrant to apprehend the father, mother, and the two daughters. The family, justly terrified at the catastrophe of Calas, and agreeably to the advice of their friends, betook themselves instantly to flight; they travelled amidst snow during a rigorous winter, and, toiling over mountain after mountain, at length arrived at those of Switzerland. The daughter, who was married and pregnant, was prematurely delivered amidst surrounding ice.

The first intelligence this family received, after reaching a place of safety, was that the father and mother were condemned to be hanged; the two daughters to remain under the gallows during the execution of their mother, and to be reconducted by the executioner out of the territory, under pain of being hanged if they returned. Such is the lesson given to contumacy!

This judgment was equally absurd and abominable. If the father, in concert with his wife, had strangled his daughter, he ought to have been broken on the wheel, like Calas, and the mother to have been burned—at least, after having been strangled—because the practice of breaking women on the wheel is not yet the custom in the country of this judge. To limit the punishment to hanging in such a case, was an acknowledgment that the crime was not proved, and that in the doubt the halter was adopted to compromise for want of evidence. This sentence was equally repugnant to law and reason. The mother died of a broken heart, and the whole family, their property having been confiscated, would have perished through want, unless they had met with assistance.

We stop here to inquire whether there be any law and any reason that can justify such a sentence? We ask the judge, "What madness has urged you to condemn a father and a mother?" "It was because they fled," he replies. "Miserable wretch, would you have had them remain to glut your insensate fury? Of what consequence could it be, whether they appeared in chains to plead before you, or whether in a distant land they lifted up their hands in an appeal to heaven against you? Could you not see the truth, which ought to have struck you, as well during their absence? Could you not see that the father was a league distant from his daughter, in the midst of twenty persons, when the unfortunate young woman withdrew from her mother's protection? Could you be ignorant that the whole family were in search of her for twenty days and nights?" To this you answer by the words, contumacy, contumacy. What! because a man is absent, therefore must he be condemned to be hanged, though his innocence be manifest? It is the jurisprudence of a fool and a monster. And the life, the property, and the honor of citizens, are to depend upon this code of Iroquois!

The Sirven family for more than eight years dragged on their misfortunes, far from their native country. At length, the sanguinary superstition which disgraced Languedoc having been somewhat mitigated, and men's minds becoming more enlightened, those who had befriended the Sirvens during their exile, advised them to return and demand justice from the parliament of Toulouse itself, now that the blood of Calas no longer smoked, and many repented of having ever shed it. The Sirvens were justified.

Erudimini, qui judicatis terram.
Be instructed, ye judges of the earth.

CROMWELL.

SECTION I.

Cromwell is described as a man who was an impostor all his life. I can scarcely believe it. I conceive that he was first an enthusiast, and that he afterwards made his fanaticism instrumental to his greatness. An ardent novice at twenty often becomes an accomplished rogue at forty. In the great game of human life, men begin with being dupes, and end in becoming knaves. A statesman engages as his almoner a monk, entirely made up of the details of his convent, devout, credulous, awkward, perfectly new to the world; he acquires information, polish, finesse, and supplants his master.

Cromwell knew not, at first, whether he should become a churchman or a soldier. He partly became both. In 1622 he made a campaign in the army of the prince of Orange, Frederick Henry, a great man and the brother of two great men; and, on his return to England, engaged in the service of Bishop Williams, and was the chaplain of his lordship, while the bishop passed for his wife's gallant. His principles were puritanical, which led him to cordially hate a bishop, and not to be partial to kingship. He was dismissed from the family of Bishop Williams because he was a Puritan; and thence the origin of his fortune. The English Parliament declared against monarchy and against episcopacy; some friends whom he had in that parliament procured him a country living. He might be said only now to have commenced his existence; he was more than forty before he acquired any distinction. He was master of the sacred Scriptures, disputed on the authority of priests and deacons, wrote some bad sermons, and some lampoons; but he was unknown. I have seen one of his sermons, which is insipid enough, and pretty much resembles the holdings forth of the Quakers; it is impossible to discover in it any trace of that power by which he afterwards swayed parliaments. The truth is, he was better fitted for the State than for the Church. It was principally in his tone and in his air that his eloquence consisted. An inclination of that hand which had gained so many battles, and killed so many royalists, was more persuasive than the periods of Cicero. It must be acknowledged that it was his incomparable valor that brought him into notice, and which conducted him gradually to the summit of greatness.

He commenced by throwing himself, as a volunteer and a soldier of fortune, into the town of Hull, besieged, by the king. He there performed some brilliant and valuable services, for which he received a gratuity of about six thousand francs from the parliament. The present, bestowed by parliament upon an adventurer, made it clear that the rebel party must prevail. The king could not give to his general officers what the parliament gave to volunteers. With money and fanaticism, everything must in the end be mastered. Cromwell was made colonel. His great talents for war became then so conspicuous that, when the parliament created the earl of Manchester general of its forces, Cromwell was appointed lieutenant-general, without his having passed through the intervening ranks. Never did any man appear more worthy of command. Never was seen more activity and skill, more daring and more resources, than in Cromwell. He is wounded at the battle of York, and, while undergoing the first dressing, is informed that his commander, the earl of Manchester, is retreating, and the battle lost. He hastens to find the earl; discovers him flying, with some officers; catches him by the arm, and, in a firm and dignified tone, he exclaims: "My lord, you mistake; the enemy has not taken that road." He reconducts him to the field of battle; rallies, during the night, more than twelve thousand men; harangues them in the name of God; cites Moses, Gideon, and Joshua; renews the battle at daybreak against the victorious royalist army, and completely defeats it. Such a man must either perish or obtain the mastery. Almost all the officers of his army were enthusiasts, who carried the New Testament on their saddle-bows. In the army, as in the parliament, nothing was spoken of but Babylon destroyed, building up the worship of Jerusalem, and breaking the image. Cromwell, among so many madmen, was no longer one himself, and thought it better to govern than to be governed by them. The habit of preaching, as by inspiration, remained with him. Figure to yourself a fakir, who, after putting an iron girdle round his loins in penance, takes it off to drub the ears of other fakirs. Such was Cromwell. He becomes as intriguing as he was intrepid. He associates with all the colonels of the army, and thus forms among the troops a republic which forces the commander to resign. Another commander is appointed, and him he disgusts. He governs the army, and through it he governs the parliament; which he at last compels to make him commander. All this is much; but the essential point is that he wins all the battles he fights in England, Scotland, and Ireland; and wins them, not consulting his own security while the fight rages, but always charging the enemy, rallying his troops, presenting himself everywhere, frequently wounded, killing with his own hands many royalist officers, like the fiercest soldier in the ranks.

In the midst of this dreadful war Cromwell made love; he went, with the Bible under his arm, to an assignation with the wife of his major-general, Lambert. She loved the earl of Holland, who served in the king's army. Cromwell took him prisoner in battle, and had the pleasure of bringing his rival to the block. It was his maxim to shed the blood of every important enemy, in the field or by the hand of the executioner. He always increased his power by always daring to abuse it; the profoundness of his plans never lessened his ferocious impetuosity. He went to the House of Commons, and drove all the members out, one after another, making them defile before him. As they passed, each was obliged to make a profound reverence; one of them was passing on with his head covered; Cromwell seized his hat and threw it down. "Learn," said he, "to respect me."

When he had outraged all kings by beheading his own legitimate king, and he began himself to reign, he sent his portrait to one crowned head, Christina, queen of Sweden. Marvel, a celebrated English poet, who wrote excellent Latin verses, accompanied his portrait with six lines, in which he introduces

Cromwell himself speaking; Cromwell corrected these two last verses:

> *At tibi submittit frontem reverentior umbra,*
> *Non sunt hi vultus regibus usque truces.*

The spirit of the whole six verses may be given thus:

> *Les armes à la main j'ai défendu les lois;*
> *D'un peuple audacieux j'ai vengé la querelle.*
> *Regardez sans frémir cette image fidèle:*
> *Mon front n'est pas toujours l'épouvante des rois.*

> 'Twas mine by arms t'uphold my country's laws;
> My sword maintained a lofty people's cause;
> With less of fear these faithful outlines trace,
> Menace of kings not always clouds my face.

This queen was the first to acknowledge him after he became protector of the three kingdoms. Almost all the sovereigns of Europe sent ambassadors *to their brother Cromwell*—to that domestic of a bishop, who had just brought to the scaffold a sovereign related to them. They emulously courted his alliance. Cardinal Mazarin, in order to please him, banished from France the two sons of Charles I., the two grandsons of Henry IV., and the two cousins-german of Louis XIV. France conquered Dunkirk for him, and the keys of it were delivered into his possession. After his death, Louis XIV. and his whole court went into mourning, except mademoiselle, who dared to appear in the circle in colors, and alone to maintain the honor of her race.

No king was ever more absolute than Cromwell. He would observe "that he had preferred governing under the name of protector rather than under that of king, because the English were aware of the limits of the prerogative of a king of England, but knew not the extent of that of a protector." This was knowing mankind, who are governed by opinion, and whose opinion depends upon a name. He had conceived a profound contempt for the religion to which he owed his success. An anecdote, preserved in the St. John family, sufficiently proves the slight regard he attached to that instrument which had produced such mighty effects in his hands. He was drinking once in company with Ireton, Fleetwood, and St. John, great grandfather of the celebrated Lord Bolingbroke; a bottle of wine was to be uncorked, and the corkscrew fell under the table; they all looked for it, and were unable to find it. In the meantime a deputation from the Presbyterian churches awaited in the ante-chamber, and an usher announced them. "Tell them," said Cromwell, "that I have retired, and *that I am seeking the Lord*." This was the expression employed by the fanatics for going to prayers. Having dismissed the troop of divines, he thus addressed his companions: "Those fellows think we are seeking the Lord, while we are only seeking a corkscrew."

There is scarcely any example in Europe of a man who, from so low a beginning, raised himself to such eminence. But with all his great talents, what did he consider absolutely essential to his happiness? Power he obtained; but was he happy? He had lived in poverty and disquiet till the age of forty-three; he afterwards plunged into blood, passed his life in trouble, and died prematurely, at the age of fifty-seven. With this life let any one compare that of a Newton, who lived fourscore years, always tranquil, always honored, always the light of all thinking beings; beholding every day an accession to his fame, his character, his fortune; completely free both from care and remorse; and let him decide whose was the happier lot.

O curas hominum! O quantim est in rebus inane!
O human cares! O mortal toil how vain!

SECTION II.

Oliver Cromwell was regarded with admiration by the Puritans and Independents of England; he is still their hero. But Richard Cromwell, his son, is the man for me. The first was a fanatic who in the present day would be hissed down in the House of Commons, on uttering any one of the unintelligible absurdities which he delivered with such confidence before other fanatics who listened to him with open mouth and staring eyes, in the name of the Lord. If he were to say that they must seek the Lord, and fight the battles of the Lord—if he were to introduce the Jewish jargon into the parliament of England, to the eternal disgrace of the human understanding, he would be much more likely to be conducted to Bedlam than to be appointed the commander of armies.

Brave he unquestionably was—and so are wolves; there are even some monkeys as fierce as tigers. From a fanatic he became an able politician; in other words, from a wolf he became a fox, and the knave, craftily mounting from the first steps where the mad enthusiasm of the times had placed him, to the summit of greatness, walked over the heads of the prostrated fanatics. He reigned, but he lived in the horrors of alarm and had neither cheerful days nor tranquil nights. The consolations of friendship and society never approached him. He died prematurely, more deserving, beyond a doubt, of public execution than the monarch whom, from a window of his own palace, he caused to be led out to the scaffold.

Richard Cromwell, on the contrary, was gentle and prudent and refused to keep his father's power at the expense of the lives of three or four factious persons whom he might have sacrificed to his ambition. He preferred becoming a private individual to being an assassin with supreme power. He relinquished the protectorship without regret, to live as a subject; and in the tranquillity of a country life he enjoyed health and possessed his soul in peace for ninety years, beloved by his neighbors, to whom he was a peacemaker and a father.

Say, reader, had you to choose between the destiny of the father and that of the son, which would you prefer?

CUISSAGE.

Dion Cassius, that flatterer of Augustus and detractor from Cicero, because Cicero was the friend of liberty—that dry and diffuse writer and gazetteer of popular rumors, Dion Cassius, reports that certain senators were of opinion that in order to recompense Cæsar for all the evil which he had brought upon the commonwealth it would be right, at the age of fifty-seven, to allow him to honor with his favors all the ladies who took his fancy. Men are still found who credit this absurdity. Even the author of the "Spirit of Laws" takes it for a truth and speaks of it as of a decree which would have passed the Roman senate but for the modesty of the dictator, who suspected that he was not altogether prepared for the accession of so much good fortune. But if the Roman emperors attained not this right by a *senatus-consultum*, duly founded upon a *plebiscitum*, it is very likely that they fully enjoyed it by the courtesy of the ladies. The Marcus Aureliuses and the Julians, to be sure, exercised not this right, but all the rest extended it as widely as they were able.

It is astonishing that in Christian Europe a kind of feudal law for a long time existed, or at least it was deemed a customary usage, to regard the virginity of a female vassal as the property of the lord. The first night of the nuptials of the daughter of his *villein* belonged to him without dispute.

This right was established in the same manner as that of walking with a falcon on the fist, and of being saluted with incense at mass. The lords, indeed, did not enact that the *wives* of their villeins belonged to them; they confined themselves to the daughters, the reason of which is obvious. Girls are bashful and sometimes might exhibit reluctance. This, however, yielded at once to the majesty of the laws, when the condescending baron deemed them worthy the honor of personally enforcing their practice.

It is asserted that this curious jurisprudence commenced in Scotland, and I willingly believe that the Scotch lords had a still more absolute power over their clans than even the German and French barons over their vassals.

It is undoubted that some abbots and bishops enjoyed this privilege in their quality of temporal lords, and it is not very long since that these prelates compounded their prerogative for acknowledgments in money, to which they have just as much right as to the virginity of the girls.

But let it be well remarked that this excess of tyranny was never sanctioned by any public law. If a lord or a prelate had cited before a regular tribunal a girl affianced to one of his vassals, in claim of her quit-rent, he would doubtless have lost his cause and costs.

Let us seize this occasion to rest assured that no partially civilized people ever established formal laws against morals; I do not believe that a single instance of it can be furnished. Abuses creep in and are borne: they pass as customs and travellers mistake them for fundamental laws. It is said that in Asia greasy Mahometan saints march in procession entirely naked and that devout females crowd round them to kiss what is not worthy to be named, but I defy any one to discover a passage in the Koran which justifies this brutality.

The phallus, which the Egyptians carry in procession, may be quoted in order to confound me, as well as the idol Juggernaut, of the Indians. I reply that these ceremonies war no more against morals than circumcision at the age of eight days. In some of our towns the holy foreskin has been borne in procession, and it is preserved yet in certain sacristies without this piece of drollery causing the least disturbance in families. Still, I am convinced that no council or act of parliament ever ordained this homage to the holy foreskin.

I call a public law which deprives me of my property, which takes away my wife and gives her to another, a law against morals; and I am certain that such a law is impossible. Some travellers maintain that in Lapland husbands, out of politeness, make an offer of their wives. Out of still greater politeness, I believe them; but I nevertheless assert, that they never found this rule of good manners in the legal code of Lapland, any more than in the constitutions of Germany, in the ordinances of the king of France, or in the "Statutes at Large" of England, any positive law, adjudging the right of *cuissage* to the barons. Absurd and barbarous laws may be found everywhere; formal laws against morals nowhere.

CURATE (OF THE COUNTRY).

A curate—but why do I say a curate?—even an imam, a talapoin, or brahmin ought to have the means of living decently. The priest in every country ought to be supported by the altar since he serves the public. Some fanatic rogue may assert that I place the curate and the brahmin on the same level and associate truth with imposture; but I compare only the services rendered to society, the labor, and the recompense.

I maintain that whoever exercises a laborious function ought to be well paid by his fellow-citizens. I do not assert that he ought to amass riches, sup with Lucullus, or be as insolent as Clodius. I pity the case of a country curate who is obliged to dispute a sheaf of corn with his parishioner; to plead against him; to exact from him the tenth of his peas and beans; to be hated and to hate, and to consume his miserable life in miserable quarrels which engross the mind as much as they embitter it.

I still more pity the inconsistent lot of a curate, whom monks, claiming the great tithes, audaciously reward with a salary of forty ducats per annum for undertaking, throughout the year, the labor of visiting for three miles round his abode, by day and by night, in hail, rain, or snow, the most disagreeable and often the most useless functions, while the abbot or great tithe-holder drinks his rich wine of Volney, Beaune, or Chambertin, eats his partridges and pheasants, sleeps upon his down bed with a fair neighbor, and builds a palace. The disproportion is too great.

It has been taken for granted since the days of Charlemagne that the clergy, besides their own lands, ought to possess a tenth of the lands of other people, which tenth is at least a quarter, computing the expense of culture. To establish this payment it is claimed on a principle of divine right. Did God descend on earth to give a quarter of His property to the abbey of Monte Cassino, to the abbey of St. Denis, to the abbey of Fulda? Not that I know, but it has been discovered that formerly, in the desert of Ethan, Horeb, and Kadesh Barnea, the Levites were favored with forty-eight cities and a tenth of all which the earth produced besides.

Very well, great tithe-holders, go to Kadesh Barnea and inhabit the forty-eight cities in that uninhabitable desert. Take the tenth of the flints which the land produces there, and great good may they do you. But Abraham having combated for Sodom, gave a tenth of the spoil to Melchizedek, priest and king of Salem. Very good, combat you also for Sodom, but, like Melchizedek, take not from me the produce of the corn which I have sowed.

In a Christian country containing twelve hundred thousand square leagues throughout the whole of the North, in part of Germany, in Holland, and in Switzerland, the clergy are paid with money from the public treasury. The tribunals resound not there with lawsuits between landlords and priests, between the great and the little tithe-holders, between the pastor, plaintiff, and the flock defendants, in consequence of the third Council of the Lateran, of which the said flocks defendant have never heard a syllable.

The king of Naples this year (1772) has just abolished tithes in one of his provinces: the clergy are better paid and the province blesses him. The Egyptian priests, it is said, claimed not this tenth, but then, it is observed that they possessed a third part of the land of Egypt as their own. Oh, stupendous miracle! oh, thing most difficult to be conceived, that possessing one-third of the country they did not quickly acquire the other two!

Believe not, dear reader, that the Jews, who were a stiff-necked people, never complained of the extortion of the tenths, or tithe. Give yourself the trouble to consult the Talmud of Babylon, and if you understand not the Chaldæan, read the translation, with notes of Gilbert Gaumin, the whole of which was printed by the care of Fabricius. You will there peruse the adventure of a poor widow with the High Priest Aaron, and learn how the quarrel of this widow became the cause of the quarrel of Koran, Dathan, and Abiram, on the one side, and Aaron on the other.

"A widow possessed only a single sheep which she wished to shear. Aaron came and took the wool for himself: 'It belongs to me,' said he, 'according to the law, thou shalt give the first of the wool to God.' The widow, in tears, implored the protection of Koran. Koran applied to Aaron but his entreaties were fruitless. Aaron replies that the wool belongs to him. Koran gives some money to the widow and retires, filled with indignation.

"Some time after, the sheep produces a lamb. Aaron returns and carries away the lamb. The widow runs weeping again to Koran, who in vain implores Aaron. The high priest answers, 'It is written in the law, every first-born male in thy flock belongs to God.' He eats the lamb and Koran again retires in a rage.

"The widow, in despair, kills her sheep; Aaron returns once more and takes away the shoulder and the breast. Koran again complains. Aaron replies: 'It is written, thou shalt give unto the priests the shoulder, the two cheeks, and the maw.'

"The widow could no longer contain her affliction and said, 'Anathema,' to the sheep, upon which Aaron observed, 'It is written, all that is anathema (cursed) in Israel belongs to thee;' and took away the sheep altogether."

What is not so pleasant, yet very remarkable, is that in a suit between the clergy of Rheims and the citizens, this instance from the Talmud was cited by the advocate of the citizens. Gaumin asserts that he witnessed it. In the meantime it may be answered that the tithe-holders do not take *all* from the people, the tax-gatherers will not suffer it. To every one his share is just.

CURIOSITY.

Suave, mari magno turbantibus aequora ventis,
E terra magnum alterius spectare laborem;
Non quia vexari quemquam est jucunda voluptas,
Sed quibus ipse malis careas, quia cernere suave
est.
Suave etiam belli certamina magna tueri
Per campos instructa tua sine parte pericli;
Sed nil dulcius est, bene quam munita tenere
Edita doctrina sapientum templa serena
Despicere unde queas alios, passimque videre
Errare, atque viam palantes quaerere vitae,
Certare ingenio, contendere nobilitate,
Noctes atque dies niti praestante labore
Ad summas emergere opes, rerumque potiri.
O miseras hominum mentes! O pectora caeca!

'Tis pleasant, when the seas are rough, to stand
And view another's danger, safe at land;
Not 'cause he's troubled, but 'tis sweet to see
Those cares and fears, from which ourselves are
free;
Tis also pleasant to behold from far
How troops engage, secure ourselves from war.
But, above all, 'tis pleasantest to get
The top of high philosophy, and set
On the calm, peaceful, nourishing head of it;
Whence we may view, deep, wondrous deep below,
How poor mistaken mortals wandering go,
Seeking the path to happiness; some aim
At learning, not nobility, or fame;

Others, with cares and dangers vie each hour
To reach the top of wealth and sovereign power.
Blind, wretched man, in what dark paths of strife
We walk this little journey of our life.
—CREECH'S *Lucretius.*

I ask your pardon, Lucretius! I suspect that you are here as mistaken in morals as you are always mistaken in physics. In my opinion it is curiosity alone that induces people to hasten to the shore to see a vessel in danger of being overwhelmed in a tempest. The case has happened to myself, and I solemnly assure you that my pleasure, mingled as it was with uneasiness and distress, did not at all arise from reflection, nor originate in any secret comparison between my own security and the danger of the unfortunate crew. I was moved by curiosity and pity.

At the battle of Fontenoy little boys and girls climbed up the surrounding trees to have a view of the slaughter. Ladies ordered seats to be placed for them on a bastion of the city of Liege that they might enjoy the spectacle at the battle of Rocoux.

When I said, "Happy they who view in peace the gathering storm," the happiness I had in view consists in tranquillity and the search of truth, and not in seeing the sufferings of thinking beings, oppressed by fanatics or hypocrites under persecution for having sought it.

Could we suppose an angel flying on six beautiful wings from the height of the Empyrean, setting out to take a view through some loophole of hell of the torments and contortions of the damned, and congratulating himself on feeling nothing of their inconceivable agonies, such an angel would much resemble the character of Beelzebub.

I know nothing of the nature of angels because I am only a man; divines alone are acquainted with them; but, as a man, I think, from my own experience and also from that of all my brother drivellers, that people do not flock to any spectacle, of whatever kind, but from pure curiosity.

This seems to me so true that if the exhibition be ever so admirable men at last get tired of it. The Parisian public scarcely go any longer to see "*Tartuffe*" the most masterly of Molière's masterpieces. Why is it? Because they have gone often; because they have it by heart. It is the same with "Andromache."

Perrin Dandin is unfortunately right when he proposes to the young Isabella to take her to see the method of "putting to the torture;" it serves, he says, to pass away an hour or two. If this anticipation of the execution, frequently more cruel than the execution itself, were a public spectacle, the whole city of Toulouse would have rushed in crowds to behold the venerable Calas twice suffering those execrable torments, at the instance of the attorney-general. Penitents, black, white, and gray, married women, girls, stewards of the floral games, students, lackeys, female servants, girls of the town, doctors of the canon law would have been all squeezed together. At Paris we must have been almost suffocated in order to see the unfortunate General Lally pass along in a dung cart, with a six-inch gag in his mouth.

But if these tragedies of cannibals, which are sometimes performed before the most frivolous of nations, and the one most ignorant in general of the principles of jurisprudence and equity; if the spectacles, like those of St. Bartholomew, exhibited by tigers to monkeys and the copies of it on a smaller scale were renewed every day, men would soon desert such a country; they would fly from it with horror; they would abandon forever the infernal land where such barbarities were common.

When little boys and girls pluck the feathers from their sparrows it is merely from the impulse of curiosity, as when they dissect the dresses of their dolls. It is this passion alone which produces the immense attendance at public executions. "Strange eagerness," as some tragic author remarks, "to behold the wretched."

I remember being in Paris when Damiens suffered a death the most elaborate and frightful that can be conceived. All the windows in the city which bore upon the spot were engaged at a high price by ladies, not one of whom, assuredly, made the consoling reflection that her own breasts were not torn by pincers; that melted lead and boiling pitch were not poured upon wounds of her own, and that her own limbs, dislocated and bleeding, were not drawn asunder by four horses. One of the executioners judged more correctly than Lucretius, for, when one of the academicians of Paris tried to get within the enclosure to examine what was passing more closely, and was forced back by one of the guards, "Let the gentleman go in," said he, "he is an amateur." That is to say, he is inquisitive; it is not through malice that he comes here; it is not from any reflex consideration of self to revel in the pleasure of not being himself quartered; it is only from curiosity, as men go to see experiments in natural philosophy.

Curiosity is natural to man, to monkeys, and to little dogs. Take a little dog with you in your carriage, he will continually be putting up his paws against the door to see what is passing. A monkey searches everywhere, and has the air of examining everything. As to men, you know how they are constituted: Rome, London, Paris, all pass their time in inquiring what's the news?

CUSTOMS—USAGES.

There are, it is said, one hundred and forty-four customs in France which possess the force of law.

These laws are almost all different in different places. A man that travels in this country changes his law almost as often as he changes his horses. The majority of these customs were not reduced to writing until the time of Charles VII., the reason of which probably was that few people knew how to write. They then copied a part of the customs of a part of Ponthieu, but this great work was not aided by the Picards until Charles VIII. There were but sixteen digests in the time of Louis XII., but our jurisprudence is so improved there are now but few customs which have not a variety of commentators, all of whom are of different opinions. There are already twenty-six upon the customs of Paris. The judges know not which to prefer, but, to put them at their ease the custom of Paris has been just turned into verse. It was in this manner that the Delphian pythoness of old declared her oracles.

Weights and measures differ as much as customs, so that which is correct in the faubourg of Montmartre, is otherwise in the abbey of St. Denis. The Lord pity us!

CYRUS.

Many learned men, and Rollin among the number, in an age in which reason is cultivated, have assured us that Javan, who is supposed to be the father of the Greeks, was the grandson of Noah. I believe it precisely as I believe that Persius was the founder of the kingdom of Persia and Niger of Nigritia. The only thing which grieves me is that the Greeks have never known anything of Noah, the venerable author of their race. I have elsewhere noted my astonishment and chagrin that our father Adam should be absolutely unknown to everybody from Japan to the Strait of Le Maire, except to a small people to whom he was known too late. The science of genealogy is doubtless in the highest degree certain, but exceedingly difficult.

It is neither upon Javan, upon Noah, nor upon Adam that my doubts fall at present; it is upon Cyrus, and I seek not which of the fables in regard to him is preferable, that of Herodotus, of Ctesias, of Xenophon, of Diodorus, or of Justin, all of which contradict one another. Neither do I ask why it is obstinately determined to give the name of Cyrus to a barbarian called Khosrou, and those of Cyropolis and Persepolis to cities that never bore them.

I drop all that has been said of the grand Cyrus, including the romance of that name, and the travels which the Scottish Ramsay made him undertake, and simply inquire into some instructions of his to the Jews, of which that people make mention.

I remark, in the first place, that no author has said a word of the Jews in the history of Cyrus, and that the Jews alone venture to notice themselves, in speaking of this prince.

They resemble, in some degree, certain people, who, alluding to individuals of a rank superior to their own say, we know the gentlemen but the gentlemen know not us. It is the same with Alexander in the narratives of the Jews. No historian of Alexander has mixed up his name with that of the Jews, but Josephus fails not to assert that Alexander came to pay his respects at Jerusalem; that he worshipped, I know not what Jewish pontiff, called Jaddus, who had formerly predicted to him the conquest of Persia in a dream. Petty people are often visionary in this way: the great dream less of their greatness.

When Tarik conquered Spain the vanquished said they had foretold it. They would have said the same thing to Genghis, to Tamerlane, and to Mahomet II.

God forbid that I should compare the Jewish prophets to the predictors of good fortune, who pay their court to conquerors by foretelling them that which has come to pass. I merely observe that the Jews produce some testimony from their nation in respect to the actions of Cyrus about one hundred and sixty years before he was born.

It is said, in the forty-fifth chapter of Isaiah, "Thus saith the Lord to His anointed—His Christ—Cyrus, whose right hand I have holden to subdue nations before him, and I will loosen the loins of kings to open before him the two-leaved gates, and the gates shall not be shut. I will go before thee and make the crooked places straight; I will break in pieces the gates of brass and cut in sunder the bars of iron. And I will give thee the treasures of darkness and hidden riches of secret places that thou mayest know that I the Lord, who call thee by thy name, am the God of Israel," etc.

Some learned men have scarcely been able to digest the fact of the Lord honoring with the name of His Christ an idolater of the religion of Zoroaster. They even dare to say that the Jews, in the manner of all the weak who flatter the powerful, invented predictions in favor of Cyrus.

These learned persons respect Daniel no more than Isaiah, but treat all the prophecies attributed to the latter with similar contempt to that manifested by St. Jerome for the adventures of Susannah, of Bel and the Dragon, and of the three children in the fiery furnace.

The sages in question seem not to be penetrated with sufficient esteem for the prophets. Many of them even pretend that to see clearly the future is metaphysically impossible. To see that which is not, say they, is a contradiction in terms, and as the future exists not, it consequently cannot be seen. They add that frauds of this nature abound in all nations, and, finally, that everything is to be doubted which is recorded in ancient history.

They observe that if there was ever a formal prophecy it is that of the discovery of America in the tragedy of Seneca:

Venient annis
Sæcula seris quibus oceanus
Vinculo rerum laxet, et ingens
Pateat tellus,...

A time may arrive when ocean will loosen the chains of nature and lay open a vast world. The four stars of the southern pole are advanced still more clearly in Dante, yet no one takes either Seneca or Dante for diviners.

As to Cyrus, it is difficult to know whether he died nobly or had his head cut off by Tomyris, but I am anxious, I confess, that the learned men may be right who claim the head of Cyrus was cut off. It is not amiss that these illustrious robbers on the highway of nations who pillage and deluge the earth with blood, should be occasionally chastised.

Cyrus has always been the subject of remark, Xenophon began and, unfortunately, Ramsay ended. Lastly, to show the sad fate which sometimes attends heroes, Danchet has made him the subject of a tragedy.

This tragedy is entirely unknown; the "Cyropædia" of Xenophon is more popular because it is in Greek. The "Travels of Cyrus" are less so, although printed in French and English, and wonderfully erudite.

The pleasantry of the romance entitled "The Travels of Cyrus," consists in its discovery of a Messiah everywhere—at Memphis, at Babylon, at Ecbatana, and at Tyre, as at Jerusalem, and as much in Plato as in the gospel. The author having been a Quaker, an Anabaptist, an Anglican, and a Presbyterian, had finally become a *Fénelonist* at Cambray, under the illustrious author of "Telemachus." Having since been made preceptor to the child of a great nobleman, he thought himself born to instruct and govern the universe, and, in consequence, gives lessons to Cyrus in order to render him at once the best king and the most orthodox theologian in existence. These two rare qualities appear to lack the grace of congruity.

Ramsay leads his pupil to the school of Zoroaster and then to that of the young Jew, Daniel, the greatest philosopher who ever existed. He not only explained dreams, which is the acme of human science, but discovered and interpreted even such as had been forgotten, which none but he could ever accomplish. It might be expected that Daniel would present the beautiful Susannah to the prince, it being in the natural manner of romance, but he did nothing of the kind.

Cyrus, in return, has some very long conversations with Nebuchadnezzar while he was an ox, during which transformation Ramsay makes Nebuchadnezzar ruminate like a profound theologian.

How astonishing that the prince for whom this work was composed preferred the chase and the opera to perusing it!

DANTE.

You wish to become acquainted with Dante. The Italians call him divine, but it is a mysterious divinity; few men understand his oracles, and although there are commentators, that may be an additional reason why he is little comprehended. His reputation will last because he is little read. Twenty pointed things in him are known by rote, which spare people the trouble of being acquainted with the remainder.

The divine Dante was an unfortunate person. Imagine not that he was divine in his own day; no one is a prophet at home. It is true he was a prior—not a prior of monks, but a prior of Florence, that is to say, one of its senators.

He was born in 1260, when the arts began to flourish in his native land. Florence, like Athens, abounded in greatness, wit, levity, inconstancy, and faction. The white faction was in great credit; it was called after a Signora Bianca. The opposing party was called the blacks, in contradistinction. These two parties sufficed not for the Florentines; they had also Guelphs and Ghibellines. The greater part of the whites were Ghibellines, attached to the party of the emperors; the blacks, on the other hand, sided with the Guelphs, the partisans of the popes.

All these factions loved liberty, but did all they could to destroy it. Pope Boniface VIII. wished to profit by these divisions in order to annihilate the power of the emperors in Italy. He declared Charles de Valois, brother of Philip the Fair, king of France, his vicar in Italy. The vicar came well armed and chased away the whites and the Ghibellines and made himself detested by blacks and Guelphs. Dante was a white and a Ghibelline; he was driven away among the first and his house razed to the ground. We may judge if he could be for the remainder of his life, favorable towards the French interest and to the popes. It is said, however, that he took a journey to Paris, and, to relieve his chagrin turned theologian and disputed vigorously in the schools. It is added that the emperor Henry VIII. did nothing for him, Ghibelline as he was, and that he repaired to Frederick of Aragon, king of Sicily, and returned as poor as he went. He subsequently died in poverty at Ravenna at the age of fifty-six. It was during these various peregrinations that he composed his divine comedy of "Hell, Purgatory, and Paradise."

[Voltaire here enters into a description of the *"Inferno,"* which it is unnecessary to insert, after the various translations into English. The conclusion, however, exhibiting our author's usual vivacity, is retained.]

Is all this in the comic style? No. In the heroic manner? No. What then is the taste of this poem? An exceedingly wild one, but it contains verses so happy and piquant that it has not lain dormant for four centuries and never will be laid aside. A poem, moreover, which puts popes into hell excites attention, and the sagacity of commentators is exhausted in correctly ascertaining who it is that Dante has damned, it being, of course, of the first consequence not to be deceived in a matter so important.

A chair and a lecture have been founded with a view to the exposition of this classic author. You ask me why the Inquisition acquiesces. I reply that in Italy the Inquisition understands raillery and knows that raillery in verse never does any harm.

DAVID.

We are called upon to reverence David as a prophet, as a king, as the ancestor of the holy spouse of Mary, as a man who merited the mercy of God from his penitence.

I will boldly assert that the article on "David," which raised up so many enemies to Bayle, the first author of a dictionary of facts and of reasonings, deserves not the strange noise which was made about it. It was not David that people were anxious to defend, but Bayle whom they were solicitous to destroy. Certain preachers of Holland, his mortal enemies, were so far blinded by their enmity as to blame him for having praised popes whom he thought meritorious, and for having refuted the unjust calumny with which they had been assailed.

This absurd and shameful piece of injustice was signed by a dozen theologians on Dec. 20, 1698, in the same consistory in which they pretended to take up the defence of King David. A great proof that the condemnation of Bayle arose from personal feeling is supplied by the fact of that which happened in 1761, to Mr. Peter Anet, in London. The doctors Chandler and Palmer, having delivered funeral sermons on the death of King George II., in which they compared him to King David, Mr. Anet, who did not regard this comparison as honorable to the deceased monarch, published his famous dissertation entitled, "The History of the Man after God's Own Heart." In that work he makes it clear that George II., a king much more powerful than David, did not fall into the errors of the Jewish sovereign, and consequently could not display the penitence which was the origin of the comparison.

He follows, step by step, the Books of Kings, examines the conduct of David with more severity than Bayle, and on it founds an opinion that the Holy Spirit does not praise actions of the nature of those attributed to David. The English author, in fact, judges the king of Judah upon the notions of justice and injustice which prevail at the present time.

He cannot approve of the assembly of a band of robbers by David to the amount of four hundred; of his being armed with the sword of Goliath, by the high priest Abimelech, from whom he received hallowed bread.

He could not think well of the expedition of David against the farmer, Nabal, in order to destroy his abode with fire and sword, because Nabal refused contributions to his troop of robbers; or of the death of Nabal a few days afterwards, whose widow David immediately espoused.

He condemned his conduct to King Achish, the possessor of a few villages in the district of Gath. David, at the head of five or six hundred banditti, made inroads upon the allies of his benefactor Achish. He pillaged the whole of them, massacred all the inhabitants, men, women, and children at the breast. And why the children at the breast? For fear, says the text, these children should carry the news to King Achish, who was deceived into a belief that these expeditions were undertaken against the Israelites, by an absolute lie on the part of David.

Again, Saul loses a battle and wishes his armor-bearer to slay him, who refuses; he wounds himself, but not effectually, and at his own desire a young man despatches him, who, carrying the news to David, is massacred for his pains.

Ishbosheth succeeds his father, Saul, and David makes war upon him. Finally Ishbosheth is assassinated.

David, possessed of the sole dominion, surprised the little town or village of Rabbah and put all the inhabitants to death by the most extraordinary devices—sawing them asunder, destroying them with harrows and axes of iron, and burning them in brick-kilns.

After these expeditions there was a famine in the country for three years. In fact, from this mode of making war, countries must necessarily be badly cultivated. The Lord was consulted as to the causes of the famine. The answer was easy. In a country which produces corn with difficulty, when laborers are baked in brick-kilns and sawed into pieces, few people remain to cultivate the earth. The Lord, however, replied that it was because Saul had formerly slain some Gibeonites.

What is David's speedy remedy? He assembles the Gibeonites, informs them that Saul had committed a great sin in making war upon them, and that Saul not being like him, a man after God's own heart, it would be proper to punish him in his posterity. He therefore makes them a present of seven grandsons of Saul to be hanged, who were accordingly hanged because there had been a famine.

Mr. Anet is so just as not to insist upon the adultery with Bathsheba and the murder of her husband, as these crimes were pardoned in consequence of the repentance of David. They were horrible and abominable, but being remitted by the Lord, the English author also absolves from them.

No one complained in England of the author, and the parliament took little interest in the history of a kinglet of a petty district in Syria.

Let justice be done to Father Calmet; he has kept within bounds in his dictionary of the Bible, in the article on "David." "We pretend not," said he, "to approve of the conduct of David, but it is to be believed that this excess of cruelty was committed before his repentance on the score of Bathsheba." Possibly he repented of all his crimes at the same time, which were sufficiently numerous.

Let us here ask what appears to us to be an important question. May we not exhibit a portion of contempt in the article on "David," and treat of his person and glory with the respect due to the sacred books? It is to the interest of mankind that crime should in no case be sanctified. What signifies what *he* is called, who massacres the wives and children of his allies; who hangs the grandchildren of his king; who saws his unhappy captives in two, tears them to pieces with harrows, or burns them in brick-kilns?

These actions we judge, and not the letters which compose the name of the criminal. His name neither augments nor diminishes the criminality.

The more David is revered after his reconciliation with God, the more are his previous qualities condemnable.

If a young peasant, in searching after she-asses finds a kingdom it is no common affair. If another peasant cures his king of insanity by a tune on the harp that is still more extraordinary. But when this petty player on the harp becomes king because he meets a village priest in secret, who pours a bottle of olive oil on his head, the affair is more marvellous still.

I know nothing either of the writers of these marvels, or of the time in which they were written, but I am certain that it was neither Polybius nor Tacitus.

I shall not speak here of the murder of Uriah, and of the adultery with Bathsheba, these facts being sufficiently well known. The ways of God are not the ways of men, since He permitted the descent of Jesus Christ from this very Bathsheba, everything being rendered pure by so holy a mystery.

I ask not now how Jurieu had the audacity to persecute the wise Bayle for not approving all the actions of the good King David. I only inquire why a man like Jurieu is suffered to molest a man like Bayle.

DECRETALS.

These are letters of the popes which regulate points of doctrine and discipline and which have the force of law in the Latin church.

Besides the genuine ones collected by Denis le Petit, there is a collection of false ones, the author of which, as well as the date, is unknown. It was an archbishop of Mentz called Riculphus who circulated it in France about the end of the eighth century; he had also brought to Worms an epistle of Pope Gregory, which had never before been heard of, but no vestige of the latter is at present remaining, while the false decretals, as we shall see, have met with the greatest success for eight centuries.

This collection bears the name of Isidore Mercator, and comprehends an infinite number of decrees falsely ascribed to the popes, from Clement I. down to Siricius. The false donation of Constantine; the Council of Rome under Sylvester; the letter of Athanasius to Mark; that of Anastasius to the bishops of Germany and Burgundy; that of Sixtus III. to the Orientals; that of Leo. I. relating to the privileges of the rural bishops; that of John I. to the archbishop Zachariah; one of Boniface II. to Eulalia of Alexandria; one of John III. to the bishops of France and Burgundy; one of Gregory, containing a privilege of the monastery of St. Médard; one from the same to Felix, bishop of Messina, and many others.

The object of the author was to extend the authority of the pope and the bishops. With this view, he lays it down as a principle that they can be definitely judged only by the pope, and he often repeats this maxim that not only every bishop but every priest, and, generally, every oppressed individual may, in any stage of a cause, appeal directly to the pope. He likewise considers it as an incontestable principle that no council, not even a provincial one, may be held without the permission of the pope.

These decretals, favoring the impunity of bishops, and still more the ambitious pretensions of the popes, were eagerly adopted by them both. In 861, Rotade, bishop of Soissons, being deprived of episcopal communion in a provincial council on account of disobedience, appeals to the pope. Hincmar of Rheims, his metropolitan, notwithstanding his appeal, deposes him in another council under the pretext that he had afterwards renounced it, and submitted himself to the judgment of the bishops.

Pope Nicholas I. being informed of this affair, wrote to Hincmar, and blamed his proceedings. "You ought," says he, "to honor the memory of St. Peter, and await our judgment, even although Rotade had not appealed." And in another letter on the same matter, he threatens Hincmar with excommunication, if he does not restore Rotade. That pope did more. Rotade having arrived at Rome, he declared him acquitted in a council held on Christmas eve, 864; and dismissed him to his see with letters. That which he addressed to all the bishops is worthy of notice, and is as follows:

"What you say is absurd, that Rotade, after having appealed to the holy see, changed his language and submitted himself anew to your judgment. Even although he had done so, it would have been your duty to set him right, and teach him that an appeal never lies from a superior judge to an inferior one. But even although he had not appealed to the holy see, you ought by no means to depose a bishop without our participation, in prejudice of so many decretals of our predecessors; for, if it be by their judgment that the writings of other doctors are approved or rejected, how much more should that be respected which they have themselves written, to decide on points of doctrine and discipline. Some tell you that these decretals are not in the book of canons; yet those same persons, when they find them favorable to their designs, use both without distinction, and reject them only to lessen the power of the holy see. If the decretals of the ancient popes are to be rejected because they are not contained in the book of canons, the writings of St. Gregory, and the rest of the fathers, must, on the same principle, be rejected also, and even the Holy Scriptures themselves."

"You say," the pope continues, "that judgments upon bishops are not among the higher causes; we maintain that they are high in proportion as bishops hold a high rank in the church. Will you assert that it is only metropolitan affairs which constitute the higher causes? But metropolitans are not of a different order from bishops, and we do not demand different witnesses or judges in the one case, from what are usual in the other; we therefore require that causes which involve either should be reserved for us. And, finally, can anyone be found so utterly unreasonable as to say that all other churches ought to preserve their privileges, and that the Roman Church alone should lose hers?" He concludes with ordering them to receive and replace Rotade.

Pope Adrian, the successor of Nicholas I., seems to have been no less zealous in a similar case relating to Hincmar of Laon. That prelate had rendered himself hateful both to the clergy and people of his diocese, by various acts of injustice and violence. Having been accused before the Council of Verberie—at which Hincmar of Rheims, his uncle and metropolitan, presided—he appealed to the pope, and demanded permission to go to Rome. This was refused him. The process against him was merely suspended, and the affair went no farther. But upon new matters of complaint brought against him by Charles the Bald and Hincmar of Rheims, he was cited at first before the Council of Attigny, where he appeared, and soon afterwards fled; and then before the Council of Douzy, where he renewed his appeal, and was deposed. The council wrote to the pope a synodal letter, on Sept. 6, 871, to request of him a confirmation of the acts which they sent him; but Adrian, far from acquiescing in the judgment of the council, expressed in the strongest terms his disapprobation of the condemnation of Hincmar; maintaining that, since Hincmar declared before the council that he appealed to the holy see, they ought not to have pronounced any sentence of condemnation upon him. Such were the terms used by that pope, in his letter to the bishops of the council, as also in that which he wrote to the king.

The following is the vigorous answer sent by Charles to Adrian: "Your letters say, 'We will and ordain, by apostolical authority, that Hincmar of Laon shall come to Rome and present himself before us, resting upon your supremacy.'

"We wonder where the writer of this letter discovered that a king, whose duty it is to chastise the guilty and be the avenger of crimes, should send to Rome a criminal convicted according to legal forms, and more especially one who, before his deposition, was found guilty, in three councils, of enterprises against the public peace; and who, after his deposition, persisted in his disobedience.

"We are compelled further to tell you, that we, kings of France, born of a royal race, have never yet passed for the deputies of bishops, but for sovereigns of the earth. And, as St. Leon and the Roman council have said, kings and emperors, whom God has appointed to govern the world, have permitted bishops to regulate their affairs according to their ordinances, but they have never been the stewards of bishops; and if you search the records of your predecessors, you will not find that they have ever written to persons in our exalted situation as you have done in the present instance."

He then adduces two letters of St. Gregory, to show with what modesty he wrote, not only to the kings of France, but to the exarchs of Italy. "Finally," he concludes, "I beg that you will never more send to me, or to the bishops of my kingdom, similar letters, if you wish that we should give to what you write that honor and respect which we would willingly grant it." The bishops of the Council of Douzy answered the pope nearly in the same strain; and, although we have not the entire letter, it appears that their object in it was to prove that Hincmar's appeal ought not to be decided at Rome, but in France, by judges delegated conformably to the canons of the Council of Sardis.

These examples are sufficient to show how the popes extended their jurisdiction by the instrumentality of these false decretals; and although Hincmar of Rheims objected to Adrian, that, not being included in the book of canons, they could not subvert the discipline established by the canons—which occasioned his being accused, before Pope John VIII., of not admitting the decretals of the popes—he constantly cited these decretals as authorities, in his letters and other writings, and his example was followed by many bishops. At first, those only were admitted which were not contrary to the more recent canons, and afterwards there was less and less scruple.

The councils themselves made use of them. Thus, in that of Rheims, held in 992, the bishops availed themselves of the decretals of Anacletus, of Julius, of Damasus, and other popes, in the cause of Arnoul. Succeeding councils imitated that of Rheims. The popes Gregory VII., Urban II., Pascal II., Urban III., and Alexander III. supported the maxims they found in them, persuaded that they constituted the discipline of the flourishing age of the church. Finally, the compilers of the canons—Bouchard of Worms, Yves of Chartres, and Gratian—introduced them into their collection. After they became publicly taught in the schools, and commented upon, all the polemical and scholastic divines, and all the expositors of the canon law, eagerly laid hold of these false decretals to confirm the Catholic dogmas, or to establish points of discipline, and scattered them profusely through their works.

It was not till the sixteenth century that the first suspicions of their authenticity were excited. Erasmus, and many others with him, called them in question upon the following grounds:

1. The decretals contained in the collection of Isidore are not in that of Denis le Petit, who cited none of the decretals of the popes before the time of Siricius. Yet he informs us that he took extreme care in collecting them. They could not, therefore, have escaped him, if they had existed in the archives of the see of Rome, where he resided. If they were unknown to the holy see, to which they were favorable, they were so to the whole church. The fathers and councils of the first eight centuries have made no mention of them. But how can this universal silence be reconciled with their authenticity?

2. These decretals do not all correspond with the state of things existing at the time in which they are supposed to have been written. Not a word is said of

the heresies of the three first centuries, nor of other ecclesiastical affairs with which the genuine works of the same period are filled. This proves that they were fabricated afterwards.

3. Their dates are almost always false. Their author generally follows the chronology of the pontifical book, which, by Baronius's own confession, is very incorrect. This is a presumptive evidence that the collection was not composed till after the pontifical book.

4. These decretals, in all the citations of Scripture passages which they contain, use the version known by the name of "Vulgate," made, or at least revised, by St. Jerome. They are, therefore, of later date than St. Jerome.

Finally, they are all written in the same style, which is very barbarous; and, in that respect, corresponding to the ignorance of the eighth century: but it is not by any means probable that all the different popes, whose names they bear, affected that uniformity of style. It may be concluded with confidence, that all the decretals are from the same hand.

Besides these general reasons, each of the documents which form Isidore's collection carries with it marks of forgery peculiar to itself, and none of which have escaped the keen criticism of David Blondel, to whom we are principally indebted for the light thrown at the present day on this compilation, now no longer known but as "The False Decretals";

but the usages introduced in consequence of it exist not the less through a considerable portion of Europe.

DELUGE (UNIVERSAL).

We begin with observing that we are believers in the universal deluge, because it is recorded in the holy Hebrew Scriptures transmitted to Christians. We consider it as a miracle:

1. Because all the facts by which God condescends to interfere in the sacred books are so many miracles.

2. Because the sea could not rise fifteen cubits, or one-and-twenty standard feet and a half, above the highest mountains, without leaving its bed dry, and, at the same time, violating all the laws of gravity and the equilibrium of fluids, which would evidently require a miracle.

3. Because, even although it might rise to the height mentioned, the ark could not have contained, according to known physical laws, all the living things of the earth, together with their food, for so long a time; considering that lions, tigers, panthers, leopards, ounces, rhinoceroses, bears, wolves, hyenas, eagles, hawks, kites, vultures, falcons, and all carnivorous animals, which feed on flesh alone, would have died of hunger, even after having devoured all the other species.

There was printed some time ago, in an appendix to Pascal's "Thoughts," a dissertation of a merchant of Rouen, called Le Peletier, in which he proposes a plan for building a vessel in which all kinds of animals might be included and maintained for the space of a year. It is clear that this merchant never superintended even a poultry-yard. We cannot but look upon M. Le Peletier, the architect of the ark, as a visionary, who knew nothing about menageries; and upon the deluge as an adorable miracle, fearful, and incomprehensible to the feeble reason of M. Le Peletier, as well as to our own.

4. Because the physical impossibility of a universal deluge, by natural means, can be strictly demonstrated. The demonstration is as follows: All the seas cover half the globe. A common measure of their depths near the shores, and in the open ocean, is assumed to be five hundred feet.

In order that they might cover both hemispheres to the depth of five hundred feet, not only would an ocean of that depth be necessary over all the land, but a new sea would, in addition, be required to envelop the ocean at present existing, without which the laws of hydrostatics would occasion the dispersion of that other new mass of water five hundred feet deep, which should remain covering the land. Thus, then, two new oceans are requisite to cover the terraqueous globe merely to the depth of five hundred feet.

Supposing the mountains to be only twenty thousand feet high, forty oceans, each five hundred feet in height, would be required to accumulate on each other, merely in order to equal the height of the mountains. Every successive ocean would contain all the others, and the last of them all would have a circumference containing forty times that of the first.

In order to form this mass of water, it would be necessary to create it out of nothing. In order to withdraw it, it would be necessary to annihilate it. The event of the deluge, then, is a double miracle, and the greatest that has ever manifested the power of the eternal Sovereign of all worlds.

We are exceedingly surprised that some learned men have attributed to this deluge some small shell found in many parts of our continent. We are still more surprised at what we find under the article on "Deluge," in the grand "Encyclopædia." An author is quoted in it, who says things so very profound that they may be considered as chimerical. This is the first characteristic of Pluche. He proves the possibility of the deluge by the history of the giants who made war against the gods!

Briareus, according to him, is clearly the deluge, for it signifies "the loss of serenity": and in what language does it signify this loss?—in Hebrew. But *Briareus* is a Greek word, which means "robust": it is not a Hebrew word. Even if, by chance, it had been so, we should beware of imitating Bochart, who derives so many Greek, Latin, and even French words from the Hebrew idiom. The Greeks certainly knew no more of the Jewish idiom than of the language of the Chinese.

The giant Othus is also in Hebrew, according to Pluche, "the derangement of the seasons." But it is also a Greek word, which does not signify anything, at least, that I know; and even if it did, what, let me ask, could it have to do with the Hebrew?

Porphyrion is "a shaking of the earth," in Hebrew; but in Greek, it is porphyry. This has nothing to do with the deluge.

Mimos is "a great rain"; for once, he does mention a name which may bear upon the deluge. But in Greek *mimos* means mimic, comedian. There are no means of tracing the deluge of such an origin. *Enceladus* is another proof of the deluge in Hebrew; for, according to Pluche, it is the fountain of time; but, unluckily, in Greek it is "noise."

Ephialtes, another demonstration of the deluge in Hebrew; for *ephialtes*, which signifies leaper, oppressor, incubus, in Greek is, according to Pluche, "a vast accumulation of clouds."

But the Greeks, having taken everything from the Hebrews, with whom they were unacquainted, clearly gave to their giants all those names which Pluche extracts from the Hebrew as well as he can, and all as a memorial of the deluge.

Such is the reasoning of Pluche. It is he who cites the author of the article on "Deluge" without refuting him. Does he speak seriously, or does he jest? I do not know. All I know is, that there is scarcely a single system to be found at which one can forbear jesting.

I have some apprehension that the article in the grand "Encyclopædia," attributed to M. Boulanger, is not serious. In that case, we ask whether it is philosophical. Philosophy is so often deceived, that we shall not venture to decide against M. Boulanger.

Still less shall we venture to ask what was that abyss which was broken up, or what were the cataracts of heaven which were opened. Isaac Vossius denies the universality of the deluge: "*Hoc est pie nugari.*" Calmet maintains it; informing us, that bodies have no weight in air, but in consequence of their being compressed by air. Calmet was not much of a natural philosopher, and the weight of the air has nothing to do with the deluge. Let us content ourselves with reading and respecting everything in the Bible, without comprehending a single word of it.

I do not comprehend how God created a race of men in order to drown them, and then substituted in their room a race still viler than the first.

How seven pairs of all kinds of clean animals should come from the four quarters of the globe, together with two pairs of unclean ones, without the wolves devouring the sheep on the way, or the kites the pigeons, etc.

How eight persons could keep in order, feed, and water, such an immense number of inmates, shut up in an ark for nearly two years; for, after the cessation of the deluge, it would be necessary to have food for all these passengers for another year, in consequence of the herbage being so scanty.

I am not like M. Le Peletier. I admire everything, and explain nothing.

DEMOCRACY.

Le pire des états, c'est l'état populaire.
That sway is worst, in which the people rule.

Such is the opinion which Cinna gave Augustus. But on the other hand, Maximus maintains, that

Le pire des états, c'est l'état monarchique.
That sway is worst, in which a monarch rules.

Bayle, in his "Philosophical Dictionary," after having repeatedly advocated both sides of the question, gives, under the article on "Pericles," a most disgusting picture of democracy, and more particularly that of Athens.

A republican, who is a stanch partisan of democracy, and one of our "proposers of questions," sends us his refutation of Bayle and his apology for Athens. We will adduce his reasons. It is the privilege of every writer to judge the living and the dead; he who thus sits in judgment will be himself judged by others, who, in their turn, will be judged also; and thus, from age to age, all sentences are, according to circumstances, reversed or reformed.

Bayle, then, after some common-place observations, uses these words: "A man would look in vain into the history of Macedon for as much tyranny as he finds in the history of Athens."

Perhaps Bayle was discontented with Holland when he thus wrote; and probably my republican friend, who refutes him, is contented with his little democratic city "for the present."

It is difficult to weigh, in an exquisitely nice balance, the iniquities of the republic of Athens and of the court of Macedon. We still upbraid the Athenians with the banishment of Cimon, Aristides, Themistocles, and Alcibiades, and the sentences of death upon Phocion and Socrates; sentences similar in absurdity and cruelty to those of some of our own tribunals.

In short, what we can never pardon in the Athenians is the execution of their six victorious generals, condemned because they had not time to bury their dead after the victory, and because they were prevented from doing so by a tempest. The sentence is at once so ridiculous and barbarous, it bears such a stamp of superstition and ingratitude, that those of the Inquisition, those delivered against Urbain Grandier, against the wife of Marshal d'Ancre, against Montrin, and against innumerable sorcerers and witches, etc., are not, in fact, fooleries more atrocious.

It is in vain to say, in excuse of the Athenians, that they believed, like Homer before them, that the souls of the dead were always wandering, unless they had received the honors of sepulture or burning. A folly is no excuse for a barbarity.

A dreadful evil, indeed, for the souls of a few Greeks to ramble for a week or two on the shores of the ocean! The evil is, in consigning living men to the executioner; living men who have won a battle for you; living men, to whom you ought to be devoutly grateful.

Thus, then, are the Athenians convicted of having been at once the most silly and the most barbarous judges in the world. But we must now place in the balance the crimes of the court of Macedon; we shall see that that court far exceeds Athens in point of tyranny and atrocity.

There is ordinarily no comparison to be made between the crimes of the great, who are always ambitious, and those of the people, who never desire, and who never can desire, anything but liberty and equality. These two sentiments, "liberty and equality," do not *necessarily* lead to calumny, rapine, assassination, poisoning, and devastation of the lands of neighbors; but, the towering ambition and thirst for power of the great precipitate them head-long into every species of crime in all periods and all places.

In this same Macedon, the virtue of which Bayle opposes to that of Athens, we see nothing but a tissue of tremendous crimes for a series of two hundred years.

It is Ptolemy, the uncle of Alexander the Great, who assassinates his brother Alexander to usurp the kingdom. It is Philip, his brother, who spends his life in guilt and perjury, and ends it by a stab from Pausanias.

Olympias orders Queen Cleopatra and her son to be thrown into a furnace of molten brass. She assassinates Aridæus. Antigonus assassinates

Eumenes. Antigonus Gonatas, his son, poisons the governor of the citadel of Corinth, marries his widow, expels her, and takes possession of the citadel. Philip, his grandson, poisons Demetrius, and defiles the whole of Macedon with murders. Perseus kills his wife with his own hand, and poisons his brother. These perfidies and cruelties are authenticated in history.

Thus, then, for two centuries, the madness of despotism converts Macedon into a theatre for every crime; and in the same space of time you see the popular government of Athens stained only by five or six acts of judicial iniquity, five or six certainly atrocious judgments, of which the people in every instance repented, and for which they made, as far as they could, honorable expiation (*amende honorable.*) They asked pardon of Socrates after his death, and erected to his memory the small temple called *Socrateion.* They asked pardon of Phocion, and raised a statue to his honor. They asked pardon of the six generals, so ridiculously condemned and so basely executed. They confined in chains the principal accuser, who, with difficulty, escaped from public vengeance. The Athenian people, therefore, appear to have had good natural dispositions, connected, as they were, with great versatility and frivolity. In what despotic state has the injustice of precipitate decrees ever been thus ingenuously acknowledged and deplored?

Bayle, then, is for this once in the wrong. My republican has reason on his side. Popular government, therefore, is in itself iniquitous, and less abominable than monarchical despotism.

The great vice of democracy is certainly not tyranny and cruelty. There have been republicans in mountainous regions wild and ferocious; but they were made so, not by the spirit of republicanism, but by nature. The North American savages were entirely republican; but they were republics of bears.

The radical vice of a civilized republic is expressed by the Turkish fable of the dragon with many heads, and the dragon with many tails. The multitude of heads become injurious, and the multitude of tails obey one single head, which wants to devour all.

Democracy seems to suit only a very small country; and even that fortunately situated. Small as it may be, it will commit many faults, because it will be composed of men. Discord will prevail in it, as in a convent of monks; but there will be no St. Bartholomews there, no Irish massacre, no Sicilian vespers, no Inquisition, no condemnation to the galleys for having taken water from the ocean without paying for it; at least, unless it be a republic of devils, established in some corner of hell.

After having taken the side of my Swiss friend against the dexterous fencing-master, Bayle, I will add: That the Athenians were warriors like the Swiss, and as polite as the Parisians were under Louis XIV.; that they excelled in every art requiring genius or execution, like the Florentine in time of the Medici; that they were the masters of the Romans in the sciences and in eloquence, even in the days of Cicero; that this same people, insignificant in number, who scarcely possessed anything of territory, and who, at the present day, consist only of a band of ignorant slaves, a hundred times less numerous than the Jews, and deprived of all but their name, yet bear away the palm from Roman power, by their ancient reputation, which triumphs at once over time and degradation.

Europe has seen a republic, ten times smaller than Athens, attract its attention for the space of one hundred and fifty years, and its name placed by the side of that of Rome, even while she still commanded kings; while she condemned one Henry, a sovereign of France, and absolved and scourged another Henry, the first man of his age; even while Venice retained her ancient splendor, and the republic of the seven United Provinces was astonishing Europe and the Indies, by its successful establishment and extensive commerce.

This almost imperceptible ant-hill could not be crushed by the royal demon of the South, and the monarch of two worlds, nor by the intrigues of the Vatican, which put in motion one-half of Europe. It resisted by words and by arms; and with the help of a Picard who wrote, and a small number of Swiss who fought for it, it became at length established and triumphant, and was enabled to say, "Rome and I." She kept all minds divided between the rich pontiffs who succeeded to the Scipios—*Romanos rerum dominos*—and the poor inhabitants of a corner of the world long unknown in a country of poverty and *goîtres*.

The main point was, to decide how Europe should think on the subject of certain questions which no one understood. It was the conflict of the human mind. The Calvins, the Bezas, and Turetins, were the Demostheneses, Platos, and Aristotles, of the day.

The absurdity of the greater part of the controversial questions which bound down the attention of Europe, having at length been acknowledged, this small republic turned our consideration to what appears of solid consequence—the acquisition of wealth. The system of law, more chimerical and less baleful than that of the supralapsarians and the sublapsarians, occupied with arithmetical calculations those who could no longer gain celebrity as partisans of the doctrine of crucified divinity. They became rich, but were no longer famous.

It is thought at present there is no republic, except in Europe. I am mistaken if I have not somewhere made the remark myself; it must, however, have been a great inadvertence. The Spaniards found in America the republic of Tlascala perfectly well established. Every part of that continent which has not been subjugated is still republican. In the whole of that vast territory, when it was first discovered, there existed no more than two kingdoms; and this may well be considered as a proof that republican government is the most natural. Men must have obtained considerable refinement, and have tried many experiments, before they submit to the government of a single individual.

In Africa, the Hottentots, the Kaffirs, and many communities of negroes, are democracies. It is pretended that the countries in which the greater part of the negroes are sold are governed by kings. Tripoli, Tunis, and Algiers are republics of soldiers and pirates. There are similar ones in India. The Mahrattas, and many other Indian hordes, have no kings: they elect chiefs when they go on their expeditions of plunder.

Such are also many of the hordes of Tartars. Even the Turkish Empire has long been a republic of janissaries, who have frequently strangled their sultan, when their sultan did not decimate them. We are every day asked, whether a republican or a kingly government is to be preferred? The dispute always ends in agreeing that the government of men is exceedingly difficult. The Jews had God himself for their master; yet observe the events of their history. They have almost always been trampled upon and enslaved; and, nationally, what a wretched figure do they make at present!

DEMONIACS.

Hypochondriacal and epileptic persons, and women laboring under hysterical affections, have always been considered the victims of evil spirits, malignant demons and divine vengeance. We have seen that this disease was called the sacred disease; and that while the physicians were ignorant, the priests of antiquity obtained everywhere the care and management of such diseases.

When the symptoms were very complicated, the patient was supposed to be possessed with many demons—a demon of madness, one of luxury, one of avarice, one of obstinacy, one of short-sightedness, one of deafness; and the exorciser could not easily miss finding a demon of foolery created, with another of knavery.

The Jews expelled devils from the bodies of the possessed, by the application of the root *barath*, and a certain formula of words; our Saviour expelled them by a divine virtue; he communicated that virtue to his apostles, but it is now greatly impaired.

A short time since, an attempt was made to renew the history of St. Paulin. That saint saw on the roof of a church a poor demoniac, who walked under, or rather upon, this roof or ceiling, with his head below and his feet above, nearly in the manner of a fly. St. Paulin clearly perceived that the man was possessed, and sent several leagues off for some relics of St. Felix of Nola, which were applied to the patient as blisters. The demon who supported the man against the roof instantly fled, and the demoniac fell down upon the pavement.

We may have doubts about this history, while we preserve the most profound respect for genuine miracles; and we may be permitted to observe that this is not the way in which we now cure demoniacs. We bleed them, bathe them, and gently relax them by medicine; we apply emollients to them. This is M. Pome's treatment of them; and he has performed more cures than the priests of Isis or Diana, or of anyone else who ever wrought by miracles. As to demoniacs who say they are possessed merely to gain money, instead of being bathed, they are at present flogged.

It often happened, that the specific gravity of epileptics, whose fibres and muscles withered away, was lighter than water, and that they floated when put into it. A miracle! was instantly exclaimed. It was pronounced that such a person must be a demoniac or sorcerer; and holy water or the executioner was immediately sent for. It was an unquestionable proof that either the demon had become master of the body of the floating person, or that the latter had voluntarily delivered himself over to the demon. On the first supposition the person was exorcised, on the second he was burned. Thus have we been reasoning and acting for a period of fifteen or sixteen hundred years, and yet we have the effrontery to laugh at the Kaffirs.

In 1603, in a small village of Franche-Comté, a woman of quality made her granddaughter read aloud the lives of the saints in the presence of her parents; this young woman, who was, in some respects, very well informed, but ignorant of orthography, substituted the word *histories* for that of *lives* (*vies*). Her step-mother, who hated her, said to her in a tone of harshness, "Why don't you read as it is there?" The girl blushed and trembled, but did not venture to say anything; she wished to avoid disclosing which of her companions had interpreted the word upon a false orthography, and prevented her using it. A monk, who was the family confessor, pretended that the devil had taught her the word. The girl chose to be silent rather than vindicate herself; her silence was considered as amounting to confession; the Inquisition convicted her of having made a compact with the devil: she was condemned to be burned, because she had a large fortune from her mother, and the confiscated property went by law to the inquisitors. She was the hundred thousandth victim of the doctrine of demoniacs, persons possessed by devils and exorcisms, and of the real devils who swayed the world.

DESTINY.

Of all the books written in the western climes of the world, which have reached our times, Homer is the most ancient. In his works we find the manners of profane antiquity, coarse heroes, and material gods, made after the image of man, but mixed up with reveries and absurdities; we also find the seeds of philosophy, and more particularly the idea of destiny, or necessity, who is the dominatrix of the gods, as the gods are of the world.

When the magnanimous Hector determines to fight the magnanimous Achilles, and runs away with all possible speed, making the circuit of the city three times, in order to increase his vigor; when Homer compares the light-footed Achilles, who pursues him, to a man that is asleep! and when Madame Dacier breaks into a rapture of admiration at the art and meaning exhibited in this passage, it is precisely then that Jupiter, desirous of saving the great Hector who has offered up to him so many sacrifices, bethinks him of consulting the destinies, upon weighing the fates of Hector and Achilles in a balance. He finds that the Trojan must inevitably be killed by the Greek, and is not only unable to oppose it, but from that moment Apollo, the guardian genius of Hector, is compelled to abandon him. It is not to be denied that Homer is frequently extravagant, and even on this very occasion displays a contradictory flow of ideas, according to the privilege of antiquity; but yet he is the first in whom we meet with the notion of destiny. It may be concluded, then, that in his days it was a prevalent one.

The Pharisees, among the small nation of Jews, did not adopt the idea of a destiny till many ages after. For these Pharisees themselves, who were the most learned class among the Jews, were but of very recent date. They mixed up, in Alexandria, a portion of the dogmas of the Stoics with their ancient Jewish ideas. St. Jerome goes so far as to state that their sect is but a little anterior to our vulgar era.

Philosophers would never have required the aid of Homer, or of the Pharisees, to be convinced that everything is performed according to immutable laws, that everything is ordained, that everything is, in fact, *necessary*. The manner in which they reason is as follows:

Either the world subsists by its own nature, by its own physical laws, or a Supreme Being has formed it according to His supreme laws: in both cases these laws are immovable; in both cases everything is necessary; heavy bodies tend towards the centre of the earth without having any power or tendency to rest in the air. Pear-trees cannot produce pine-apples. The instinct of a spaniel cannot be the instinct of an ostrich; everything is arranged, adjusted, and fixed.

Man can have only a certain number of teeth, hairs, and ideas; and a period arrives when he necessarily loses his teeth, hair, and ideas.

It is contradictory to say that yesterday should not have been; or that to-day does not exist; it is just as contradictory to assert that that which is to come will not inevitably be.

Could you derange the destiny of a single fly there would be no possible reason why you should not control the destiny of all other flies, of all other animals, of all men, of all nature. You would find, in fact, that you were more powerful than God.

Weak-minded persons say: "My physician has brought my aunt safely through a mortal disease; he has added ten years to my aunt's life." Others of more judgment say, the prudent man makes his own destiny.

> *Nullum numen abest, si sit Prudentia, sed te*
> *Nos facimus, Fortuna, deam cœoque locamus.*
> —JUVENAL, *Sat*. x. v. 365.

We call on Fortune, and her aid implore, While Prudence is the goddess to adore.

But frequently the prudent man succumbs under his destiny instead of making it; it is destiny which makes men prudent. Profound politicians assure us that if Cromwell, Ludlow, Ireton, and a dozen other parliamentary leaders, had been assassinated eight days before Charles I. had his head cut off, that king would have continued alive and have died in his bed; they are right; and they may add, that if all England had been swallowed up in the sea, that king would not have perished on a scaffold before Whitehall. But things were so arranged that Charles was to have his head cut off.

Cardinal d'Ossat was unquestionably more clever than an idiot of the *petites maisons*; but is it not evident that the organs of the wise d'Ossat were differently formed than those of that idiot?—Just as the organs of a fox are different from those of a crane or a lark.

Your physician saved your aunt, but in so doing he certainly did not contradict the order of nature, but followed it. It is clear that your aunt could not prevent her birth in a certain place, that she could not help being affected by a certain malady, at a certain time; that the physician could be in no other place than where he was, that your aunt could not but apply to him, that he could not but prescribe medicines which cured her, or were thought to cure her, while nature was the sole physician.

A peasant thinks that it hailed upon his field by chance; but the philosopher knows that there was no chance, and that it was absolutely impossible, according to the constitution of the world, for it not to have hailed at that very time and place.

There are some who, being shocked by this truth, concede only half of it, like debtors who offer one moiety of their property to their creditors, and ask remission for the other. There are, they say, some events which are necessary, and others which are not so. It would be curious for one part of the world to be changed and the other not; that one part of what happens should happen inevitably, and another fortuitously. When we examine the question closely, we see that the doctrine opposed to that of destiny is absurd; but many men are destined to be bad reasoners, others not to reason at all, and others to persecute those who reason well or ill.

Some caution us by saying, "Do not believe in fatalism, for, if you do, everything appearing to you unavoidable, you will exert yourself for nothing; you will sink down in indifference; you will regard neither wealth, nor honors, nor praise; you will be careless about acquiring anything whatever; you will consider yourself meritless and powerless; no talent will be cultivated, and all will be overwhelmed in apathy."

Do not be afraid, gentlemen; we shall always have passions and prejudices, since it is our destiny to be subjected to prejudices and passions. We shall very well know that it no more depends upon us to have great merit or superior talents than to have a fine head of hair, or a beautiful hand; we shall be convinced that we ought to be vain of nothing, and yet vain we shall always be.

I have necessarily the passion for writing as I now do; and, as for you, you have the passion for censuring me; we are both equally fools, both equally the sport of destiny. Your nature is to do ill, mine is to love truth, and publish it in spite of you.

The owl, while supping upon mice in his ruined tower, said to the nightingale, "Stop your singing there in your beautiful arbor, and come to my hole that I may eat you." The nightingale replied, "I am born to sing where I am, and to laugh at you."

You ask me what is to become of liberty: I do not understand you; I do not know what the liberty you speak of really is. You have been so long disputing about the nature of it that you do not understand it. If you are willing, or rather, if you are able to examine with me coolly what it is, turn to the letter L.

DEVOTEE.

The word devout (*dévot*) signifies devoted (*dévoué*), and, in the strict sense of the term, can only be applicable to monks, and to females belonging to some religious order and under vows. But as the gospel makes no mention of vows or devotees, the title should not, in fact, be given to any person: the whole world ought to be equally just. A man who calls himself devout is like a plebeian who calls himself a marquis; he arrogates a quality which does not belong to him; he thinks himself a better man than his neighbor. We pardon this folly in women; their weakness and frivolity render them excusable; they pass, poor things, from a lover to a spiritual director with perfect sincerity, but we cannot pardon the knaves who direct them, who abuse their ignorance, and establish the throne of their pride on the credulity of the sex. They form a snug mystical harem, composed of seven or eight elderly beauties subjugated by the weight of inoccupation, and almost all these subjects pay tribute to their new master. No young women without lovers; no elderly devotee without a director.—Oh, how much more shrewd are the Orientals than we! A pasha never says, "We supped last night with the aga of the janissaries, who is my sister's lover; and with the vicar of the mosque, who is my wife's director."

DIAL.

Dial of Ahaz.

It is well known that everything is miraculous in the history of the Jews; the miracle performed in favor of King Hezekiah on the dial of Ahaz is one of the greatest that ever took place: it is evident that the whole earth must have been deranged, the course of the stars changed forever, and the periods of the eclipses of the sun and moon so altered as to confuse all the ephemerides. This was the second time the prodigy happened. Joshua had stopped the sun at noon on Gibeon, and the moon on Ascalon, in order to get time to kill a troop of Amorites already crushed by a shower of stones from heaven.

The sun, instead of stopping for King Hezekiah, went back, which is nearly the same thing, only differently described.

In the first place Isaiah said to Hezekiah, who was sick, "Thus saith the Lord, set thine house in order; for thou shalt die and not live."

Hezekiah wept and God was softened; He signified to him, through Isaiah, that he should still live fifteen years, and that in three days he should go to the temple; then Isaiah brought a plaster of figs and put it on the king's ulcers, and he was cured—"*et curatus est.*"

Hezekiah demanded a sign to convince him that he should be cured. Isaiah said to him, "Shall the shadow go forward ten degrees, or go back ten degrees?" And Hezekiah answered, "It is a light thing for the shadow to go down ten degrees; let the shadow return backward ten degrees." And Isaiah the prophet cried unto the Lord, and He brought the shadow ten degrees backwards from the point to which it had gone down on the dial of Ahaz.

We should like to know what this dial of Ahaz was; whether it was the work of a dialmaker named Ahaz, or whether it was a present made to a king of that name, it is an object of curiosity. There have been many disputes on this dial; the learned have proved that the Jews never knew either clocks or dials before their captivity in Babylon—the only time, say they, in which they learned anything of the Chaldæans, or the greater part of the nation began to read or write. It is even known that in their language they had no words to express clock, dial, geometry, or astronomy; and in the Book of Kings the dial of Ahaz is called the hour of the stone.

But the grand question is to know how King Hezekiah, the possessor of this clock, or dial of the sun—this hour of stone—could tell that it was easy to advance the sun ten degrees. It is certainly as difficult to make it advance against its ordinary motion as to make it go backward.

The proposition of the prophet appears as astonishing as the discourse of the king: Shall the shadow go forward ten degrees, or go back ten degrees? That would have been well said in some town of Lapland, where the longest day of the year is twenty hours; but at Jerusalem, where the longest day of the year is about fourteen hours and a half, ii was absurd. The king and the prophet deceived each other grossly. We do not deny the miracle, we firmly believe it; we only remark that Hezekiah and Isaiah knew not what they said. Whatever the hour, it was a thing equally impossible to make the shadow of the dial advance or recede ten hours. If it were two hours after noon, the prophet could, no doubt, have very well made the shadow of the dial go back to four o'clock in the morning; but in this case he could not have advanced it ten hours, since then it would have been midnight, and at that time it is not usual to have a shadow of the sun in perfection.

It is difficult to discover when this strange history was written, but perhaps it was towards the time in which the Jews only confusedly knew that there were clocks and sun-dials. In that case it is true that they got but a very imperfect knowledge of these sciences until they went to Babylon. There is a still greater difficulty of which the commentators have not thought; which is that the Jews did not count by hours as we do.

The same miracle happened in Greece, the day that Atreus served up the children of Thyestes for their father's supper.

The same miracle was still more sensibly performed at the time of Jupiter's intrigue with Alcmena. It required a night double the natural length to form Hercules. These adventures are common in antiquity, but very rare in our days, in which all things have degenerated.

DICTIONARY.

The invention of dictionaries, which was unknown to antiquity, is of the most unquestionable utility; and the "Encyclopædia," which was suggested by Messrs. d'Alembert and Diderot, and so successfully completed by them and their associates, notwithstanding all its defects, is a decisive evidence of it. What we find there under the article "Dictionary" would be a sufficient instance; it is done by the hand of a master.

I mean to speak here only of a new species of historical dictionaries, which contain a series of lies and satires in alphabetical order; such is the "Historical Literary and Critical Dictionary," containing a summary of the lives of celebrated men of every description, and printed in 1758, in six volumes, octavo, without the name of the author.

The compilers of that work begin with declaring that it was undertaken by the advice of the author of the "Ecclesiastical Gazette," "a formidable writer," they add, "whose arrow," which had already been compared to that of Jonathan, "never returned back, and was always steeped in the blood of the slain, in the carnage of the valiant."—"*A sanguine interfectorum ab adipe fortium sagitta Jonathæ nunquam abiit retrorsum.*"

It will, no doubt, be easily admitted that the connection between Jonathan, the son of Saul, who was killed at the battle of Gilboa, and a Parisian convulsionary, who scribbles ecclesiastical notices in his garret, in 1758, is wonderfully striking.

The author of this preface speaks in it of the great Colbert. We should conceive, at first, that the great statesman who conferred such vast benefits on France is alluded to; no such thing, it is a bishop of Montpellier. He complains that no other dictionary has bestowed sufficient praise on the celebrated Abbé d'Asfeld, the illustrious Boursier, the famous Genes, the immortal Laborde, and that the lash of invective on the other hand has not been sufficiently applied to Languet, archbishop of Sens, and a person of the name of Fillot, all, as he pretends, men well known from the Pillars of Hercules to the frozen ocean. He engages to be "animated, energetic, and sarcastic, on a principle of religion"; that he will make his countenance "sterner than that of his enemies, and his front harder than their front, according to the words of Ezekiel," etc.

He declares that he has put in contribution all the journals and all the anas; and he concludes with hoping that heaven will bestow a blessing on his labors.

In dictionaries of this description, which are merely party works, we rarely find what we are in quest of, and often what we are not. Under the word "Adonis," for example, we learn that Venus fell in love with him; but not a word about the worship of Adonis, or Adonai among the Phœnicians—nothing about those very ancient and celebrated festivals, those lamentations succeeded by rejoicings, which were manifest allegories, like the feasts of Ceres, of Isis, and all the mysteries of antiquity.

But, in compensation, we find *Adkichomia* a devotee, who translated David's psalms in the sixteenth century; and *Adkichomus*, apparently her relation, who wrote the life of Jesus Christ in low German.

We may well suppose that all the individuals of the faction which employed this person are loaded with praise, and their enemies with abuse. The author, of the crew of authors who have put together this vocabulary of trash, say of Nicholas Boindin, attorney-general of the treasures of France, and a member of the Academy of Belles-lettres, that he was a poet and an atheist.

That magistrate, however, never printed any verses, and never wrote anything on metaphysics or religion.

He adds that Boindin will be ranked by posterity among the Vaninis, the Spinozas, and the Hobbeses. He is ignorant that Hobbes never professed atheism—that he merely subjected religion to the sovereign power, which he denominates the Leviathan. He is ignorant that Vanini was not an atheist; that the term "atheist" is not to be found even in the decree which condemned him; and that he was accused of impiety for having strenuously opposed the philosophy of Aristotle, and for having disputed with indiscretion and acrimony against a counsellor of the parliament of Toulouse, called Francon, or Franconi, who had the credit of getting him burned to death; for the latter burn whom they please; witness the Maid of Orleans, Michael Servetus, the Counsellor Dubourg, the wife of Marshal d'Ancre, Urbain Grandier, Morin, and the books of the Jansenists. See, moreover, the apology for Vanini by the learned Lacroze, and the article on "Atheism."

The vocabulary treats Boindin as a miscreant; his relations were desirous of proceeding at law and punishing an author, who himself so well deserved the appellation which he so infamously applied to a man who was not merely a magistrate, but also learned and estimable; but the calumniator concealed himself, like most libellers, under a fictitious name.

Immediately after having applied such shameful language to a man respectable compared with himself, he considers him as an irrefragable witness, because Boindin—whose unhappy temper was well known—left an ill-written and exceedingly ill-advised memorial, in which he accuses La Motte— one of the worthiest men in the world, a geometrician, and an ironmonger—with having written the infamous verses for which Jean Baptiste Rousseau was convicted. Finally, in the list of Boindin's works, he altogether omits his excellent dissertations printed in the collection of the Academy of Belles-lettres, of which he was a highly distinguished member.

The article on "Fontenelle" is nothing but a satire upon that ingenious and learned academician, whose science and talents are esteemed by the whole of literary Europe. The author has the effrontery to say that "his 'History of Oracles' does no honor to his religion." If Van Dale, the author of the "History of Oracles," and his abridger, Fontenelle, had lived in the time of the Greeks and of the Roman republic, it might have been said with reason that they were rather good philosophers than good pagans; but, to speak sincerely, what injury do they do to Christianity by showing that the pagan priests were a set of knaves? Is it not evident that the authors of the libel, miscalled a dictionary, are pleading their own cause? "*Jam proximus ardet Ucalegon*" But would it be offering an insult to the Christian religion to prove the knavery of the Convulsionaries? Government has done more; it has punished them without being accused of irreligion.

The libeller adds that he suspects that Fontenelle never performed the duties of a Christian but out of contempt for Christianity itself. It is a strange species of madness on the part of these fanatics to be always proclaiming that a philosopher cannot be a Christian. They ought to be excommunicated and punished for this alone; for assuredly it implies a wish to destroy Christianity to assert that it is impossible for a man to be a good reasoner and at the same time believe a religion so reasonable and holy.

Des Yveteaux, preceptor of Louis XIV., is accused of having lived and died without religion. It seems as if these compilers had none; or at least as if, while violating all the precepts of the true one, they were searching about everywhere for accomplices.

The very gentlemanly writer of these articles is wonderfully pleased with exhibiting all the bad verses that have been written on the French Academy, and various anecdotes as ridiculous as they are false. This also is apparently out of zeal for religion.

I ought not to lose an opportunity of refuting an absurd story which has been much circulated, and which is repeated exceedingly malapropos under the article of the "Abbé Gedoyn," upon whom the writer falls foul with great satisfaction, because in his youth he had been a Jesuit; a transient weakness, of which I know he repented all his life.

The devout and scandalous compiler of the dictionary asserts that the Abbé Gedoyn slept with the celebrated Ninon de l'Enclos on the very night of her completing her eightieth year. It certainly was not exactly befitting in a priest to relate this anecdote in a pretended dictionary of illustrious men. Such a foolery, however, is in fact highly improbable; and I can take upon me to assert that nothing can be more false. The same anecdote was formerly put down to the credit of the Abbé Chateauneuf, who was not very difficult in his amours, and who, it was said, had received Ninon's favors when she was of the age of sixty, or, rather, had conferred upon her his own. In early life I saw a great deal of the Abbé Gedoyn, the Abbé Chateauneuf, and Mademoiselle de l'Enclos; and I can truly declare that at the age of eighty years her countenance bore the most hideous marks of old age—that her person was afflicted with all the infirmities belonging to that stage of life, and that her mind was under the influence of the maxims of an austere philosophy.

Under the article on "Deshoulières" the compiler pretends that lady was the same who was designated under the term prude (*précieuse*) in Boileau's satire upon women. Never was any woman more free from such weakness than Madame Deshoulières; she always passed for a woman of the best society, possessed great simplicity, and was highly agreeable in conversation.

The article on "La Motte" abounds with atrocious abuse of that academician, who was a man of very amiable manners, and a philosophic poet who produced excellent works of every description. Finally the author, in order to secure the sale of his book of six volumes, has made of it a slanderous libel.

His hero is Carré de Montgeron, who presented to the king a collection of the miracles performed by the Convulsionaries in the cemetery of St. Médard; who became mad and died insane.

The interest of the republic of literature and reason demands that those libellers should be delivered up to public indignation, lest their example, operating upon the sordid love of gain, should stimulate others to imitation; and the more so, as nothing is so easy as to copy books in alphabetical order, and add to them insipidities, calumnies, and abuse.

Extract from the Reflections of an Academician on the "Dictionary of the French Academy."

It would be desirable to state the natural and incontestable etymology of every word, to compare the application, the various significations, the extent of the word, with use of it; the different acceptations, the strength or weakness of correspondent terms in foreign languages; and finally, to quote the best authors who have used the word, to show the greater or less extent of meaning which they have given to it and to remark whether it is more fit for poetry than prose.

For example, I have observed that the "inclemency" of the weather is ridiculous in history, because that term has its origin in the anger of heaven, which is supposed to be manifested by the intemperateness, irregularities, and rigors of the seasons, by the violence of the cold, the disorder of the atmosphere, by tempests, storms, and pestilential exhalations. Thus then inclemency, being a metaphor, is consecrated to poetry.

I have given to the word "impotence" all the acceptations which it receives. I showed the correctness of the historian, who speaks of the impotence of King Alphonso, without explaining whether he referred to that of resisting his brother, or that with which he was charged by his wife.

I have endeavored to show that the epithets "irresistible" and "incurable" require very delicate management. The first who used the expression, "the irresistible impulse of genius," made a very fortunate hit; because, in fact, the question was in relation to a great genius throwing itself upon its own resources in spite of all difficulties. Those imitators who have employed the expression in reference to very inferior men are plagiarists who know not how to dispose of what they steal.

As soon as the man of genius has made a new application of any word in the language, copyists are not wanting to apply it, very malapropos, in twenty places, without giving the inventor any credit.

I do not know that a single one of these words, termed by Boileau "foundlings" (*des mots trouvés*) a single new expression of genius, is to be found in any tragic author since Racine, until within the last few years. These words are generally lax, ineffective, stale, and so ill placed as to produce a barbarous style. To the disgrace of the nation, these Visigothic and Vandal productions were for a certain time extolled, panegyrized, and admired in the journals, especially as they came out under the protection of a certain lady of distinction, who knew nothing at all about the subject. We have recovered from all this now; and, with one or two exceptions, the whole race of such productions is extinct forever.

I did not in the first instance intend to make all these reflections, but to put the reader in a situation to make them. I have shown at the letter E that our *e* mute, with which we are reproached by an Italian, is precisely what occasions the delicious harmony of our language:—*empire, couronne, diadème, épouvantable, sensible*. This *e* mute, which we make perceptible without articulating it, leaves in the ear a melodious sound like that of a bell which still resounds although it is no longer struck. This we have already stated in respect to an Italian, a man of letters, who came to Paris to teach his own language, and who, while there, ought not to decry ours.

He does not perceive the beauty or necessity of our feminine rhymes; they are only *e*'s mute. This interweaving of masculine and feminine rhymes constitutes the charm of our verse.

Similar observations upon the alphabet, and upon words generally, would not have been without utility; but they would have made the work too long.

DIOCLETIAN.

After several weak or tyrannic reigns, the Roman Empire had a good emperor in Probus, whom the legions massacred, and elected Carus, who was struck dead by lightning while making war against the Persians. His son, Numerianus, was proclaimed by the soldiers. The historians tell us seriously that he lost his sight by weeping for the death of his father, and that he was obliged to be carried along with the army, shut up in a close litter. His father-in-law Aper killed him in his bed, to place himself on the throne; but a druid had predicted in Gaul to Diocletian, one of the generals of the army, that he would become emperor after having killed a boar. A boar, in Latin, is *aper*. Diocletian assembled the army, killed Aper with his own hands in the presence of the soldiers, and thus accomplished the prediction of the druid. The historians who relate this oracle deserve to be fed on the fruit of the tree which the druids revered. It is certain that Diocletian killed the father-in-law of the emperor, which was his first right to the throne. Numerianus had a brother named Carinus, who was also emperor, but being opposed to the elevation of Diocletian, he was killed by one of the tribunes of his army, which formed his second pretension to the purple. These were Diocletian's rights to the throne, and for a long time he had no other.

He was originally of Dalmatia, of the little town of Dioclea, of which he took the name. If it be true that his father was a laborer, and that he himself in his youth had been a slave to a senator named Anulinus, the fact forms his finest eulogium. He could have owed his elevation to himself alone; and it is very clear that he had conciliated the esteem of his army, since they forgot his birth to give him the diadem. Lactantius, a Christian authority, but rather partial, pretends that Diocletian was the greatest poltroon of the empire. It is not very likely that the Roman soldiers would have chosen a poltroon to govern them, or that this poltroon would have passed through all the degrees of the army. The zeal of Lactantius against a pagan emperor is very laudable, but not judicious.

Diocletian continued for twenty years the master of those fierce legions, who dethroned their emperors with as much facility as they created them; which is another proof, notwithstanding Lactantius, that he was as great a prince as he was a brave soldier. The empire under him soon regained its pristine splendor. The Gauls, the Africans, Egyptians, and British, who had revolted several times, were all brought under obedience to the empire; even the Persians were vanquished. So much success without; a still more happy administration within; laws as humane as wise, which still exist in the Justinian code; Rome, Milan, Autun, Nicomedia, Carthage, embellished by his munificence; all tended to gain him the love and respect both of the East and West; so that, two hundred and forty years after his death, they continued to reckon and date from the first year of his reign, as they had formerly dated from the foundation of Rome. This is what is called the era of Diocletian; it has also been called the era of martyrs;

but this is a mistake of eighteen years, for it is certain that he did not persecute any Christian for eighteen years. So far from it, the first thing he did, when emperor, was to give a company of prætorian guards to a Christian named Sebastian, who is in the list of the saints.

He did not fear to give a colleague to the empire in the person of a soldier of fortune, like himself; it was Maximian Hercules, his friend. The similarity of their fortunes had caused their friendship. Maximian was also born of poor and obscure parents, and had been elevated like Diocletian, step by step, by his own courage. People have not failed to reproach this Maximian with taking the surname of Hercules, and Diocletian with accepting that of Jove. They do not condescend to perceive that we have clergymen every day who call themselves Hercules, and peasants denominated Cæsar and Augustus.

Diocletian created two Cæsars; the first was another Maximian, surnamed Galerius, who had formerly been a shepherd. It seemed that Diocletian, the proudest of men and the first introducer of kissing the imperial feet, showed his greatness in placing Cæsars on the throne from men born in the most abject condition. A slave and two peasants were at the head of the empire, and never was it more flourishing.

The second Cæsar whom he created was of distinguished birth. He was Constantius Chlorus, great-nephew, on his mother's side, to the emperor Claudius II. The empire was governed by these four princes; an association which might have produced four civil wars a year, but Diocletian knew so well how to be master of his colleagues, that he obliged them always to respect him, and even to live united among themselves. These princes, with the name of Cæsars were in reality no more than his subjects. It is seen that he treated them like an absolute sovereign; for when the Cæsar Galerius, having been conquered by the Persians, went into Mesopotamia to give him the account of his defeat, he let him walk for the space of a mile near his chariot, and did not receive him into favor until he had repaired his fault and misfortune.

Galerius retrieved them the year after, in 297, in a very signal manner. He vanquished the king of Persia in person.

These kings of Persia had not been cured, by the battle of Arbela, of carrying their wives, daughters, and eunuchs along with their armies. Galerius, like Alexander, took his enemy's wife and all his family, and treated them with the same respect. The peace was as glorious as the victory. The vanquished ceded five provinces to the Romans, from the sands of Palmyra to Armenia.

Diocletian and Galerius went to Rome to dazzle the inhabitants with a triumph till then unheard of. It was the first time that the Roman people had seen the wife and children of a king of Persia in chains. All the empire was in plenty and prosperity. Diocletian went through all the provinces, from Rome to Egypt, Syria, and Asia Minor. His ordinary residence was not at Rome, but at Nicomedia, near the Euxine Sea, either to watch over the Persians and the barbarians, or because he was attached to a retreat which he had himself embellished. It was in the midst of this prosperity that Galerius commenced the persecution against the Christians. Why had he left them in repose until then, and why were they then ill treated? Eusebius says that a centurion of the Trajan legion, named Marcellus, who served in Mauritania, assisting with his troop at a feast given in honor of the victory of Galerius, threw his military sash, his arms, and his branch of vine, on the ground, and cried out loudly that he was a Christian and that he would no longer serve pagans—a desertion which was punished with death by the council of war. This was the first known example of the famous persecution of Diocletian. It is true that there were a great number of Christians in the armies of the empire, and the interest of the state demanded that such a desertion should not be allowed. The zeal of Marcellus was pious, but not reasonable. If at the feast given in Mauritania, viands offered to the gods of the empire were eaten, the law did not command Marcellus to eat of them, nor did Christianity order him to set the example of sedition. There is not a country in the world in which so rash an action would not have been punished.

However, after the adventure of Marcellus, it does not appear that the Christians were thought of until the year 303. They had, at Nicomedia, a superb church, next to the palace, which it exceeded in loftiness. Historians do not tell us the reasons why Galerius demanded of Diocletian the instant destruction of this church; but they tell us that Diocletian was a long time before he determined upon it, and that he resisted for almost a year. It is very strange that after this he should be called the *persecutor*. At last the church was destroyed and an edict was affixed by which the Christians were deprived of all honors and dignities. Since they were then deprived of them, it is evident that they possessed them. A Christian publicly tore the imperial edict in pieces—that was not an act of religion, it was an incitement to revolt. It is, therefore, very likely that an indiscreet and unreasonable zeal drew down this fatal persecution. Some time afterwards the palace of Galerius was burned down; he accused the Christians, and they accused Galerius of having himself set fire to it, in order to get a pretext for calumniating them. The accusation of Galerius appeared very unjust; that which they entered against him was no less so, for the edict having been already issued, what new pretext could he want? If he really wanted a new argument to engage Diocletian to persecute, this would only form a new proof of the reluctance of Diocletian to abandon the Christians, whom he had always protected; it would evidently show that he wanted new additional reasons to determine him to so much severity.

It appears certain that there were many Christians tormented in the empire, but it is difficult to reconcile with the Roman laws the alleged reported tortures, the mutilations, torn-out tongues, limbs cut and broiled, and all the insults offered against modesty and public decency. It is certain that no Roman law ever ordered such punishments; the aversion of the people to the Christians might carry them to horrible excesses, but we do not anywhere find that these excesses were ordered, either by the emperors or the senate.

It is very likely that the suffering of the Christians spread itself in exaggerated complaints: the "*Acta Sincera*" informs us that the emperor, being at Antioch, the prætor condemned a Christian child named Romanus to be burned; that the Jews present at the punishment began to laugh, saying: "We had formerly three children, Shadrach, Meshach, and Abednego, who did not burn in the fiery furnace but these do burn." At that instant, to confound the Jews, a great rain extinguished the pile and the little boy walked out safe and sound, asking, "Where then is the fire?" The account goes on to say that the emperor commanded him to be set free, but that the judge ordered his tongue to be cut out. It is scarcely possible to believe that the judge would have the tongue of a boy cut out, whom the emperor had pardoned.

That which follows is more singular. It is pretended that an old Christian physician named Ariston, who had a knife ready, cut the child's tongue out to pay his court to the prætor. The little Romanus was then carried back to prison; the jailer asked him the news. The child related at length how the old surgeon had cut out his tongue. It should be observed that before this operation the child stammered very much but that now he spoke with wonderful volubility. The jailer did not fail to relate this miracle to the emperor. They brought forward the old surgeon who swore that the operation had been performed according to the rules of his art and showed the child's tongue which he had properly preserved in a box as a relic. "Bring hither another person," said he, "and I will cut his tongue out in your majesty's presence, and you will see if he can speak." The proposition was accepted; they took a poor man whose tongue the surgeon cut out as he had done the child's, and the man died on the spot.

I am willing to believe that the "Acts" which relate this fact are as veracious as their title pretends, but they are still more simple than sincere, and it is very strange that Fleury, in his "Ecclesiastical History," relates such a prodigious number of similar incidents, being much more conducive to scandal than edification.

You will also remark that in this year 303, in which it is pretended that Diocletian was present at this fine affair in Antioch, he was at Rome and passed all that year in Italy. It is said that it was at Rome, and in his presence, that St. Genestus, a comedian, was converted on the stage while playing in a comedy against the Christians. This play shows clearly that the taste of Plautus and Terence no longer existed; that which is now called comedy, or Italian farce, seems to have originated at this time. St. Genestus represented an invalid; the physician asked him what was the matter with him. "I am too unwieldy," said Genestus. "Would you have us exorcise you to make you lighter?" said the physician. "No," replied Genestus, "I will die a

Christian, to be raised again of a finer stature." Then the actors, dressed as priests and exorcists, came to baptize him, at which moment Genestus really became a Christian, and, instead of finishing his part, began to preach to the emperor and the people. The "*Acta Sincera*" relate this miracle also.

It is certain that there were many true martyrs, but it is not true that the provinces were inundated with blood, as it is imagined. Mention is made of about two hundred martyrs towards the latter days of Diocletian in all the extent of the Roman Empire, and it is averred, even in the letters of Constantine, that Diocletian had much less part in the persecution than Galerius.

Diocletian fell ill this year and feeling himself weakened he was the first who gave the world the example of the abdication of empire. It is not easy to know whether this abdication was forced or not; it is true, however, that having recovered his health he lived nine years equally honored and peaceable in his retreat of Salonica, in the country of his birth. He said that he only began to live from the day of his retirement and when he was pressed to remount the throne he replied that the throne was not worth the tranquillity of his life, and that he took more pleasure in cultivating his garden than he should' have in governing the whole earth. What can be concluded from these facts but that with great faults he reigned like a great emperor and finished his life like a philosopher!

DIONYSIUS, ST. (THE AREOPAGITE),

AND THE FAMOUS ECLIPSE.

The author of the article "Apocrypha" has neglected to mention a hundred works recognized for such, and which, being entirely forgotten, seem not to merit the honor of being in his list. We have thought it right not to omit St. Dionysius, surnamed the Areopagite, who is pretended to have been for a long time the disciple of St. Paul, and of one Hierotheus, an unknown companion of his. He was, it is said, consecrated bishop of Athens by St. Paul himself. It is stated in his life that he went to Jerusalem to pay a visit to the holy Virgin and that he found her so beautiful and majestic that he was strongly tempted to adore her.

After having a long time governed the Church of Athens he went to confer with St. John the evangelist, at Ephesus, and afterwards with Pope Clement at Rome; thence he went to exercise his apostleship in France; and knowing, says the historian, that Paris was a rich, populous, and abundant town, and like other capitals, he went there to plant a citadel, to lay hell and infidelity in ruins.

He was regarded for a long time as the first bishop of Paris. Harduinus, one of his historians, adds that at Paris he was exposed to wild beasts, but, having made the sign of the cross on them, (they crouched at his feet. The pagan Parisians then threw him into a hot oven from which he walked out fresh and in perfect health; he was crucified and he began to preach from the top of the cross.

They imprisoned him with his companions Rusticus and Eleutherus. He there said mass, St. Rusticus performing the part of deacon and Eleutherus that of subdeacon. Finally they were all three carried to Montmartre, where their heads were cut off, after which they no longer said mass.

But, according to Harduinus, there appeared a still greater miracle. The body of St. Dionysius took its head in its hands and accompanied by angels singing "*Gloria tibi, Domine, alleluia*!" carried it as far as the place where they afterwards built him a church, which is the famous church of St. Denis.

Mestaphrastus, Harduinus, and Hincmar, bishop of Rheims, say that he was martyred at the age of ninety-one years, but Cardinal Baronius proves that he was a hundred and ten, in which opinion he is supported by Ribadeneira, the learned author of "Flower of the Saints." For our own part we have no opinion on the subject.

Seventeen works are attributed to him, six of which we have unfortunately lost; the eleven which remain to us have been translated from the Greek by Duns Scotus, Hugh de St. Victor, Albert Magnus, and several other illustrious scholars.

It is true that since wholesome criticism has been introduced into the world it has been discovered that all the books attributed to Dionysius were written by an impostor in the year 362 of our era, so that there no longer remains any difficulty on that head.

Of the Great Eclipse Noticed by Dionysius.

A fact related by one of the unknown authors of the life of Dionysius has, above all, caused great dissension among the learned. It is pretended that this first bishop of Paris, being in Egypt in the town of Diospolis, or No-Amon, at the age of twenty-five years, before he was a Christian, he was there, with one of his friends, witness of the famous eclipse of the sun which happened at the full moon, at the death of Jesus Christ and that he cried in Greek, "Either God suffers or is afflicted at the sufferings of the criminal."

These words have been differently related by different authors, but in the time of Eusebius of Cæsarea it is pretended that two historians—the one named Phlegon and the other Thallus—had made mention of this miraculous eclipse. Eusebius of Cæsarea quotes Phlegon, but we have none of his works now existing. He said—at least it is pretended so—that this eclipse happened in the fourth year of the two hundredth Olympiad, which would be the eighteenth year of Tiberius's reign. There are several versions of this anecdote; we distrust them all and much more so, if it were possible to know whether they reckoned by Olympiads in the time of Phlegon, which is very doubtful.

This important calculation interested all the astronomers. Hodgson, Whiston, Gale, Maurice, and the famous Halley, demonstrated that there was no eclipse of the sun in this first year, but that on November 24th in the year of the hundred and second Olympiad an eclipse took place which obscured the sun for two minutes, at a quarter past one, at Jerusalem.

It has been carried still further: a Jesuit named Greslon pretended that the Chinese preserved in their annals the account of an eclipse which happened near that time, contrary to the order of nature. They desired the mathematicians of Europe to make a calculation of it; it was pleasant enough to desire the astronomists to calculate an eclipse which was not natural. Finally it was discovered that these Chinese annals do not in any way speak of this eclipse.

It appears from the history of St. Dionysius the Areopagite, the passage from Phlegon, and from the letter of the Jesuit Greslon that men like to impose upon one another. But this prodigious multitude of lies, far from harming the Christian religion, only serves, on the contrary, to show its divinity, since it is more confirmed every day in spite of them.

DIODORUS OF SICILY, AND HERODOTUS.

We will commence with Herodotus as the most ancient. When Henry Stephens entitled his comic rhapsody "The Apology of Herodotus," we know that his design was not to justify the tales of this father of history; he only sports with us and shows that the enormities of his own times were worse than those of the Egyptians and Persians. He made use of the liberty which the Protestants assumed against those of the Catholic, Apostolic, and Roman churches. He sharply reproaches them with their debaucheries, their avarice, their crimes expiated by money, their indulgences publicly sold in the taverns, and the false relics manufactured by their own monks, calling them idolaters. He ventures to say that if the Egyptians adored cats and onions, the Catholics adore the bones of the dead. He dares to call them in his preliminary discourses, "theophages," and even "theokeses." We have fourteen editions of this book, for we relish general abuse, just as much as we resent that which we deem special and personal.

Henry Stephens made use of Herodotus only to render us hateful and ridiculous; we have quite a contrary design. We pretend to show that the modern histories of our good authors since Guicciardini are in general as wise and true as those of Herodotus and Diodorus are foolish and fabulous.

1. What does the father of history mean by saying in the beginning of his work, "the Persian historians

relate that the Phoenicians were the authors of all the wars. From the Red Sea they entered ours," etc.? It would seem that the Phœnicians, having embarked at the Isthmus of Suez, arrived at the straits of Babel-Mandeb, coasted along Ethiopia, passed the line, doubled the Cape of Tempests, since called the Cape of Good Hope, returned between Africa and America, repassed the line and entered from the ocean into the Mediterranean by the Pillars of Hercules, a voyage of more than four thousand of our long marine leagues at a time when navigation was in its infancy.

2. The first exploit of the Phœnicians was to go towards Argos to carry off the daughter of King Inachus, after which the Greeks, in their turn, carried off Europa, the daughter of the king of Tyre.

3. Immediately afterwards comes Candaules, king of Lydia, who, meeting with one of his guards named Gyges, said to him, "Thou must see my wife quite naked; it is absolutely essential." The queen, learning that she had been thus exposed, said to the soldier, "You shall either die or assassinate my husband and reign with me." He chose the latter alternative, and the assassination was accomplished without difficulty.

4. Then follows the history of Arion, carried on the back of a dolphin across the sea from the skirts of Calabria to Cape Matapan, an extraordinary voyage of about a hundred leagues.

5. From tale to tale—and who dislikes tales?—we arrive at the infallible oracle of Delphi, which

somehow foretold that Crœsus would cook a quarter of lamb and a tortoise in a copper pan and that he would be dethroned by a mullet.

6. Among the inconceivable absurdities with which ancient history abounds is there anything approaching the famine with which the Lydians were tormented for twenty-eight years? This people, whom Herodotus describes as being richer in gold than the Peruvians, instead of buying food from foreigners, found no better expedient than that of amusing themselves every other day with the ladies without eating for eight-and-twenty successive years.

7. Is there anything more marvellous than the history of Cyrus? His grandfather, the Mede Astyages, with a Greek name, dreamed that his daughter Mandane—another Greek name— inundated all Asia; at another time, that she produced a vine, of which all Asia ate the grapes, and thereupon the good man Astyages ordered one Harpagos, another Greek, to murder his grandson Cyrus—for what grandfather would not kill his posterity after dreams of this nature?

8. Herodotus, no less a good naturalist than an exact historian, does not fail to tell us that near Babylon the earth produced three hundred ears of wheat for one. I know a small country which yields three for one. I should like to have been transported to Diabek when the Turks were driven from it by Catherine II. It has fine corn also but returns not three hundred ears for one.

9. What has always seemed to me decent and edifying in Herodotus is the fine religious custom established in Babylon of which we have already spoken—that of all the married women going to prostitute themselves in the temple of Mylitta for money, to the first stranger who presented himself. We reckon two millions of inhabitants in this city; the devotion must have been ardent. This law is very probable among the Orientals who have always shut up their women, and who, more than six ages before Herodotus, instituted eunuchs to answer to them for the chastity of their wives. I must no longer proceed numerically; we should very soon indeed arrive at a hundred.

All that Diodorus of Sicily says seven centuries after Herodotus is of the same value in all that regards antiquities and physics. The Abbé Terrasson said, "I translate the text of Diodorus in all its coarseness." He sometimes read us part of it at the house of de Lafaye, and when we laughed, he said, "You are resolved to misconstrue; it was quite the contrary with Dacier."

The finest part of Diodorus is the charming description of the island of Panchaica—"Panchaica Tellus," celebrated by Virgil: "There were groves of odoriferous trees as far as the eye could see, myrrh and frankincense to furnish the whole world without exhausting it; fountains, which formed an infinity of canals, bordered with flowers, besides unknown birds, which sang under the eternal shades; a temple of marble four thousand feet long, ornamented with columns, colossal statues," etc.

This puts one in mind of the Duke de la Ferté, who, to flatter the taste of the Abbé Servien, said to him one day, "Ah, if you had seen my son who died at fifteen years of age! What eyes! what freshness of complexion! what an admirable stature! the Antinous of Belvidere compared to him was only like a Chinese baboon, and as to sweetness of manners, he had the most engaging I ever met with." The Abbé Servien melted, the duke of Ferté, warmed by his own words, melted also, both began to weep, after which he acknowledged that he never had a son.

A certain Abbé Bazin, with his simple common sense, doubts another tale of Diodorus. It is of a king of Egypt, Sesostris, who probably existed no more than the island of Panchaica. The father of Sesostris, who is not named, determined on the day that he was born that he would make him the conqueror of all the earth as soon as he was of age. It was a notable project. For this purpose he brought up with him all the boys who were born on the same day in Egypt, and, to make them conquerors, he did not suffer them to have their breakfasts until they had run a hundred and eighty stadia, which is about eight of our long leagues.

When Sesostris was of age he departed with his racers to conquer the world. They were then about seventeen hundred and probably half were dead, according to the ordinary course of nature—and, above all, of the nature of Egypt, which was desolated by a destructive plague at least once in ten years.

There must have been three thousand four hundred boys born in Egypt on the same day as Sesostris, and as nature produces almost as many girls as boys, there must have been six thousand persons at least born on that day. But women were confined every day, and six thousand births a day produce, at the end of the year, two millions one hundred and ninety thousand children. If you multiply by thirty-four, according to the rule of Kersseboom, you would have in Egypt more than seventy-four millions of inhabitants in a country which is not so large as Spain or France.

All this appeared monstrous to the Abbé Bazin, who had seen a little of the world, and who judged only by what he had seen.

But one Larcher, who was never outside of the college of Mazarin arrayed himself with great animation on the side of Sesostris and his runners. He pretends that Herodotus, in speaking of the Greeks, does not reckon by the stadia of Greece, and that the heroes of Sesostris only ran four leagues before breakfast. He overwhelms poor Abbé Bazin with injurious names such as no scholar in *us* or *es* had ever before employed. He does not hold with the seventeen hundred boys, but endeavors to prove by the prophets that the wives, daughters, and nieces of the king of Babylon, of the satraps, and the magi, resorted, out of pure devotion, to sleep for money in the aisles of the temple of Babylon with all the camel-drivers and muleteers of Asia. He treats all those who defend the honor of the ladies of Babylon as bad Christians, condemned souls, and enemies to the state.

He also takes the part of the goat, so much in the good graces of the young female Egyptians. It is said that his great reason was that he was allied, by the female side, to a relation of the bishop of Meaux, Bossuet, the author of an eloquent discourse on "Universal History"; but this is not a peremptory reason.

Take care of the extraordinary stories of all kinds. Diodorus of Sicily was the greatest compiler of these tales. This Sicilian had not a grain of the temper of his countryman Archimedes, who sought and found so many mathematical truths.

Diodorus seriously examines the history of the Amazons and their queen Theaestris; the history of the Gorgons, who fought against the Amazons; that of the Titans, and that of all the gods. He searches into the history of Priapus and Hermaphroditus. No one could give a better account of Hercules: this hero wandered through half the earth, sometimes on foot and alone like a pilgrim, and sometimes like a general at the head of a great army, and all his labors are faithfully discussed, but this is nothing in comparison with the gods of Crete.

Diodorus justifies Jupiter from the reproach which other grave historians have passed upon him, of having dethroned and mutilated his father. He shows how Jupiter fought the giants, some in his island, others in Phrygia, and afterwards in Macedonia and Italy; the number of children which he had by his sister Juno and his favorites are not omitted.

He describes how he afterwards became a god, and the supreme god. It is thus that all the ancient histories have been written. What is more remarkable, they were sacred; if they had not been sacred, they would never have been read.

It is clear that it would be very useful if in all they were all different, and from province to province, and island to island, each had a different history of the gods, demi-gods, and heroes, from that of their neighbors. But it should also be observed that the people never fought for this mythology.

The respectable history of Thucydides, which has several glimmerings of truth, begins at Xerxes, but, before that epoch how much time was wasted.

DIRECTOR.

It is neither of a director of finances, a director of hospitals, nor a director of the royal buildings that I pretend to speak, but of a director of conscience, for that directs all the others: it is the preceptor of human kind; it knows and teaches all that should be done or omitted in all possible cases.

It is clear that it would be very useful if in all courts there were one conscientious man whom the monarch secretly consulted on most occasions, and who would boldly say, "*Non licet.*" Louis the Just would not then have begun his mischievous and unhappy reign by assassinating his first minister and imprisoning his mother. How many wars, unjust as fatal, a few good dictators would have spared! How many cruelties they would have prevented!

But often, while intending to consult a lamb, we consult a fox. Tartuffe was the director of Orgon. I should like to know who was the conscientious director of the massacre of St. Bartholomew.

The gospel speaks no more of directors than of confessors. Among the people whom our ordinary courtesy calls Pagans we do not see that Scipio, Fabricius, Cato, Titus, Trajan, or the Antonines had directors. It is well to have a scrupulous friend to remind you of your duty. But your conscience ought to be the chief of your council.

A Huguenot was much surprised when a Catholic lady told him that she had a confessor to absolve her from her sins and a director to prevent her committing them. "How can your vessel so often go astray, madam," said he, "having two such good pilots?"

The learned observe that it is not the privilege of every one to have a director. It is like having an equerry; it only belongs to ladies of quality. The Abbé Gobelin, a litigious and covetous man, directed Madame de Maintenon only. The directors of Paris often serve four or five devotees at once; they embroil them with their husbands, sometimes with their lovers, and occasionally fill the vacant places.

Why have the women directors and the men none? It was possibly owing to this distinction that Mademoiselle de la Vallière became a Carmelite when she was quitted by Louis XIV., and that M. de Turenne, being betrayed by Madame de Coetquin, did *not* make himself a monk.

St. Jerome, and Rufinus his antagonist, were great directors of women and girls. They did not find a Roman senator or a military tribune to govern. These people profited by the devout facility of the feminine gender. The men had too much beard on their chins and often too much strength of mind for them. Boileau has given the portrait of a director in his "Satire on Women," but might have said something much more to the purpose.

DISPUTES.

There have been disputes at all times, on all subjects:—"*Mundum tradidit disputationi eorum.*" There have been violent quarrels about whether the whole is greater than a part; whether a body can be in several places at the same time; whether the whiteness of snow can exist without snow, or the sweetness of sugar without sugar; whether there can be thinking without a head, etc.

I doubt not that as soon as a Jansenist shall have written a book to demonstrate that one and two are three, a Molinist will start up and demonstrate that two and one are five.

We hope to please and instruct the reader by laying before him the following verses on "Disputation." They are well known to every man of taste in Paris, but they are less familiar to those among the learned who still dispute on gratuitous predestination, concomitant grace, and that momentous question—whether the mountains were produced by the sea.

ON DISPUTATION.

Each brain its thought, each season has its mode;
Manners and fashions alter every day;
Examine for yourself what others say;—
This privilege by nature is bestowed;—
But, oh! dispute not—the designs of heaven
To mortal insight never can be given.
What is the knowledge of this world worth

knowing?
What, but a bubble scarcely worth the blowing?
"Quite full of errors was the world before;"
Then, to preach reason is but one error more.

Viewing this earth from Luna's elevation,
Or any other convenient situation,
What shall we see? The various tricks of man.
Here is a synod—*there* is a divan;
Behold the mufti, dervish, iman, bonze,
The lama and the pope on equal thrones.
The modern doctor and the ancient rabbi,
The monk, the priest, and the expectant abbé:
If you are disputants, my friends, pray travel—
When you come home again, you'll cease to cavil.

That wild Ambition should lay waste the earth,
Or Beauty's glance give civil discord birth;
That, in our courts of equity, a suit
Should hang in doubt till ruin is the fruit;
That an old country priest should deeply groan,
To see a benefice he'd thought his own
Borne off by a court abbé; that a poet
Should feel most envy when he least should show
it;
And, when another's play the public draws,
Should grin damnation while he claps applause;
With this, and more, the human heart is fraught—
But whence the rage to rule another's thought;
Say, wherefore—in what way—can you design
To make *your* judgment give the law to *mine*?

But chiefly I detest those tiresome elves,

Half-learned critics, worshipping themselves,
Who, with the utmost weight of all their lead,
Maintain against you what yourself have said;
Philosophers—and poets—and musicians—
Great statesmen—deep in third and fourth
editions—
They know all—read all—and (the greatest curse)
They *talk* of all—from politics to verse;
On points of taste they'll contradict Voltaire;
In law e'en Montesquieu they will not spare;
They'll tutor Broglio in affairs of arms;
And teach the charming d'Egmont higher charms.
See them, alike in great and small things clever,
Replying constantly, though answering never;
Hear them assert, repeat, affirm, aver,
Wax wroth. And wherefore all this mighty stir?
This the great theme that agitates their breast—
Which of two wretched rhymesters rhymes the
best?

Pray, gentle reader, did you chance to know
One Monsieur d'Aube, who died not long ago?
One whom the disputatious mania woke
Early each morning? If, by chance, you spoke
Of your own part in some well-fought affair,
Better than you he knew how, when, and where;
What though your own the deed and the renown?
His "letters from the army" put you down;
E'en Richelieu he'd have told—if he attended—
How Mahon fell, or Genoa was defended.
Although he wanted neither wit nor sense,
His every visit gave his friends offence;
I've seen him, raving in a hot dispute,

Exhaust their logic, force them to be mute,
Or, if their patience were entirely spent,
Rush from the room to give their passion vent.
His kinsmen, whom his property allured,
At last were wearied, though they long endured.
His neighbors, less athletic than himself,
For health's sake laid him wholly on the shelf.
Thus, 'midst his many virtues, this one failing
Brought his old age to solitary wailing;—
For solitude to him was deepest woe—
A sorrow which the peaceful ne'er can know
At length, to terminate his cureless grief,
A mortal fever came to his relief,
Caused by the great, the overwhelming pang,
Of hearing in the church a long harangue
Without the privilege of contradiction;
So, yielding to this crowning dire affliction,
His spirit fled. But, in the grasp of death,
'Twas some small solace, with his parting breath,
To indulge once more his ruling disposition
By arguing with the priest and the physician.

Oh! may the Eternal goodness grant him now
The rest *he* ne'er to mortals would allow!
If, even there, he like not disputation
Better than uncontested, calm salvation.

But see, my friends, this bold defiance made
To every one of the disputing trade,
With a young bachelor their skill to try;
And God's own essence shall the theme supply.

Come and behold, as on the theatric stage,
The pitched encounter, the contending rage;
Dilemmas, enthymemes, in close array—
Two-edged weapons, cutting either way;
The strong-built syllogism's pondering might,
The sophism's vain ignis fatuus light;
Hot-headed monks, whom all the doctors dread,
And poor Hibernians arguing for their bread,
Fleeing their country's miseries and morasses
To live at Paris on disputes and masses;
While the good public lend their strict attention
To what soars far above their sober comprehension.

Is, then, all arguing frivolous or absurd?
Was Socrates himself not sometimes heard
To hold an argument amidst a feast?
E'en naked in the bath he hardly ceased.
Was this a failing in his mental vision?
Genius is sure discovered by collision;
The cold hard flint by one quick blow is fired;—
Fit emblem of the close and the retired,
Who, in the keen dispute struck o'er and o'er,
Acquire a sudden warmth unfelt before.

All this, I grant, is good. But mark the ill:
Men by disputing have grown blinder still.
The crooked mind is like the squinting eye:
How can you make it see *itself* awry?
Who's in the wrong? Will any answer "I"?
Our words, our efforts, are an idle breath;
Each hugs his darling notion until death;
Opinions ne'er are altered; all we do
Is, *to arouse conflicting passions, too.*

Not truth itself should always find a tongue;
"To be too stanchly right, is to be wrong."

In earlier days, by vice and crime unstained,
Justice and Truth, two naked sisters, reigned;
But long since fled—as every one can tell—
Justice to heaven and Truth into a well.

Now vain Opinion governs every age,
And fills poor mortals with fantastic rage.
Her airy temple floats upon the clouds;
Gods, demons, antic sprites, in countless crowds,
Around her throne—a strange and motley mask—
Ply busily their never-ceasing task,
To hold up to mankind's admiring gaze
A thousand nothings in a thousand ways;
While, wafted on by all the winds that blow,
Away the temple and the goddess go.
A mortal, as her course uncertain turns,
To-day is worshipped, and to-morrow burns.
We scoff, that young Antinous once had priests;
We think our ancestors were worse than beasts;
And he who treats each modern custom ill,
Does but what future ages surely will.
What female face has Venus smiled upon?
The Frenchman turns with rapture to Brionne,
Nor can believe that men were wont to bow
To golden tresses and a narrow brow.
And thus is vagabond Opinion seen
To sway o'er Beauty—this world's other queen!
How can we hope, then, that she e'er will quit

Her vapory throne, to seek some sage's feet,
And Truth from her deep hiding-place remove,
Once more to witness what is done above?

And for the learned—even for the wise—
Another snare of false delusion lies;
That rage for systems, which, in dreamy thought,
Frames magic universes out of naught;
Building ten errors on one truth's foundation.
So he who taught the art of calculation,
In one of these illusive mental slumbers,
Foolishly sought the Deity in numbers;
The first mechanic, from as wild a notion,
Would rule man's freedom by the laws of motion.
This globe, says one, is an extinguished sun;

No, says another, 'tis a globe of glass;
And when the fierce contention's once begun,

Book upon book—a vast and useless mass—On
Science's altar are profusely strewn,
While Disputation sits on Wisdom's throne.

And then, from contrarieties of speech,
What countless feuds have sprung! For you may
teach,
In the same words, two doctrines different quite
As day from darkness, or as wrong from right.
This has indeed been man's severest curse;
Famine and pestilence have not been worse,
Nor e'er have matched the ills whose aggravations

Have scourged the world through
misinterpretations.

How shall I paint the conscientious strife?
The holy transports of each heavenly soul—
Fanaticism wasting human life
With torch, with dagger, and with poisoned bow;
The ruined hamlet and the blazing town,
Homes desolate, and parents massacred,
And temples in the Almighty's honor reared
The scene of acts that merit most his frown!
Rape, murder, pillage, in one frightful storm,
Pleasure with carnage horribly combined,
The brutal ravisher amazed to find
A sister in his victim's dying form!

Sons by their fathers to the scaffold led;
The vanquished always numbered with the dead.
Oh, God, permit that all the ills we know
May one day pass for merely fabled woe!

But see, an angry disputant steps forth—
His humble mien a proud heart ill conceals
In holy guise inclining to the earth,
Offering to God the venom he distils.
"Beneath all this a dangerous poison lies;
So—every man is neither right nor wrong,
And, since we never can be truly wise,
By instinct only should be driven along."
"Sir, I've not said a word to that effect."
"It's true, you've artfully disguised your meaning."

"But, Sir, my judgment ever is correct."
"Sir, in this case, 'tis rather overweening.
Let truth be sought, but let all passion yield;
'Discussion's right, and disputation's wrong;'
This have I said—and that at court, in field,
Or town, one often should restrain one's tongue."
"But, my dear Sir, you've still a double sense;
I can distinguish—" "Sir, with all my heart;
I've told my thoughts with all due deference,
And crave the like indulgence on your part."
"My son, all 'thinking' is a grievous crime;
So I'll denounce you without loss of time."

Blest would be they who, from fanatic power,
From carping censors, envious critics, free,
O'er Helicon might roam in liberty,
And unmolested pluck each fragrant flower!
So does the farmer, in his healthy fields,
Far from the ills in swarming towns that spring,
Taste the pure joys that our existence yields,
Extract the honey and escape the sting.

DISTANCE.

A man who knows how to reckon the paces from one end of his house to the other might imagine that nature had all at once taught him this distance and that he has only need of a *coup d'œil*, as in the case of colors. He is deceived; the different distances of objects can be known only by experience, comparison, and habit. It is that which makes a sailor, on seeing a vessel afar off, able to say without hesitation what distance his own vessel is from it, of which distance a passenger would only form a very confused idea.

Distance is only the line from a given object to ourselves. This line terminates at a point; and whether the object be a thousand leagues from us or only a foot, this point is always the same to our eyes.

We have then no means of directly perceiving distances, as we have of ascertaining by the touch whether a body is hard or soft; by the taste, if it is bitter or sweet; or by the ear, whether of two sounds the one is grave and the other lively. For if I duly notice, the parts of a body which give way to my fingers are the immediate cause of my sensation of softness, and the vibrations of the air, excited by the sonorous body, are the immediate cause of my sensation of sound. But as I cannot have an immediate idea of distance I must find it out by means of an intermediate idea, but it is necessary that this intermediate idea be clearly understood, for it is only by the medium of things known that we can acquire a notion of things unknown.

I am told that such a house is distant a mile from such a river, but if I do not know where this river is I certainly do not know where the house is situated. A body yields easily to the impression of my hand: I conclude immediately that it is soft. Another resists, I feel at once its hardness. I ought therefore to feel the angles formed in my eye in order to determine the distance of objects. But most men do not even know that these angles exist; it is evident, therefore, that they cannot be the immediate cause of our ascertaining distances.

He who, for the first time in his life, hears the noise of a cannon or the sound of a concert, cannot judge whether the cannon be fired or the concert be performed at the distance of a league or of twenty paces. He has only the experience which accustoms him to judge of the distance between himself and the place whence the noise proceeds. The vibrations, the undulations of the air carry a sound to his ears, or rather to his sensorium, but this noise no more carries to his sensorium the place whence it proceeds than it teaches him the form of the cannon or of the musical instruments. It is the same thing precisely with regard to the rays of light which proceed from an object, but which do not at all inform us of its situation.

Neither do they inform us more immediately of magnitude or form. I see from afar a little round tower. I approach, perceive, and touch a great quadrangular building. Certainly, this which I now see and touch cannot be that which I saw before. The little round tower which was before my eyes cannot be this large, square building. One thing in relation to us is the measurable and tangible object; another, the visible object. I hear from my chamber the noise of a carriage, I open my window and see it. I descend and enter it. Yet this carriage that I have heard, this carriage that I have seen, and this carriage which I have touched are three objects absolutely distinct to three of my senses, which have no immediate relation to one another.

Further; it is demonstrated that there is formed in my eye an angle a degree larger when a thing is near, when I see a man four feet from me than when I see the same man at a distance of eight feet. However, I always see this man of the same size. How does my mind thus contradict the mechanism of my organs? The object is really a degree smaller to my eyes, and yet I see it the same. It is in vain that we attempt to explain this mystery by the route which the rays follow or by the form taken by the crystalline humor of the eye. Whatever may be supposed to the contrary, the angle at which I see a man at four feet from me is always nearly double the angle at which I see him at eight feet. Neither geometry nor physics will explain this difficulty.

These geometrical lines and angles are not really more the cause of our seeing objects in their proper places than that we see them of a certain size and at a certain distance. The mind does not consider that if this part were to be painted at the bottom of the eye it could collect nothing from lines that it saw not. The eye looks down only to see that which is near the ground, and is uplifted to see that which is above the earth. All this might be explained and placed beyond dispute by any person born blind, to whom the sense of sight was afterwards attained. For if this blind man, the moment that he opens his eyes, can correctly judge of distances, dimensions, and situations, it would be true that the optical angles suddenly formed in his retina were the immediate cause of his decisions. Doctor Berkeley asserts, after Locke—going even further than Locke—that neither situation, magnitude, distance, nor figure would be discerned by a blind man thus suddenly gifted with sight.

In fact, a man born blind was found in 1729, by whom this question was indubitably decided. The famous Cheselden, one of those celebrated surgeons who join manual skill to the most enlightened minds, imagined that he could give sight to this blind man by couching, and proposed the operation. The patient was with great difficulty brought to consent to it. He did not conceive that the sense of sight could much augment his pleasures, except that he desired to be able to read and to write, he cared indeed little about seeing. He proved by this indifference that it is impossible to be rendered unhappy by the privation of pleasures of which we have never formed an idea—a very important truth. However this may be, the operation was performed, and succeeded. This young man at fourteen years of age saw the light for the first time, and his experience confirmed all that Locke and Berkeley had so ably foreseen. For a long time he distinguished neither dimensions, distance, nor form. An object about the size of an inch, which was placed before his eyes, and which concealed a house from him, appeared as large as the house itself.

All that he saw seemed to touch his eyes, and to touch them as objects of feeling touch the skin. He could not at first distinguish that which, by the aid of his hands, he had thought round from that which he had supposed square, nor could he discern with his eyes if that which his hands had felt to be tall and short were so in reality. He was so far from knowing anything about magnitude that after having at last conceived by his sight that his house was larger than his chamber, he could not conceive how sight could give him this idea. It was not until after two months' experience he could discover that pictures represented existing bodies, and when, after this long development of his new sense in him, he perceived that bodies, and not surfaces only, were painted in the pictures, he took them in his hands and was astonished at not finding those solid bodies of which he had begun to perceive the representation, and demanded which was the deceived, the sense of feeling or that of sight.

Thus was it irrevocably decided that the manner in which we see things follows not immediately from the angles formed in the eye. These mathematical angles were in the eyes of this man the same as in our own and were of no use to him without the help of experience and of his other senses.

The adventure of the man born blind was known in France towards the year 1735. The author of the "Elements of Newton," who had seen a great deal of Cheselden, made mention of this important discovery, but did not take much notice of it. And even when the same operation of the cataract was performed at Paris on a young man who was said to have been deprived of sight from his cradle, the operators neglected to attend to the daily development of the sense of sight in him and to the progress of nature. The fruit of this operation was therefore lost to philosophy.

How do we represent to ourselves dimensions and distances? In the same manner that we imagine the passions of men by the colors with which they vary their countenances, and by the alteration which they make in their features. There is no person who cannot read joy or grief on the countenance of another. It is the language that nature addresses to all eyes, but experience only teaches this language. Experience alone teaches us that, when an object is too far, we see it confusedly and weakly, and thence we form ideas, which always afterwards accompany the sensation of sight. Thus every man who at ten paces sees his horse five feet high, if, some minutes after, he sees this horse of the size of a sheep, by an involuntary judgment immediately concludes that the horse is much farther from him.

It is very true that when I see my horse of the size of a sheep a much smaller picture is formed in my eye—a more acute angle; but it is a fact which accompanies, not causes, my opinion. In like manner, it makes a different impression on my brain, when I see a man blush from shame and from anger; but these different impressions would tell me nothing of what was passing in this man's mind, without experience, whose voice alone is attended to.

So far from the angle being the immediate cause of my thinking that a horse is far off when I see it very small, it happens that I see my horse equally large at ten, twenty, thirty, or forty paces, though the angle at ten paces may be double, treble, or quadruple. I see at a distance, through a small hole, a man posted on the top of a house; the remoteness and fewness of the rays at first prevent me from distinguishing that it is a man; the object appears to me very small. I think I see a statue two feet high at most; the object moves; I then judge that it is a man; and from that instant the man appears to me of his ordinary size. Whence come these two judgments so different? When I believed that I saw a statue, I imagined it to be two feet high, because I saw it at such an angle; experience had not led my mind to falsify the traits imprinted on my retina; but as soon as I judged that it was a man, the association established in my mind by experience between a man and his known height of five or six feet, involuntarily obliged me to imagine that I saw one of a certain height; or, in fact, that I saw the height itself.

It must therefore be absolutely concluded, that distance, dimension, and situation are not, properly speaking, visible things; that is to say, the proper and immediate objects of sight. The proper and immediate object of sight is nothing but colored light; all the rest we only discover by long acquaintance and experience. We learn to see precisely as we learn to speak and to read. The difference is, that the art of seeing is more easy, and that nature is equally mistress of all.

The sudden and almost uniform judgments which, at a certain age, our minds form of distance, dimension, and situation, make us think that we have only to open our eyes to see in the manner in which we do see. We are deceived; it requires the help of the other senses. If men had only the sense of sight, they would have no means of knowing extent in length, breadth, and depth, and a pure spirit perhaps would not know it, unless God revealed it to him. It is very difficult, in our understanding, to separate the extent of an object from its color. We never see anything but what is extended, and from that we are led to believe that we really see the extent. We can scarcely distinguish in our minds the yellow that we see in a *louis d'or* from the *louis d'or* in which we see the yellow. In the same manner, as when we hear the word *"louis d'or"* pronounced, we cannot help attaching the idea of the money to the word which we hear spoken.

If all men spoke the same language, we should be always ready to believe in a necessary connection between words and ideas. But all men in fact do possess the same language of imagination. Nature says to them all: When you have seen colors for a certain time, imagination will represent the bodies to which these colors appear attached to all alike. This prompt and summary judgment once attained will be of use to you during your life; for if to estimate the distances, magnitudes, and situations of all that surrounds you, it were necessary to examine the visual angles and rays, you would be dead before you had ascertained whether the things of which you have need were ten paces from you or a hundred thousand leagues, and whether they were of a size of a worm or of a mountain. It would be better to be born blind.

We are then, perhaps, very wrong, when we say that our senses deceive us. Every one of our senses performs the function for which it was destined by nature. They mutually aid one another to convey to our minds, through the medium of experience, the measure of knowledge that our being allows. We ask from our senses what they are not made to give us. We would have our eyes acquaint us with solidity, dimension, distance, etc.; but it is necessary for the touch to agree for that purpose with the sight, and that experience should second both. If Father Malebranche had looked at this side of nature, he would perhaps have attributed fewer errors to our senses, which are the only sources of all our ideas.

We should not, however, extend this species of metaphysics to every case before us. We should only call it to our aid when the mathematics are insufficient.

DIVINITY OF JESUS.

The Socinians, who are regarded as blasphemers, do not recognize the divinity of Jesus Christ. They dare to pretend, with the philosophers of antiquity, with the Jews, the Mahometans, and most other nations, that the idea of a god-man is monstrous; that the distance from God to man is infinite; and that it is impossible for a perishable body to be infinite, immense, or eternal.

They have the confidence to quote Eusebius, bishop of Cæsarea, in their favor, who, in his "Ecclesiastical History," i., 9, declares that it is absurd to imagine the uncreated and unchangeable nature of Almighty God taking the form of a man. They cite the fathers of the Church, Justin and Tertullian, who have said the same thing: Justin, in his "Dialogue with Triphonius"; and Tertullian, in his "Discourse against Praxeas."

They quote St. Paul, who never calls Jesus Christ "God," and who calls Him "man" very often. They carry their audacity so far as to affirm that the Christians passed three entire ages in forming by degrees the apotheosis of Jesus; and that they only raised this astonishing edifice by the example of the pagans, who had deified mortals. At first, according to them, Jesus was only regarded as a man inspired by God, and then as a creature more perfect than others. They gave Him some time after a place above the angels, as St. Paul tells us. Every day added to His greatness. He in time became an emanation, proceeding from God. This was not enough; He was even born before time. At last He was made God consubstantial with God. Crellius, Voquelsius, Natalis Alexander, and Horneck have supported all these blasphemies by arguments which astonish the wise and mislead the weak. Above all, Faustus Socinus spread the seeds of this doctrine in Europe; and at the end of the sixteenth century a new species of Christianity was established. There were already more than three hundred.

DIVORCE.

In the article on "Divorce," in the "Encyclopædia," it is said that the custom of divorce having been brought into Gaul by the Romans, it was therefore that Basine, or Bazine, quitted the king of Thuringia, her husband, in order to follow Childeric, who married her. Why not say that because the Trojans established the custom of divorce in Sparta, Helen repudiated Menelaus according to law, to run away with Paris into Phrygia?

The agreeable fable of Paris, and the ridiculous one of Childeric, who never was king of France, and who it is pretended carried off Bazine, the wife of Bazin, have nothing to do with the law of divorce.

They all quote Cheribert, ruler of the little town of Lutetia, near Issay—Lutetia Parisiorum—who repudiated his wife. The Abbé Velly, in his "History of France," says that this Cheribert, or Caribert, divorced his wife Ingoberg to espouse Mirefleur, the daughter of an artisan; and afterwards Theudegild, the daughter of a shepherd, who was raised to the first throne of the French Empire.

There was at that time neither first nor second throne among these barbarians whom the Roman Empire never recognized as kings. There was no French Empire. The empire of the French only commenced with Charlemagne. It is very doubtful whether the word "mirefleur" was in use either in the Welsh or Gallic languages, which were a *patois* of the Celtic jargon. This *patois* had no expressions so soft.

It is also said that the ruler or governor Chilperic, lord of the province of Soissonnais, whom they call king of France, divorced his queen Andovere, or Andove; and here follows the reason of this divorce.

This Andovere, after having given three male children to the lord of Soissons, brought forth a daughter. The Franks having been in some manner Christians since the time of Clovis, Andovere, after her recovery, presented her daughter to be baptized. Chilperic of Soissons, who was apparently very tired of her, declared that it was an unpardonable crime in her to be the godmother of her infant, and that she could no longer be his wife by the laws of the Church. He therefore married Fredegond, whom he subsequently put away also, and espoused a Visigoth. To conclude, this scrupulous husband ended by taking Fredegond back again.

There was nothing legal in all this, and it ought no more to be quoted than anything which passed in Ireland or the Orcades. The Justinian code, which we have adopted in several points, authorizes divorce; but the canonical law, which the Catholics have placed before it, does not permit it.

The author of the article says that divorce is practised in the states of Germany, of the confession of Augsburg. He might have added that this custom is established in all the countries of the North, among the reformed of all professions, and among all the followers of the Greek Church.

Divorce is probably of nearly the same date as marriage. I believe, however, that marriage is some weeks more ancient; that is to say, men quarrelled with their wives at the end of five days, beat them at the end of a month, and separated from them after six weeks' cohabitation.

Justinian, who collected all the laws made before him, to which he added his own, not only confirms that of divorce, but he extends it still further; so that every woman, whose husband is not a slave, but simply a prisoner of war during five years, may, after the five years have expired, contract another marriage.

Justinian was a Christian, and even a theologian; how is it, then, that the Church derogates from his laws? It was when the Church became the sovereign and the legislator. The popes had not much trouble to substitute their decretals instead of the civil code in the West, which was plunged in ignorance and barbarism. They took, indeed, so much advantage of the prevailing ignorance, that Honorius III., Gregory IX., and Innocent III., by their bulls, forbade the civil law to be taught. It may be said of this audacity, that it is not creditable, but true.

As the Church alone took cognizance of marriages, so it alone judged of divorce. No prince effected a divorce and married a second wife without previously obtaining the consent of the pope. Henry VIII., king of England, did not marry without his consent, until after having a long time solicited his divorce in the court of Rome in vain.

This custom, established in ignorant times, is perpetuated in enlightened ones only because it exists. All abuse eternizes itself; it is an Augean stable, and requires a Hercules to cleanse it.

Henry IV. could not be the father of a king of France without the permission of the pope; which must have been given, as has already been remarked, not by pronouncing a *divorce*, but a *lie*; that is to say, by pretending that there had not been previous marriage with Margaret de Valois.

DOG.

It seems as if nature had given the dog to man for his defence and pleasure; it is of all animals the most faithful; it is the best possible friend of man.

It appears that there are several species absolutely different. How can we believe that a greyhound comes originally from a spaniel? It has neither its hair, legs, shape, ears, voice, scent, nor instinct. A man who has never seen any dogs but barbets or spaniels, and who saw a greyhound for the first time, would take it rather for a dwarf horse than for an animal of the spaniel race. It is very likely that each race was always what it now is, with the exception of the mixture of a small number of them.

It is astonishing that, in the Jewish law, the dog was considered unclean, as well as the griffin, the hare, the pig, and the eel; there must have been some moral or physical reason for it, which we have not yet discovered.

That which is related of the sagacity, obedience, friendship, and courage of dogs, is as extraordinary as true. The military philosopher, Ulloa, assures us that in Peru the Spanish dogs recognize the men of the Indian race, pursue them, and tear them to pieces; and that the Peruvian dogs do the same with the Spaniards. This would seem to prove that each species of dogs still retained the hatred which was inspired in it at the time of the discovery, and that each race always fought for its master with the same valor and attachment.

Why, then, has the word "dog" become an injurious term? We say, for tenderness, my sparrow, my dove, my chicken; we even say my kitten, though this animal is famed for treachery; and, when we are angry, we call people dogs! The Turks, when not even angry, speak with horror and contempt of the Christian dogs. The English populace, when they see a man who, by his manner or dress, has the appearance of having been born on the banks of the Seine or of the Loire, commonly call him a French dog—a figure of rhetoric which is neither just to the dog nor polite to the man.

The delicate Homer introduces the divine Achilles telling the divine Agamemnon that he is as impudent as a dog—a classical justification of the English populace.

The most zealous friends of the dog must, however, confess that this animal carries audacity in its eyes; that some are morose; that they often bite strangers whom they take for their master's enemies, as sentinels assail passengers who approach too near the counterscarp. These are probably the reasons which have rendered the epithet "dog" insulting; but we dare not decide.

Why was the dog adored and revered—as has been seen—by the Egyptians? Because the dog protects man. Plutarch tells us that after Cambyses had killed their bull Apis, and had had it roasted, no animal except the dog dared to eat the remains of the feast, so profound was the respect for Apis; the dog, not so scrupulous, swallowed the god without hesitation. The Egyptians, as may be imagined, were exceedingly scandalized at this want of reverence, and Anubis lost much of his credit.

The dog, however, still bears the honor of being always in the heavens, under the names of the great and little dog. We regularly record the dog-days.

But of all dogs, Cerberus has had the greatest reputation; he had three heads. We have remarked that, anciently, all went by threes—Isis, Osiris, and Orus, the three first Egyptian divinities; the three brother gods of the Greek world—Jupiter, Neptune, and Pluto; the three Fates, the three Furies, the three Graces, the three judges of hell, and the three heads of this infernal dog.

We perceive here with grief that we have omitted the article on "Cats"; but we console ourselves by referring to their history. We will only remark that there are no cats in the heavens, as there are goats, crabs, bulls, rams, eagles, lions, fishes, hares, and dogs; but, in recompense, the cat has been consecrated, or revered, or adored, as partaking of divinity or saintship in several towns, and as altogether divine by no small number of women.

DOGMAS.

We know that all belief taught by the Church is a dogma which we must embrace. It is a pity that there are dogmas received by the Latin Church, and rejected by the Greek. But if unanimity is wanting, charity replaces it. It is, above all, between hearts that union is required. I think that we can relate a dream to the purpose, which has already found favor in the estimation of many peaceably disposed persons.

"On Feb. 18, 1763, of the vulgar era, the sun entering the sign of the fishes, I was transported to heaven, as all my friends can bear witness. The mare Borac, of Mahomet, was not my steed, neither was the fiery chariot of Elijah my carriage. I was not carried on the elephant of Somonocodom, the Siamese; on the horse of St. George, the patron of England; nor on St. Anthony's pig. I avow with frankness that my journey was made I know not how.

"It will be easily believed that I was dazzled; but it will not so easily be credited that I witnessed the judgment of the dead. And who were the judges? They were—do not be displeased at it—all those who have done good to man. Confucius, Solon, Socrates, Titus, Antoninus, Epictetus, Charron, de Thou, Chancellor de L' Hôpital, and all the great men who, having taught and practised the virtues that God requires, seemed to be the only persons possessing the right of pronouncing his devrees.

"I shall not describe on what thrones they were seated, nor how many celestial beings were prostrated before the eternal architect of all worlds, nor what a crowd of the inhabitants of these innumerable worlds appeared before the judges. I shall not even give an account of several little interesting peculiarities which were exceedingly striking.

"I remarked that every spirit who pleaded his cause and displayed his specious pretensions had beside him all the witnesses of his actions. For example, when Cardinal Lorraine boasted of having caused some of his opinions to be adopted by the Council of Trent, and demanded eternal life as the price of his orthodoxy, there immediately appeared around him twenty ladies of the court, all bearing on their foreheads the number of their interviews with the cardinal. I also saw those who had concerted with him the foundations of the infamous league. All the accomplices of his wicked designs surrounded him.

"Over against Cardinal Lorraine was John Calvin, who boasted, in his gross *patois*, of having trampled upon the papal idol, after others had overthrown it. 'I have written against painting and sculpture,' said he; 'I have made it apparent that good works are of no avail, and I have proved that it is diabolical to dance a minuet. Send away Cardinal Lorraine quickly, and place me by the side of St. Paul.'

"As he spoke there appeared by his side a lighted pile; a dreadful spectre, wearing round his neck a Spanish frill, arose half burned from the midst of the flames, with dreadful shrieks. 'Monster,' cried he; 'execrable monster, tremble! recognize that Servetus, whom you caused to perish by the most cruel torments, because he had disputed with you on the manner in which three persons can form one substance.' Then all the judges commanded that Cardinal Lorraine should be thrown into the abyss, but that Calvin should be punished still more rigorously.

"I saw a prodigious crowd of spirits, each of which said, 'I have believed, I have believed!' but on their forehead it was written, 'I have acted,' and they were condemned.

"The Jesuit Letellier appeared boldly with the bull Unigenitus in his hand. But there suddenly arose at his side a heap, consisting of two thousand *lettres-de-cachet*. A Jansenist set fire to them, and Letellier was burned to a cinder; while the Jansenist, who had no less caballed than the Jesuit, had his share of the flames.

"I saw approach, from right and left, troops of fakirs, talapoins, bonzes, and black, white, and gray monks, who all imagined that, to make their court to the Supreme Being, they must either sing, scourge themselves, or walk quite naked. 'What good have you done to men?' was the query. A dead silence succeeded to this question. No one dared to answer; and they were all conducted to the mad-houses of the universe, the largest buildings imaginable.

"One cried out that he believed in the metamorphoses of Xaca, another in those of Somonocodom. 'Bacchus stopped the sun and moon!' said this one. 'The gods resuscitated Pelops!' said the other. 'Here is the bull *in cœna Domini!*' said a newcomer—and the officer of the court exclaimed, 'To Bedlam, to Bedlam!'

"When all these causes were gone through, I heard this proclamation: 'By the Eternal Creator, Preserver, Rewarder, Revenger, Forgiver, etc., be it known to all the inhabitants of the hundred thousand millions of millions of worlds that it hath pleased us to form, that we never judge any sinners in reference to their own shallow ideas, but only as to their actions. Such is our Justice.'

"I own that this was the first time I ever heard such an edict; all those which I had read, on the little grain of dust on which I was born, ended with these words: 'Such is our *pleasure*.'"

DONATIONS.

The Roman Republic, which seized so many states, also gave some away. Scipio made Massinissa king of Numidia.

Lucullus, Sulla, and Pompey, each gave away half a dozen kingdoms. Cleopatra received Egypt from Cæsar. Antony, and afterwards Octavius, gave the little kingdom of Judæa to Herod.

Under Trajan, the famous medal of *regna assignata* was struck and kingdoms bestowed.

Cities and provinces given in sovereignty to priests and to colleges, for the greater glory of God, or of the gods, are seen in every country. Mahomet, and the caliphs, his vicars, took possession of many states in the propagation of their faith, but they did not make donations of them. They held by nothing but their Koran and their sabre.

The Christian religion, which was at first a society of poor people, existed for a long time on alms alone. The first donation was that of Ananias and Sapphira his wife. It was in ready money and was not prosperous to the donors.

The Donation of Constantine.

The celebrated donation of Rome and all Italy to Pope Sylvester by the emperor Constantine, was maintained as a part of the creed of Rome until the sixteenth century. It was believed that Constantine, being at Nicomedia, was cured of leprosy at Rome by the baptism which he received from Bishop Sylvester, though he was not baptized at all; and that by way of recompense he gave forthwith the city of Rome and all its western provinces to this Sylvester. If the deed of this donation had been drawn up by the doctor of the Italian comedy, it could not have been more pleasantly conceived. It is added that Constantine declared all the canons of Rome consuls and patricians—"*patricios et consules effici*" —that he himself held the bridle of the mare on which the new bishop was mounted—"*tenentes frenum equi illius*."

It is astonishing to reflect that this fine story was held an article of faith and respected by the rest of Europe for eight centuries, and that the Church persecuted as heretics all those who doubted it.

Donation of Pepin.

At present people are no longer persecuted for doubting that Pepin the usurper gave, or was able to give, the exarchate of Ravenna to the pope. It is at most an evil thought, a venial sin, which does not endanger the loss of body or of soul.

The reasoning of the German lawyers, who have scruples in regard to this donation, is as follows:

1. The librarian Anastatius, whose evidence is always cited, wrote one hundred and forty years after the event.

2. It is not likely that Pepin, who was not firmly established in France, and against whom Aquitaine

made war, could give away, in Italy, states which already belonged to the emperor, resident at Constantinople.

3. Pope Zacharias recognized the Roman-Greek emperor as the sovereign of those lands, disputed by the Lombards, and had administered the oath to him; as may be seen by the letters of this bishop, Zacharias of Rome to Bishop Boniface of Mentz. Pepin could not give to the pope the imperial territories.

4. When Pope Stephen II. produced a letter from heaven, written in the hand of St. Peter, to Pepin, to complain of the grievances of the king of the Lombards, Astolphus, St. Peter does not mention in his letter that Pepin had made a present of the exarchate of Ravenna to the pope; and certainly St. Peter would not have failed to do so, even if the thing had been only equivocal; he understands his interest too well.

Finally, the deed of this donation has never been produced; and what is still stronger, the fabrication of a false one cannot be ventured. The only proofs are vague recitals, mixed up with fables. Instead of certainty, there are only the absurd writings of monks, copied from age to age, from one another.

The Italian advocate who wrote in 1722 to prove that Parma and Placentia had been ceded to the holy see as a dependency of the exarchate, asserts that the Greek emperors were justly despoiled of their rights because they had excited the people against God. Can lawyers write thus in our days? Yes, it appears, but only at Rome. Cardinal Bellarmine goes still farther. "The first Christians," says he, "supported the emperors only because they were not the strongest." The avowal is frank, and I am persuaded that Bellarmine is right.

The Donation of Charlemagne.

At a time when the court of Rome believed itself deficient in titles, it pretended that Charlemagne had confirmed the donation of the exarchate, and that he added to it Sicily, Venice, Benevento, Corsica, and Sardinia. But as Charlemagne did not possess any of these states, he could not give them away; and as to the town of Ravenna, it is very clear that he kept it, since in his will he made a legacy to his city of Ravenna as well as to his city of Rome. It is surprising enough that the popes have obtained Ravenna and Rome; but as to Venice, it is not likely that the diploma which granted them the sovereignty will be found in the palace of St. Mark.

All these acts, instruments, and diplomas have been subjects of dispute for ages. But it is a confirmed opinion, says Giannone, that martyr to truth, that all these pieces were forged in the time of Gregory VII. "*E costante opinione presso i piu gravi scrittori che tutti questi istromenti e diplomi furono supposti ne tempi d'Ildebrando.*"

Donation of Benevento by the Emperor Henry III.

The first well attested donation which was made to the see of Rome was that of Benevento, and that was an exchange of the Emperor Henry III. with the pope. It wanted only one formality, which was that the emperor who gave away Benevento was not the owner of it. It belonged to the dukes of Benevento, and the Roman-Greek emperors reclaimed their rights on this duchy. But history supplies little beyond a list of those who have accommodated themselves with the property of others.

Donation of the Countess Mathilda.

The most authentic and considerable of these donations was that of all the possessions of the famous Countess Mathilda to Gregory VII. She was a young widow, who gave all to her spiritual director. It is supposed that the deed was twice executed and afterwards confirmed by her will.

However, there still remains some difficulty. It was always believed at Rome that Mathilda had given all her states, all her possessions, present and to come, to her friend Gregory VII. by a solemn deed, in her castle of Canossa, in 1077, for the relief of her own soul and that of her parents. And to corroborate this precious instrument a second is shown to us, dated in the year 1102, in which it is said that it is to Rome that she made this donation; that she recalled it, and that she afterwards renewed it; and always for the good of her soul.

How could so important a deed be recalled? Was the court of Rome so negligent? How could an instrument written at Canossa have been written at Rome? What do these contradictions mean? All that is clear is that the souls of the receivers fared better than the soul of the giver, who to save it was obliged to deprive herself of all she possessed in favor of her physicians.

In short, in 1102, a sovereign was deprived of the power of disposing of an acre of land; yet after this deed, and to the time of her death, in 1115, there are still found considerable donations of lands made by this same Mathilda to canons and monks. She had not, therefore, given all. Finally, this deed was very likely made by some ingenious person after her death.

The court of Rome still includes among its titles the testament of Mathilda, which confirmed her donations. The popes, however, never produce this testament. It should also be known whether this rich countess had the power to dispose of her possessions, which were most of them fiefs of the empire.

The Emperor Henry V., her heir, possessed himself of all, and recognized neither testament, donation, deed, nor right. The popes, in temporizing, gained more than the emperors in exerting their authority; and in time these Cæsars became so weak that the popes finally obtained the succession of Mathilda, which is now called the patrimony of St. Peter.

Donation of the Sovereignty of Naples to the Popes.

The Norman gentlemen who were the first instruments of the conquests of Naples and Sicily achieved the finest exploit of chivalry that was ever heard of. From forty to fifty men only delivered

Salerno at the moment it was taken by an army of Saracens. Seven other Norman gentlemen, all brothers, sufficed to chase these same Saracens from all the country, and to take prisoner the Greek emperor, who had treated them ungratefully. It was quite natural that the people, whom these heroes had inspired with valor, should be led to obey them through admiration and gratitude.

Such were the first rights to the crown of the two Sicilies. The bishops of Rome could no more give those states in fief than the kingdoms of Boutan or Cachemire. They could not even grant the investiture which would have been demanded of them; for, in the time of the anarchy of the fiefs, when a lord would hold his free land as a fief for his protection, he could only address himself to the sovereign or the chief of the country in which it was situated. And certainly the pope was neither the sovereign of Naples, Apulia, nor Calabria.

Much has been written about this pretended vassalage, but the source has never been discovered. I dare say that it is as much the fault of the lawyers as of the theologians. Every one deduces from a received principle consequences the most favorable to himself or his party. But is the principle true? Is the first fact by which it is supported incontestable? It is this which should be examined. It resembles our ancient romance writers, who all take it for granted that Francus brought the helmet of Hector to France. This casque was impenetrable, no doubt; but had Hector really worn it? The holy Virgin's milk is also very respectable; but do the twenty sacristies, who boast of having a gill of it, really possess it?

Men of the present time, as wicked as foolish, do not shrink from the greatest crimes, and yet fear an excommunication, which would render them execrable to people still more wicked and foolish than themselves.

Robert and Richard Guiscard, the conquerors of Apulia and Calabria, were excommunicated by Pope Leo IX. They were declared vassals of the empire; but the emperor, Henry III., discontented with these feudatory conquerors, engaged Leo IX. to launch the excommunication at the head of an army of Germans. The Normans, who did not fear these thunderbolts like the princes of Italy, beat the Germans and took the pope prisoner. But to prevent the popes and emperors hereafter from coming to trouble them in their possessions, they offered their conquests to the Church under the name of *oblata*. It was thus that England paid the Peter's pence; that the first kings of Spain and Portugal, on recovering their states from the Saracens, promised two pounds of gold a year to the Church of Rome. But England, Spain, nor Portugal never regarded the pope as their sovereign master.

Duke Robert, *oblat* of the Church, was therefore no feudatory of the pope; he could not be so, since the popes were not the sovereigns of Rome. This city was then governed by its senate, and the bishop possessed only influence. The pope was at Rome precisely what the elector is at Cologne. There is a prodigious difference between the *oblat* of a saint and the feudatory of a bishop.

Baronius, in his "Acts," relates the pretended homage done by Robert, duke of Apulia and Calabria, to Nicholas II.; but this deed is suspected, like many others; it has never been seen, it has never been found in any archives. Robert entitled himself "duke by the grace of God and St. Peter"; but certainly St. Peter had given him nothing, nor was that saint king of Rome.

The other popes, who were kings no more than St. Peter, received without difficulty the homage of all the princes who presented themselves to reign over Naples, particularly when these princes were the most powerful.

Donation of England and Ireland to the Popes by King John.

In 1213, King John, vulgarly called Lackland, or more properly Lackvirtue, being excommunicated and seeing his kingdom laid under an interdict, gave it away to Pope Innocent III. and his successors. "Not constrained with fear, but with my full consent and the advice of my barons, for the remission of my sins against God and the Church, I resign England and Ireland to God, St. Peter, St. Paul, and our lord the Pope Innocent, and to his successors in the apostolic chair."

He declared himself feudatory lieutenant of the pope, paid about eight thousand pounds sterling in ready money to the legate Pandulph, promised to pay a thousand more every year, gave the first year in advance to the legate who trampled upon him, and swore on his knees that he submitted to lose all in the event of not paying at the time appointed. The jest of this ceremony was that the legate departed with the money and forgot to remove the excommunication.

Examination of the Vassalage of Naples and England.

It may be asked which was the more valuable, the donation of Robert Guiscard or that of John Lackland; both had been excommunicated, both had given their states to St. Peter and became only the farmers of them. If the English barons were indignant at the infamous bargain of their king with the pope, and cancelled it, the Neapolitan barons could have equally cancelled that of Baron Robert; and that which they could have done formerly they certainly can do at present.

Were England and Apulia given to the pope, according to the law of the Church or of the fiefs, as to a bishop or a sovereign? If to a bishop, it is precisely contrary to the law of Jesus, who so often forbids his disciples to take anything, and who declares to them that His kingdom is not of this world.

If as to a sovereign, it was high treason to his imperial majesty; the Normans had already done homage to the emperor. Thus no right, spiritual or temporal, belonged to the popes in this affair. When the principle is erroneous, all the deductions are so of course. Naples no more belonged to the pope than England.

There is still another method of providing against this ancient bargain; it is the right of the people, which is stronger than the right of the fiefs. The people's right will not suffer one sovereign to belong to another, and the most ancient law is to be master of our own, at least when we are not the weakest.

Of Donations Made by the Popes.

If principalities have been given to the bishops of Rome, they have given away many more. There is not a single throne in Europe to which they have not made a present. As soon as a prince had conquered a country, or even wished to do it, the popes granted it in the name of St. Peter. Sometimes they even made the first advances, and it may be said that they have given away every kingdom but that of heaven.

Few people in France know that Julius II. gave the states of King Louis XII. to the Emperor Maximilian, who could not put himself in possession of them. They do not sufficiently remember that Sixtus V., Gregory XIV., and Clement VIII., were ready to make a present of France to whomsoever Philip II. would have chosen for the husband of his daughter Clara Eugenia.

As to the emperors, there is not one since Charlemagne that the court of Rome has not pretended to nominate. This is the reason why Swift, in his "Tale of a Tub," says "that Lord Peter became suddenly mad, and that Martin and Jack, his brothers, confined him by the advice of their relations." We simply relate this drollery as a pleasant blasphemy of an English priest against the bishop of Rome.

All these donations disappear before that of the East and West Indies, with which Alexander VI. of his divine power and authority invested Spain and Portugal. It was giving almost all the earth. He could in the same manner have given away the globes of Jupiter and Saturn with their satellites.

Particular Donations.

The donations of citizens are treated quite differently. The codes are unanimously agreed that no one can give away the property of another as well as that no person can take it. It is a universal law.

In France, jurisprudence was uncertain on this object, as on almost all others, until the year 1731, when the equitable Chancellor d'Aguesseau, having conceived the design of making the law uniform, very weakly began the great work by the edict on donations. It is digested in forty-seven articles, but, in wishing to render all the formalities concerning donations uniform, Flanders was excepted from the general law, and in excepting Flanders, Artois was forgotten, which should have enjoyed the same exception; so that in six years after the general law, a particular one was obliged to be made for Artois.

These new edicts concerning donations and testaments were principally made to do away with all the commentators who had considerably embroiled the laws, having already compiled six commentaries upon them.

It may be remarked that donations, or deeds of gift, extend much farther than to the particular person to whom a present is made. For every present there must be paid to the farmers of the royal domain—the duty of control, the duty of "*insinuation*" the duty of the hundredth penny, the tax of two sous in the livre, the tax of eight sous in the livre, etc.

So that every time you make a present to a citizen you are much more liberal than you imagine. You have also the pleasure of contributing to the enriching of the farmers-general, but, after all, this money does not go out of the kingdom like that which is paid to the court of Rome.

DRINKING HEALTHS.

What was the origin of this custom? Has it existed since drinking commenced? It appears natural to drink wine for our own health, but not for the health of others.

The "*propino*" of the Greeks, adopted by the Romans, does not signify "I drink to your good health," but "I drink first that you may drink afterwards"—I invite you to drink.

In their festivals they drink to celebrate a mistress, not that she might have good health. See in Martial: "*Naevia sex cyathis, septem Justina bibatur*"—"Six cups for Naevia, for Justina seven."

The English, who pique themselves upon renewing several ancient customs, drink to the honor of the ladies, which they call toasting, and it is a great subject of dispute among them whether a lady is toastworthy or not—whether she is worthy to be toasted.

They drank at Rome for the victories of Augustus, and for the return of his health. Dion Cassius relates that after the battle of Actium the senate decreed that, in their repasts, libations should be made to him in the second service. It was a strange decree. It is more probable that flattery had voluntarily introduced this meanness. Be it as it may, we read in Horace:

Hinc ad vina redit lætus, et alteris
Te mensis adhibet Deum,

Te multa prece; te prosequitur nero
Defuso pateris; et labiis tuum
Miscet numen; uti Graecia Castoris
Et magni nemore Herculis.
Longas o utinam, dux bone ferias
Praestes Hesperiae; dicimus integro
Sicci mane die, dicimus uvidi,
Quum sol oceano subest.

To thee he chants the sacred song,
To thee the rich libation pours;
Thee placed his household gods among,
With solemn daily prayer adores;
So Castor and great Hercules of old
Were with her gods by graceful Greece enrolled.
Gracious and good, beneath thy reign
May Rome her happy hours employ,
And grateful hail thy just domain
With pious hymn and festal joy.
Thus, with the rising sun we sober pray,
Thus, in our wine beneath his setting ray.

It is very likely that hence the custom arose among barbarous nations of drinking to the health of their guests, an absurd custom, since we may drink four bottles without doing them the least good.

The dictionary of Trévoux tells us that we should not drink to the health of our superiors in their presence. This may be the case in France or Germany, but in England it is a received custom. The distance is not so great from one man to another at London as at Vienna.

It is of importance in England to drink to the health of a prince who pretends to the throne; it is to declare yourself his partisan. It has cost more than one Scotchman and Hibernian dear for having drank to the health of the Stuarts.

All the Whigs, after the death of King William, drank not to his health, but to his memory. A Tory named Brown, bishop of Cork in Ireland, a great enemy to William in Ireland, said, "that he would put a *cork* in all those bottles which were drunk to the glory of this monarch." He did not stop at this silly pun; he wrote, in 1702, an episcopal address to show the Irish that it was an atrocious impiety to drink to the health of kings, and, above all, to their memory; that the latter, in particular, is a profanation of these words of Jesus Christ: "Drink this in remembrance of me."

It is astonishing that this bishop was not the first who conceived such a folly. Before him, the Presbyterian Prynne had written a great book against the impious custom of drinking to the health of Christians.

Finally, there was one John Geza, vicar of the parish of St. Faith, who published "The Divine Potion to Preserve Spiritual Health, by the Cure of the Inveterate Malady of Drinking Healths; with Clear and Solid Arguments against this Criminal Custom, all for the Satisfaction of the Public, at the Request of a Worthy Member of Parliament, in the Year of Our Salvation 1648."

Our reverend Father Garasse, our reverend Father Patouillet, and our reverend Father Nonnotte are nothing superior to these profound Englishmen. We have a long time wrestled with our neighbors for the superiority—To which is it due?

THE DRUIDS.

The Scene is in Tartarus. The Furies Entwined with Serpents, and Whips in Their Hands.

Come along, Barbaquincorix, Celtic druid, and thou, detestable Grecian hierophant, Calchas, the moment of your just punishment has returned again; the hour of vengeance has arrived—the bell has sounded!

THE DRUID AND CALCHAS.

Oh, heavens! my head, my sides, my eyes, my ears! pardon, ladies, pardon!

CALCHAS.

Mercy! two vipers are penetrating my eye-balls!

DRUID.

A serpent is devouring my entrails!

CALCHAS.

Alas, how am I mangled! And must my eyes be every day restored, to be torn again from my head?

DRUID.

Must my skin be renewed only to dangle in ribbons from my lacerated body?

TISIPHONE.

It will teach you how to palm off a miserable parasitical plant for a universal remedy another time. Will you still sacrifice boys and girls to your god Theutates, priest? still burn them in osier baskets to the sound of a drum?

DRUID.

Never, never; dear lady, a little mercy, I beseech you.

TISIPHONE.

You never had any yourself. Seize him, serpents, and now another lash!

ALECTO.

Let them curry well this Calchas, who advances towards us, "With cruel eye, dark mien, and bristled hair."

CALCHAS.

My hair is torn away; I am scorched, flayed, impaled!

ALECTO.

Wretch! Will you again cut the throat of a beautiful girl, in order to obtain a favorable gale, instead of uniting her to a good husband?

CALCHAS AND THE DRUID.

Oh, what torments! and yet we die not.

TISIPHONE.

Hey-dey! God forgive me, but I hear music! It is Orpheus; why our serpents, sister, have become as gentle as lambs!

CALCHAS.

My sufferings cease; how very strange!

THE DRUID.

I am altogether recovered. Oh, the power of good music! And who are you, divine man, who thus cures wounds, and rejoices hell itself?

ORPHEUS.

My friends, I am a priest like yourselves, but I never deceived anyone, nor cut the throat of either boy or girl in my life. When on earth, instead of making the gods hated, I rendered them beloved, and softened the manners of the men whom you made ferocious. I shall exert myself in the like manner in hell. I met, just now, two barbarous priests whom they were scourging beyond measure; one of them formerly hewed a king in pieces before the Lord, and the other cut the throat of his queen and sovereign at the horse gate. I have terminated their punishment, and, having played to them a tune on the violin, they have promised me that when they return into the world they will live like honest men.

DRUID AND CALCHAS.

We promise the same thing, on the word of a priest.

ORPHEUS.

Yes, but "*Passato il pericolo, gabbato il santo.*" [*The scene closes with a-figure Dance, performed by Orpheus, the Condemned, and the Furies, to light and agreeable music.*]

EASE.

Easy applies not only to a thing easily done, but also to a thing which appears to be so. The pencil of Correggio is easy, the style of Quinault is much more easy than that of Despréaux, and the style of Ovid surpasses in facility that of Persius.

This facility in painting, music, eloquence, and poetry, consists in a natural and spontaneous felicity, which admits of nothing that implies research, strength, or profundity. Thus the pictures of Paul Veronese have a much more easy and less finished air than those of Michel Angelo. The symphonies of Rameau are superior to those of Lulli, but appear less easy. Bossuet is more truly eloquent and more easy than Fléchier. Rousseau, in his epistles, has not near the facility and truth of Despréaux.

The commentator of Despréaux says that "this exact and laborious poet taught the illustrious Racine to make verses with difficulty, and that those which appear easy are those which have been made with the most difficulty."

It is true that it often costs much pains to express ourselves with clearness, as also that the natural may be arrived at by effort; but it is also true that a happy genius often produces easy beauties without any labor, and that enthusiasm goes much farther than art.

Most of the impassioned expressions of our good poets have come finished from their pen, and appear easy, as if they had in reality been composed without labor; the imagination, therefore, often conceives and brings forth easily. It is not thus with didactic works, which require art to make them appear easy. For example, there is much less ease than profundity in Pope's "Essay on Man."

Bad works may be rapidly constructed, which, having no genius, will appear easy, and it is often the lot of those who, without genius, have the unfortunate habit of composing. It is in this sense that a personage of the old comedy, called the "Italian," says to another: "Thou makest bad verses admirably well."

The term "easy" is an insult to a woman, but is sometimes in society praise for a man; it is, however, a fault in a statesman. The manners of Atticus were easy; he was the most amiable of the Romans; the easy Cleopatra gave herself as easily to Antony as to Cæsar; the easy Claudius allowed himself to be governed by Agrippina; easy applied to Claudius is only a lenitive, the proper expression is *weak*.

An easy man is in general one possessed of a mind which easily gives itself up to reason and remonstrance—a heart which melts at the prayers which are made to it; while a weak man is one who allows too much authority over him.

ECLIPSE.

In the greatest part of the known world every extraordinary phenomenon was for a long time believed to be the presage of some happy or miserable event. Thus the Roman historians have not failed to observe that an eclipse of the sun accompanied the birth of Romulus, that another announced his death, and that a third attended the foundation of the city of Rome.

We have already spoken of the article entitled "The Vision of Constantine," of the apparition of the cross which preceded the triumph of Christianity, and under the article on "Prophecy," we shall treat of the new star which enlightened the birth of Jesus. We will, therefore, here confine ourselves to what has been said of the darkness with which all the earth was covered when He gave up the ghost.

The writers of the Greek and Romish Churches have quoted as authentic two letters attributed to Dionysius the Areopagite, in which he relates that being at Heliopolis in Egypt, with his friend Apollophanes, he suddenly saw, about the sixth hour, the moon pass underneath the sun, which caused a great eclipse. Afterwards, in the ninth hour, they perceived the moon quitting the place which she occupied and return to the opposite side of the diameter. They then took the rules of Philip Aridæus, and, having examined the course of the stars, they found that the sun could not have been naturally eclipsed at that time. Further, they observed that the moon, contrary to her natural motion, instead of going to the west to range herself under the sun, approached on the eastern side and that she returned behind on the same side, which caused Apollophanes to say, "These, my dear Dionysius, are changes of Divine things," to which Dionysius replied, "Either the author of nature suffers, or the machine of the universe will be soon destroyed."

Dionysius adds that having remarked the exact time and year of this prodigy, and compared them with what Paul afterwards told him, he yielded up to the truth as well as his friend. This is what led to the belief that the darkness happening at the death of Jesus Christ was caused by a supernatural eclipse; and what has extended this opinion is that Maldonat says it is that of almost all the Catholics. How is it possible to resist the authority of an ocular, enlightened, and disinterested witness, since it was supposed that when he saw this eclipse Dionysius was a pagan?

As these pretended letters of Dionysius were not forged until towards the fifteenth or sixteenth century, Eusebius of Cæsarea was contented with quoting the evidence of Phlegon, a freed man of the emperor Adrian. This author was also a pagan, and had written "The History of the Olympiads," in sixteen books, from their origin to the year 140 of the vulgar era. He is made to say that in the fourth year of the two hundred and second Olympiad there was the greatest eclipse of the sun that had ever been seen; the day was changed to night at the sixth hour, the stars were seen, and an earthquake overthrew several edifices in the city of Nicæa in Bithynia.

Eusebius adds that the same events are related in the ancient monuments of the Greeks, as having happened in the eighteenth year of Tiberius. It is thought that Eusebius alluded to Thallus, a Greek historian already cited by Justin, Tertullian, and Julius Africanus, but neither the work of Thallus, nor that of Phlegon having reached us, we can only judge of the accuracy of these two quotations of reasoning.

It is true that the Paschal "Chronicle of the Greeks," as well as St. Jerome Anastatius, the author of the "*Historia Miscella*," and Freculphus of Luxem, among the Latins, all unite in representing the fragment of Phlegon in the same manner. But it is known that these five witnesses, so uniform in their dispositions, translated or copied the passage, not from Phlegon himself, but from Eusebius; while John Philoponus, who had read Phlegon, far from agreeing with Eusebius, differs from him by two years. We could also name Maximus and Maleba, who lived when the work of Phlegon still existed, and the result of an examination of the whole is that five of the quoted authors copy Eusebius. Philoponus, who really saw the work of Phlegon, gives a second reading, Maximus a third, and Maleba a fourth, so that they are far from relating the passage in the same manner.

In short, the calculations of Hodgson, Halley, Whiston, and Gale Morris have demonstrated that Phlegon and Thallus speak of a natural eclipse which happened November 24, in the first year of the two hundred and second Olympiad, and not in the fourth year, as Eusebius pretends. Its size at Nicæa in

Bithynia, was, according to Whiston, only from nine to ten digits, that is to say, two-thirds and a half of the sun's disc. It began at a quarter past eight, and ended at five minutes past ten, and between Cairo in Egypt, and Jerusalem, according to Mr. Gale Morris, the sun was totally obscured for nearly two minutes. At Jerusalem the middle of the eclipse happened about an hour and a quarter after noon.

But what ought to spare all this discussion is that Tertullian says the day became suddenly dark while the sun was in the midst of his career; that the pagans believed that it was an eclipse, not knowing that it had been predicted by the prophet Amos in these words: "I will cause the sun to go down at noon, and I will darken the earth in the clear day." "They," adds Tertullian, "who have sought for the cause of this event and could not discover it, have denied it; but the fact is certain, and you will find it noted in your archives."

Origen, on the contrary, says that it is not astonishing foreign authors have said nothing about the darknesses of which the evangelists speak, since they only appeared in the environs of Jerusalem; Judæa, according to him, being designated under the name of all the earth in more than one place in Scripture. He also avows that the passage in the Gospel of St. Luke, in which we read that in his time all the earth was covered with darkness, on account of an eclipse of the sun, had been thus falsified by some ignorant Christian who thought thereby to throw a light on the text of the evangelist, or by some ill-intentioned enemy who wished a pretext to calumniate the Church, as if the evangelists had remarked an eclipse at a time when it was very evident that it could not have happened. "It is true," adds he, "that Phlegon says that there was one under Tiberius, but as he does not say that it happened at the full moon there is nothing wonderful in that."

"These obscurations," continues Origen, "were of the nature of those which covered Egypt in the time of Moses, and were not felt in the quarter in which the Israelites dwelt. Those of Egypt lasted three days, while those of Jerusalem only lasted three hours; the first were after the manner of the second, and even as Moses raised his hands to heaven and invoked the Lord to draw them down on Egypt, so Jesus Christ, to cover Jerusalem with darkness, extended his hands on the cross against an ungrateful people who had cried: 'Crucify him, crucify him!'"

We may, in this case, exclaim with Plutarch, that the darkness of superstition is more dangerous than that of eclipses.

ECONOMY (RURAL).

The primitive economy, that which is the foundation of all the rest, is rural. In early times it was exhibited in the patriarchal life and especially in that of Abraham, who made a long journey through the arid deserts of Memphis to buy corn. I shall continue, with due respect, to discard all that is divine in the history of Abraham, and attend to his rural economy alone.

I do not learn that he ever had a house; he quitted the most fertile country of the universe and towns in which there were commodious houses, to go wandering in countries, the languages of which he did not understand.

He went from Sodom into the desert of Gerar without forming the least establishment. When he turned away Hagar and the child Ishmael it was still in a desert and all the food he gave them was a morsel of bread and a cruse of water. When he was about to sacrifice his son Isaac to the Lord it was again in a desert. He cut the wood himself to burn the victim and put it on the back of Isaac, whom he was going to immolate.

His wife died in a place called Kirgath-arba, or Hebron; he had not six feet of earth in which to bury her, but was obliged to buy a cave to deposit her body. This was the only piece of land which he ever possessed.

However, he had many children, for, without reckoning Isaac and his posterity, his second wife Keturah, at the age of one hundred and forty years, according to the ordinary calculation, bore him five male children, who departed towards Arabia.

It is not said that Isaac had a single piece of land in the country in which his father died; on the contrary, he went into the desert of Gerar with his wife, Rebecca, to the same Abimelech, king of Gerar, who had been in love with his mother.

The king of the desert became also amorous of Rebecca, whom her husband caused to pass for his sister, as Abraham had acted with regard to Sarah and this same King Abimelech forty years before. It is rather astonishing that in this family the wife always passed for the sister when there was anything to be gained, but as these facts are consecrated, it is for us to maintain a respectful silence.

Scripture says that Abraham enriched himself in this horrible country, which became fertile for his benefit, and that he became extremely powerful. But it is also mentioned that he had no water to drink; that he had a great quarrel with the king's herdsmen for a well; and it is easy to discover that he still had not a house of his own.

His children, Esau and Jacob, had not a greater establishment than their father. Jacob was obliged to seek his fortune in Mesopotamia, whence Abraham came; he served seven years for one of the daughters of Laban, and seven other years to obtain the second daughter. He fled with his wives and the flocks of his father-in-law, who pursued him. A precarious fortune, that of Jacob.

Esau is represented as wandering like Jacob. None of the twelve patriarchs, the children of Jacob, had any fixed dwelling, or a field of which they were the proprietors. They reposed in their tents like Bedouin Arabs.

It is clear that this patriarchal life would not conveniently suit the temperature of our atmosphere. A good cultivator, such as Pignoux of Auvergne, must have a convenient house with an aspect towards the east, large barns and stables, stalls properly built, the whole amounting to about fifty thousand francs of our present money in value. He must sow a hundred acres with corn, besides having good pastures; he should possess some acres of vineyard, and about fifty for inferior grain and herbs, thirty acres of wood, a plantation of mulberries, silkworms, and bees. With all these advantages well economized, he can maintain a family in abundance. His land will daily improve; he will support them without fearing the irregularity of the seasons and the weight of taxes, because one good year repairs the damages of two bad ones. He will enjoy in his domain a real sovereignty, which will be subject only to the laws. It is the most natural state of man, the most tranquil, the most happy, and, unfortunately, the most rare.

The son of this venerable patriarch, seeing himself rich, is disgusted with paying the humiliating tax of the taille. Having unfortunately learned some Latin he repairs to town, buys a post which exempts him from the tax and which bestows nobility. He sells his domain to pay for his vanity, marries a girl brought up in luxury who dishonors and ruins him; he dies in beggary, and his only son wears a livery in Paris.

ECONOMY OF SPEECH—

TO SPEAK BY ECONOMY.

This is an expression consecrated in its appropriation by the fathers of the Church and even by the primitive propagators of our holy religion. It signifies the application of oratory to circumstances.

For example: St. Paul, being a Christian, comes to the temple of the Jews to perform the Judaic rites, in order to show that he does not forsake the Mosaic law; he is recognized at the end of a week and accused of having profaned the temple. Loaded with blows, he is dragged along by the mob; the tribune of the cohort—*tribunis cohortis* —arrives, and binds him with a double chain. The next day this tribune assembles the council and carries Paul before it, when the High Priest Ananias commences proceedings by giving him a box on the ear, on which Paul salutes him with the epithet of "a whited wall."

"But when Paul perceived that the one part were Sadducees and the other Pharisees, he cried out in the council, 'Men and brethren, I am a Pharisee, the son of a Pharisee, of the hope and resurrection of the dead I am called in question.' And when he had so said there arose a discussion between the Pharisees and the Sadducees, and the multitude was divided. For the Sadducees say that there is no resurrection, neither angel nor spirit, but the Pharisees confess both."

It is very evident from the text that Paul was not a Pharisee after he became a Christian and that there was in this affair no question either of resurrection or hope, of angel or spirit.

The text shows that Paul spoke thus only to embroil the Pharisees and Sadducees. This was speaking with economy, that is to say, with prudence; it was a pious artifice which, perhaps, would not have been permitted to any but an apostle.

It is thus that almost all the fathers of the Church have spoken "with economy." St. Jerome develops this method admirably in his fifty-fourth letter to Pammachus. Weigh his words. After having said that there are occasions when it is necessary to present a loaf and to throw a stone, he continues thus:

"Pray read Demosthenes, read Cicero, and if these rhetoricians displease you because their art consists in speaking of the seeming rather than the true, read Plato, Theophrastus, Xenophon, Aristotle, and all those who, having dipped into the fountain of Socrates, drew different waters from it. Is there among them any candor, any simplicity? What terms among them are not ambiguous, and what sense do they not make free with to bear away the palm of victory? Origen, Methodius, Eusebius, Apollinarus, have written a million of arguments against Celsus and Porphyry. Consider with what artifice, with what problematic subtlety they combat the spirit of the devil. They do not say what they think, but what it is expedient to say: *Non quod sentiunt, sed quod necesse est dicunt*. And not to mention other Latins—Tertullian, Cyprian, Minutius, Victorinus, Lactantius, and Hilarius—whom I will not cite here;

I will content myself with relating the example of the Apostle Paul," etc.

St. Augustine often writes with economy. He so accommodates himself to time and circumstances that in one of his epistles he confesses that he explained the Trinity only because he must say something.

Assuredly this was not because he doubted the Holy Trinity, but he felt how ineffable this mystery is and wished to content the curiosity of the people.

This method was always received in theology. It employed an argument against the Eucratics, which was the cause of triumph to the Carpocratians; and when it afterwards disputed with the Carpocratians its arms were changed.

It is asserted that Jesus Christ died for many when the number of rejected is set forth, but when his universal bounty is to be manifested he is said to have died for all. Here you take the real sense for the figurative; there the figurative for the real, as prudence and expediency direct.

Such practices are not admitted in justice. A witness would be punished who told the *pour* and *contre* of a capital offence. But there is an infinite difference between vile human interests, which require the greatest clearness, and divine interests, which are hidden in an impenetrable abyss. The same judges who require indubitable demonstrative proofs will be contented in sermons with moral proofs, and even with declamations exhibiting no proofs at all.

St. Augustine speaks with economy, when he says, "I believe, because it is absurd; I believe, because it is impossible." These words, which would be extravagant in all worldly affairs, are very respectable in theology. They signify that what is absurd and impossible to mortal eyes is not so to the eyes of God; God has revealed to me these pretended absurdities, these apparent impossibilities, therefore I ought to believe them.

An advocate would not be allowed to speak thus at the bar. They would confine in a lunatic asylum a witness who might say, "I assert that the accused, while shut up in a country house in Martinique, killed a man in Paris, and I am the more certain of this homicide because it is absurd and impossible." But revelations, miracles, and faith are quite a distinct order of things.

The same St. Augustine observes in his one hundred and fifty-third letter, "It is written that the whole world belongs to the faithful, and infidels have not an obolus that they possess legitimately."

If upon this principle a brace of bankers were to wait upon me to assure me that they were of the faithful, and in that capacity had appropriated the property belonging to me, a miserable worldling, to themselves, it is certain that they would be committed to the Châtelet, in spite of the economy of the language of St. Augustine.

St. Irenæus asserts that we must not condemn the incest of the two daughters of Lot, nor that of Thamar with her father-in-law, because the Holy Scripture has not expressly declared them criminal. This verbal economy prevents not the legal punishment of incest among ourselves. It is true that if the Lord expressly ordered people to commit incest it would not be sinful, which is the economy of Irenæus. His laudable object is to make us respect everything in the Holy Scriptures, but as God has not expressly praised the foregoing doings of the daughters of Lot and of Judah we are permitted to condemn them.

All the first Christians, without exception, thought of war like the Quakers and Dunkards of the present day, and the Brahmins, both ancient and modern. Tertullian is the father who is most explicit against this legal species of murder, which our vile human nature renders expedient. "No custom, no rule," says he, "can render this criminal destruction legitimate."

Nevertheless, after assuring us that no Christian can carry arms, he says, "by economy," in the same book, in order to intimidate the Roman Empire, "although of such recent origin, we fill your cities and your *armies*."

It is in the same spirit that he asserts that Pilate was a Christian in his heart, and the whole of his apology is filled with similar assertions, which redoubled the zeal of his proselytes.

Let us terminate these examples of the economical style, which are numberless, by a passage of St. Jerome, in his controversy with Jovian upon second marriages. The holy Jerome roundly asserts that it is plain, by the formation of the two sexes—in the description of which he is rather particular—that they are destined for each other, and for propagation. It follows, therefore, that they are to make love without ceasing, in order that their respective faculties may not be bestowed in vain. This being the case, why should not men and women marry again? Why, indeed, is a man to deny his wife to his friend if a cessation of attention on his own part be personally convenient? He may present the wife of another with a loaf of bread if she be hungry, and why may not her other wants be supplied, if they are urgent? Functions are not given to lie dormant, etc.

After such a passage it is useless to quote any more, but it is necessary to remark, by the way, that the economical style, so intimately connected with the polemical, ought to be employed with the greatest circumspection, and that it belongs not to the profane to imitate the things hazarded by the saints, either as regards the heat of their zeal or the piquancy of their delivery.

ELEGANCE.

According to some authors this word comes from "*electus*," chosen; it does not appear that its etymology can be derived from any other Latin word, since all is choice that is elegant. Elegance is the result of regularity and grace.

This word is employed in speaking of painting and sculpture. *Elegans signum* is opposed to *signum rigens*—a proportionate figure, the rounded outlines of which are expressed with softness, to a cold and badly-finished figure.

The severity of the ancient Romans gave an odious sense to the word "*elegantia*." They regarded all kinds of elegance as affectation and far-fetched politeness, unworthy the gravity of the first ages. "*Vitæ non laudi fuit*," says Aulus Gellius. They call him an "elegant man," whom in these days we designate a *petit-maître (bellus homuncio),* and which the English call a "beau"; but towards the time of Cicero, when manners received their last degree of refinement, *elegans* was always deemed laudatory. Cicero makes use of this word in a hundred places to describe a man or a polite discourse. At that time even a repast was called elegant, which is scarcely the case among us.

This term among the French, as among the ancient Romans, is confined to sculpture, painting, eloquence, and still more to poetry; it does not precisely mean the same thing as grace.

The word "grace" applies particularly to the countenance, and we do not say an elegant face, as we say elegant contours; the reason is that grace always relates to something in motion, and it is in the countenance that the mind appears; thus we do not say an elegant gait, because gait includes motion.

The elegance of a discourse is not its eloquence; it is a part of it; it is neither the harmony nor metre alone; it is clearness, metre, and choice of words, united.

There are languages in Europe in which nothing is more scarce than an elegant expression. Rude terminations, frequent consonants, and auxiliary-verbs grammatically repeated in the same sentence, offend the ears even of the natives themselves.

A discourse may be elegant without being good, elegance being, in reality, only a choice of words; but a discourse cannot be absolutely good without being elegant. Elegance is still more necessary to poetry than eloquence, because it is a part of that harmony so necessary to verse.

An orator may convince and affect even without elegance, purity, or number; a poet cannot really do so without being elegant: it is one of the principal merits of Virgil. Horace is much less elegant in his satires and epistles, so that he is much less of a poet *sermoni proprior*.

The great point in poetry and the oratorical art is that the elegance should never appear forced; and the poet in that, as in other things, has greater difficulties than the orator, for harmony being the base of his art, he must not permit a succession of harsh syllables. He must even sometimes sacrifice a little of the thought to elegance of expression, which is a constraint that the orator never experiences.

It should be remarked that if elegance always appears easy, all that is easy and natural is not, however, elegant.

It is seldom said of a comedy that it is elegantly written. The simplicity and rapidity of a familiar dialogue exclude this merit, so proper to all other poetry. Elegance would seem inconsistent with the comic. A thing elegantly said would not be laughed at, though most of the verses of Molière's *"Amphitryon,"* with the exception of those of mere pleasantry, are elegantly written. The mixture of gods and men in this piece, so unique in its kind, and the irregular verses, forming a number of madrigals, are perhaps the cause.

A madrigal requires to be more elegant than an epigram, because the madrigal bears somewhat the nature of the ode, and the epigram belongs to the comic. The one is made to express a delicate sentiment, and the other a ludicrous one.

Elegance should not be attended to in the sublime: it would weaken it. If we read of the elegance of the Jupiter Olympus of Phidias, it would be a satire. The elegance of the "Venus of Praxiteles" may be properly alluded to.

ELIAS OR ELIJAH, AND ENOCH.

Elias and Enoch are two very important personages of antiquity. They are the only mortals who have been taken out of the world without having first tasted of death. A very learned man has pretended that these are allegorical personages. The father and mother of Elias are unknown. He believes that his country, Gilead, signifies nothing but the circulation of time. He proves it to have come from Galgala, which signifies revolution. But what signifies the name of the village of Galgala!

The word Elias has a sensible relation to that of Elios, the sun. The burned sacrifice offered by Elias, and lighted by fire from heaven, is an image of that which can be done by the united rays of the sun. The rain which falls, after great heats, is also a physical truth.

The chariot of fire and the fiery horses, which bore Elias to heaven, are a lively image of the four horses of the sun. The return of Elias at the end of the world seems to accord with the ancient opinion, that the sun would extinguish itself in the waters, in the midst of the general destruction that was expected, for almost all antiquity was for a long time persuaded that the world would sooner or later be destroyed.

We do not adopt these allegories; we only stand by those related in the Old Testament.

Enoch is as singular a personage as Elias, only that Genesis names his father and son, while the family of Elias is unknown. The inhabitants of both East and West have celebrated this Enoch.

The Holy Scripture, which is our infallible guide, informs us that Enoch was the father of Methuselah, or Methusalem, and that he only dwelt on the earth three hundred and sixty-five years, which seems a very short life for one of the first patriarchs. It is said that he walked in the way of God and that he appeared no longer because God carried him away. "It is that," says Calmet, "which makes the holy fathers and most of the commentators assure us that Enoch still lives; that God has borne him out of the world as well as Elias; that both will come before the last judgment to oppose the antichrist; that Elias will preach to the Jews, and Enoch to the Gentiles."

St. Paul, in his Epistle to the Hebrews—which has been contested—says expressly, "by faith Enoch was translated, that he should not see death, because death had translated him."

St. Justin, or somebody who had taken his name, says that Elias and Enoch are in a terrestrial paradise, and that they there wait the second coming of Jesus Christ.

St. Jerome, on the contrary, believes that Enoch and Elias are in heaven. It is the same Enoch, the seventh man after Adam, who is pretended to have written the book quoted by St. Jude.

Tertullian says that this work was preserved in the ark, and even that Enoch made a second copy of it after the deluge.

This is what the Holy Scripture and the holy fathers relate of Enoch; but the profane writers of the East tell us much more. They believe that there really was an Enoch, and that he was the first who made slaves of prisoners of war; they sometimes call him Enoc, and sometimes Edris. They say that he was the same who gave laws to the Egyptians under the name of Thaut, called by the Greeks Hermes Trismegistus. They give him a son named Sabi, the author of the religion of the Sabæans.

There was a tradition in Phrygia on a certain Anach, the same whom the Hebrews call Enoch. The Phrygians held this tradition from the Chaldæans or Babylonians, who also recognized an Enoch, or Anach, as the inventor of astronomy.

They wept for Enoch one day in the year in Phrygia, as they wept for Adonis among the Phœnicians.

The ingenious and profound writer, who believes Elias a person purely allegorical, thinks the same of Enoch. He believes that Enoch, Anach, Annoch, signified the year; that the Orientals wept for it, as for Adonis, and that they rejoiced at the commencement of the new year; that Janus, afterwards known in Italy, was the ancient Anach, or Annoch, of Asia; that not only Enoch formerly signified, among all nations, the beginning and end of the year, but the last day of the week; that the names of Anne, John, Januarius, Janvier, and January, all come from the same source.

It is difficult to penetrate the depths of ancient history. When we seize truth in the dark, we are never sure of retaining her. It is absolutely necessary for a Christian to hold by the Scriptures, whatever difficulty he may have in understanding them.

ELOQUENCE.

Eloquence was created before the rules of rhetoric, as the languages are formed before grammar.

Nature renders men eloquent under the influence of great interests or passions. A person much excited sees things with a different eye from other men. To him all is the object of rapid comparison and metaphor. Without premeditation, he vivifies all, and makes all who listen to him partake of his enthusiasm.

A very enlightened philosopher has remarked that people often express themselves by figures; that nothing is more common or more natural than the turns called tropes.

Thus, in all languages, the heart burns, courage is kindled, the eyes sparkle; the mind is oppressed, it is divided, it is exhausted; the blood freezes, the head is turned upside down; we are inflated with pride, intoxicated with vengeance. Nature is everywhere painted in these strong images, which have become common.

It is from her that instinct learns to assume a modest tone and air, when it is necessary. The natural desire of captivating our judges and masters; the concentrated energies of a profoundly stricken soul, which prepares to display the sentiments which oppress it, are the first teachers of this art.

It is the same nature which sometimes inspires lively and animated sallies; a strong impulse or a pressing danger prompts the imagination suddenly. Thus a captain of the first caliphs, seeing the Mussulmans fly from the field of battle, cried out, "Where are you running to? Your enemies are not there."

This speech has been given to many captains; it is attributed to Cromwell. Strong minds much oftener accord than fine wits.

Rasi, a Mussulman, captain of the time of Mahomet, seeing his Arabs frightened at the death of their general, Derar, said to them, "What does it signify that Derar is dead? God is living, and observes your actions."

Where is there a more eloquent man than that English sailor who decided the war against Spain in 1740? "When the Spaniards, having mutilated me, were going to kill me, I recommended my soul to God, and my vengeance to my country!"

Nature, then, elicits eloquence; and if it be said that poets are created and orators formed, it is applicable only when eloquence is forced to study the laws, the genius of the judges, and the manners of the times. Nature alone is spontaneously eloquent.

The precepts always follow the art. Tisias was the first who collected the laws of eloquence, of which nature gives the first rules. Plato afterwards said, in his "*Gorgias*," that an orator should have the subtlety of the logician, the science of the philosopher, almost the diction of the poet, and the voice and gesture of the greatest actors.

Aristotle, also, showed that true philosophy is the secret guide to perfection in all the arts. He discovered the sources of eloquence in his "Book of Rhetoric." He showed that logic is the foundation of the art of persuasion, and that to be eloquent is to know how to demonstrate.

He distinguished three kinds of eloquence: the deliberative, the demonstrative, and the judiciary. The deliberative is employed to exhort those who deliberate in taking a part in war, in peace, etc.; the demonstrative, to show that which is worthy of praise or blame; the judiciary, to persuade, absolve, condemn, etc.

He afterwards treats of the manners and passions with which all orators should be acquainted.

He examines the proofs which should be employed in these three species of eloquence, and finally he treats of elocution, without which all would languish. He recommends metaphors, provided they are just and noble; and, above all, he requires consistency and decorum.

All these precepts breathe the enlightened precision of a philosopher, and the politeness of an Athenian; and, in giving the rules of eloquence, he is eloquent with simplicity.

It is to be remarked, that Greece was the only country in the world in which the laws of eloquence were then known, because it was the only one in which true eloquence existed.

The grosser art was known to all men; sublime traits have everywhere escaped from nature at all times; but to rouse the minds of the whole of a polished nation—to please, convince, and affect at the same time, belonged only to the Greeks.

The Orientals were almost all slaves; and it is one of the characteristics of servitude to exaggerate everything. Thus the Asiatic eloquence was monstrous. The West was barbarous in the time of Aristotle.

True eloquence began to show itself in the time of the Gracchi, and was not perfected until the time of Cicero. Mark Antony, the orator Hortensius, Curion, Cæsar, and several others, were eloquent men.

This eloquence perished with the republic, like that of Athens. Sublime eloquence, it is said, belongs only to liberty; it consists in telling bold truths, in displaying strong reasons and representations. A man often dislikes truth, fears reason, and likes a well-turned compliment better than the sublimest eloquence.

Cicero, after having given the examples in his harangues, gave the precepts in his "Book of the Orator"; he followed almost all the methods of Aristotle, and explained himself in the style of Plato.

It distinguishes the simple species, the temperate, and the sublime.

Rollin has followed this division in his "Treatise on Study"; and he pretends that which Cicero does not, that the "temperate" is a beautiful river, shaded with green forests on both sides; the "simple," a properly-served table, of which all the meats are of excellent flavor, and from which all refinement is banished; that the "sublime" thunders forth, and is an impetuous current which overthrows all that resists it.

Without sitting down to this table, without following this thunderbolt, this current, or this river, every man of sense must see that simple eloquence is that which has simple things to expose, and that clearness and elegance are all that are necessary to it.

There is no occasion to read Aristotle, Cicero, and Quintilian, to feel that an advocate who begins by a pompous exordium on the subject of a partition wall is ridiculous; it was, however, the fault of the bar until the middle of the seventeenth century; they spoke with emphasis of the most trivial things. Volumes of these examples may be compiled; but all might be reduced to this speech of a witty advocate, who, observing that his adversary was speaking of the Trojan war and of Scamander, interrupted him by saying, "The court will observe that my client is not called Scamander, but Michaut." The sublime species can only regard powerful interests, treated of in a great assembly.

There may still be seen lively traces of it in the Parliament of England': several harangues partook of it which were pronounced there in 1739, when they debated about declaring war against Spain. The spirits of Cicero and Demosthenes seem to have dictated several passages in their speeches; but they will not descend to posterity like those of the Greeks and Romans, because they want the art and charm of diction, which place the seal of immortality on good works.

The temperate species is that of those preparatory discourses, of those public speeches, and of those studied compliments, in which the deficiency of matter must be concealed with flowers.

These three species are often mingled, as also the three objects of eloquence, according to Aristotle: the great merit of the orator consists in uniting them with judgment.

Great eloquence can scarcely be known to the bar in France, because it does not conduct to honors, as in Athens, Rome, and at present in London; neither has it great public interests for its object; it is confined to funeral orations, in which it borders a little upon poetry.

Bossuet, and after him Fléchier, seem to have obeyed that precept of Plato, which teaches us that the elocution of an orator may sometimes be the same as that of a poet.

Pulpit oratory had been almost barbarous until P. Bourdaloue; he was one of the first who caused reason to be spoken there.

The English did not arrive at that art until a later date, as is avowed by Burnet, bishop of Salisbury. They knew not the funeral oration; they avoided, in their sermons, all those vehement turns which appeared not to them consistent with the simplicity of the Gospel; and they were diffident of using those far-fetched divisions which are condemned by Archbishop Fénelon, in his dialogues "*Sur l'Éloquence.*"

Though our sermons turn on the most important subjects to man, they supply few of those striking parts which, like the fine passages of Cicero and Demosthenes, are fit to become the models of all the western nations. The reader will therefore be glad to learn the effect produced by M. Massillon, since bishop of Clermont, the first time that he preached his famous sermon on the small number of the elect. A kind of transport seized all the audience; they rose involuntarily; the murmurs of acclamation and surprise were so great as to disturb the orator; and this confusion only served to augment the pathos of his discourse. The following is the passage:

"I will suppose that this is our last hour, that the heavens open over our heads, that time is past, and that eternity commences; that Jesus Christ is going to appear to judge us according to our works, and that we are all here to receive from Him the sentence of eternal life or death: I ask you, overwhelmed with terror like yourselves, without separating my lot from your own, and putting myself in the same situation in which we must all one day appear before God our judge—if Jesus Christ were now to make the terrible separation of the just from the unjust, do you believe that the greater part would be saved? Do you believe that the number of the righteous would be in the least degree equal to the number of the sinners? Do you believe that, if He now discussed the works of the great number who are in this church, He would find ten righteous souls among us? Would He find a single one?"

There are several different editions of this discourse, but the substance is the same in all of them.

This figure, the boldest which was ever employed, and the best timed, is one of the finest turns of eloquence which can be read either among the ancients or moderns; and the rest of the discourse is not unworthy of this brilliant appeal.

Preachers who cannot imitate these fine models would do well to learn them by heart, and deliver them to their congregations—supposing that they have the rare talent of declamation—instead of preaching to them, in a languishing style, things as common-place as they are useless.

It is asked, if eloquence be permitted to historians? That which belongs to them consists in the art of arranging events, in being always elegant in their expositions, sometimes lively and impressive, sometimes elaborate and florid; in being strong and true in their pictures of general manners and principal personages, and in the reflections naturally incorporated with the narrative, so that they should not appear to be obtruded. The eloquence of Demosthenes belongs not to Thucydides; a studied harangue, put into the mouth of a hero who never pronounced it is, in the opinion of many enlightened minds, nothing more than a splendid defect.

If, however, these licences be permitted, the following is an occasion in which Mézeray, in his great history, may obtain grace for a boldness so approved by the ancients, to whom he is equal, at least on this occasion. It is at the commencement of the reign of Henry IV., when that prince, with very few troops, was opposed near Dieppe by an army of thirty thousand men, and was advised to retire into England, Mézeray excels himself in making a speech for Marshal Biron, who really was a man of genius, and might have said a part of that which the historian attributes to him:

"What, sire, are you advised to cross the sea, as if there was no other way of preserving your kingdom than by quitting it? If you were not in France, your friends would have you run all hazards and surmount all obstacles to get there; and now you are here, they would have you depart—would have you voluntarily do that to which the greatest efforts of your enemies ought not to constrain you! In your present state, to go out of France only for four-and-twenty hours would be to banish yourself from it forever. As to the danger, it is not so great as represented; those who think to overcome us are either the same whom we shut up so easily in Paris, or people who are not much better, and will rapidly have more subjects of dispute among themselves than against us. In short, sire, we are in France, and we must remain here; we must show ourselves worthy of it; we must either conquer it or die for it; and even when there is no other safety for your sacred person than in flight, I well know that you would a thousand times rather die planted in the soil, than save yourself by such means. Your majesty would never suffer it to be said that a younger brother of the house of Lorraine had made you retire, and, still less, that you had been seen to beg at the door of a foreign prince. No, no, sire—there is neither crown nor honor for you across the sea; if you thus demand the succor of England, it will not be granted; if you present yourself at the port of Rochelle, as a man anxious to save himself, you will only meet with reproaches and contempt. I cannot believe that you would rather trust your person to the inconstancy of the waves, or the mercy of a stranger, than to so many brave gentlemen and old soldiers, who are ready to serve you as ramparts and bucklers; and I am too much devoted to your majesty to conceal from you, that if you seek your safety elsewhere than in their virtue, they will be obliged to seek theirs in a different party from your own."

This fine speech which Mézeray puts into the mouth of Marshal Biron is no doubt what Henry IV. felt in his heart.

Much more might be said upon the subject; but the books treating of eloquence have already said too much; and in an enlightened age, genius, aided by examples, knows more of it than can be taught by all the masters in the world.

EMBLEMS.

FIGURES, ALLEGORIES, SYMBOLS, ETC.

In Antiquity, everything is emblematical and figurative. The Chaldæans began with placing a ram, two kids, and a bull among the constellations, to indicate the productions of the earth in spring. In Persia, fire is the emblem of the divinity; the celestial dog gives notice to the Egyptians of the inundations of the Nile; the serpent, concealing its tail in its head, becomes the image of eternity. All nature is painted and disguised.

There are still to be found in India many of those gigantic and terrific statues which we have already mentioned, representing virtue furnished with ten arms, with which it may successfully contend against the vices, and which our poor missionaries mistook for representations of the devil; taking it for granted, that all those who did not speak French or Italian were worshippers of the devil.

Show all these symbols devised by antiquity to a man of clear sense, but who has never heard them at all mentioned or alluded to, and he will not have the slightest idea of their meaning. It would be to him a perfectly new language.

The ancient poetical theologians were under the necessity of ascribing to the deity eyes, hands, and feet; of describing him under the figure of a man.

St. Clement of Alexandria quotes verses from Xenophanes the Colophonian, which state that every species of animal supplies metaphor to aid the imagination in its ideas of the deity—the wings of the bird, the speed of the horse, and the strength of the lion. It is evident, from these verses of Xenophanes, that it is by no means a practice of recent date for men to represent God after their own image. The ancient Thracian Orpheus, the first theologian among the Greeks, who lived long before Homer, according to the same Clement of Alexandria, describes God as seated upon the clouds, and tranquilly ruling the whirlwind and the storm. His feet reach the earth, and His hands extend from one ocean to the other. He is the beginning, middle, and end of all things.

Everything being thus represented by figure and emblem, philosophers, and particularly those among them who travelled to India, employed the same method; their precepts were emblems, were enigmas.

"Stir not the fire with a sword:" that is, aggravate not men who are angry.

"Place not a lamp under a bushel:" conceal not the truth from men.

"Abstain from beans:" frequent not popular assemblies, in which votes were given by white or black beans.

"Have no swallows about your house:" keep away babblers.

"During a tempest, worship the echo:" while civil broils endure, withdraw into retirement.

"Never write on snow:" throw not away instruction upon weak and imbecile minds.

"Never devour either your heart or your brains:" never give yourself up to useless anxiety or intense study.

Such are the maxims of Pythagoras, the meaning of which is sufficiently obvious.

The most beautiful of all emblems is that of God, whom Timæus of Locris describes under the image of "A circle whose centre is everywhere and circumference nowhere." Plato adopted this emblem, and Pascal inserted it among his materials for future use, which he entitled his "Thoughts."

In metaphysics and in morals, the ancients have said everything. We always encounter or repeat them. All modern books of this description are merely repetitions.

The farther we advance eastward, the more prevalent and established we find the employment of emblems and figures: but, at the same time, the images in use are more remote from our own manners and customs.

The emblems which appear most singular to us are those which were in frequent if not in sacred use among the Indians, Egyptians, and Syrians. These people bore aloft in their solemn processions, and with the most profound respect, the appropriate organs for the perpetuation of the species—the symbols of life. We smile at such practices, and consider these people as simple barbarians. What would they have said on seeing us enter our temples wearing at our sides the weapons of destruction?

At Thebes, the sins of the people were represented by a goat. On the coast of Phœnicia, a naked woman with the lower part of her body like that of a fish was the emblem of nature.

We cannot be at all surprised if this employment of symbols extended to the Hebrews, as they constituted a people near the Desert of Syria.

Of Some Emblems Used by the Jewish Nation.

One of the most beautiful emblems in the Jewish books, is the following exquisite passage in Ecclesiastes:

"When the grinders shall cease because they are few; when those that look out of the windows shall be darkened; when the almond tree shall flourish; when the grasshopper shall become a burden; when desire shall fail; the silver cord be loosed; the golden bowl be fractured: and the pitcher broken at the fountain."

The meaning is, that the aged lose their teeth; that their sight becomes impaired; that their hair becomes white, like the blossom of the almond tree; that their feet become like the grasshopper; that their hair drops off like the leaves of the fir tree; that they have lost the power of communicating life; and that it is time for them to prepare for their long journey.

The "Song of Songs," as is well known, is a continued emblem of the marriage of Jesus Christ with the church.

"Let him kiss me with a kiss of his mouth, for thy breasts are better than wine. Let him put his left hand under my head, and embrace me with his right hand. How beautiful art thou, my love: thy eyes are like those of the dove; thy hair is as a flock of goats; thy lips are like a ribbon of scarlet, and thy cheeks like pomegranates; how beautiful is thy neck! how thy lips drop honey! my beloved put in his hand by the hole of the door, and my bowels were moved for him; thy navel is like a round goblet; thy belly is like a heap of wheat set about with lilies; thy two breasts are like two young roes that are twins; thy neck is like a tower of ivory; thy nose is as the tower of Lebanon; thy head is like Mount Carmel; thy stature is that of a palm tree. I said, I will ascend the palm tree and will gather of its fruits. What shall we do for our little sister? she has no breasts. If she be a wall, we will build upon her a tower of silver; if she be a door, we will enclose her with boards of cedar."

It would be necessary to translate the whole canticle, in order to see that it is an emblem from beginning to end. The ingenious Calmet, in particular, demonstrates that the palm tree which the lover ascended is the cross to which our Lord Jesus Christ was condemned. It must however be confessed, that sound and pure moral doctrine is preferable to these allegories.

We find in the books of this people a great number of emblems and types which shock at the present day, and excite at once our incredulity and ridicule, but which, to the Asiatics, appear clear, natural, and unexceptionable.

God appeared to Isaiah, the son of Amos, and said to him, "Go take thy girdle from thy loins and thy shoes from thy feet," and he did so, walking naked and barefoot. And the Lord said, "Like as my servant Isaiah hath walked naked and barefoot for three years for a sign upon Egypt and Ethiopia, so shall the king of Assyria lead away the Egyptian and Ethiopian prisoners, young and old, naked and barefoot, with their hind parts uncovered, to the shame of Egypt."

This appears to us exceedingly strange: but let us inform ourselves a little about what is passing in our own times among Turks, and Africans, and in India, where we go to trade with so much avidity and so little success. We shall learn that it is by no means unusual to see the santons there absolutely naked, and not only in that state preaching to women, but permitting them to salute particular parts of their body, yet neither indulging or inspiring the slightest portion of licentious or unchaste feeling. We shall see on the banks of the Ganges an innumerable company both of men and women naked from head to foot, extending their arms towards heaven, and waiting for the moment of an eclipse to plunge into the river. The citizens of Paris and Rome should not be too ready to think all the rest of the world bound down to the same modes of living and thinking as themselves.

Jeremiah, who prophesied in the reign of Jehoiakim, king of Jerusalem, in favor of the king of Babylon, puts chains and cords about his neck, by order of the Lord, and sends them to the kings of Edom, Ammon, Tyre and Sidon, by their ambassadors who had been sent to Zedekiah at Jerusalem. He commands them to address their master in these words:

"Thus saith the Lord of Hosts the God of Israel, thus shall ye say unto your masters: I have made the earth, the men, and the beasts of burden which are upon the ground, by my great power and by my outstretched arm, and have given it unto whom it seemed good unto me. And now have I given all these lands into the hands of Nebuchadnezzar, the king of Babylon, my servant, and all the beasts of the field have I given him besides, that they may serve him. I spake also all these words to Zedekiah, king of Judah, saying unto him, submit your neck to the yoke of the king of Babylon, serve him, him and his people, and you shall live," etc.

Accordingly, Jeremiah was accused of betraying his king, and of prophesying in favor of the enemy for the sake of money. It has even been asserted that he was stoned. It is clear that the cords and chains were the emblem of that servitude to which Jeremiah was desirous that the nation should submit.

In a similar manner we are told by Herodotus, that one of the kings of Scythia sent Darius a present of a bird, a mouse, a frog, and five arrows. This emblem implied that, if Darius did not fly as fast as a bird, a mouse, or a frog, he would be pierced by the arrows of the Scythians. The allegory of Jeremiah was that of weakness; the emblem of the Scythians was that of courage.

Thus, also, when Sextus Tarquinius consulted his father, whom we call Tarquinius Superbus, about the policy he should adopt to the Gabii, Tarquin, who was walking in his garden, answered only by striking off the heads of the tallest poppies. His son caught his meaning, and put to death the principal citizens among them. This was the emblem of tyranny.

Many learned men have been of opinion that the history of Daniel, of the dragon, of the den of seven lions who devoured every day two sheep and two men, and the history of the angel who transported Habakkuk by the hair of his head to dine with Daniel in the lion's den, are nothing more than a visible allegory, an emblem of the continual vigilance with which God watches over his servants. But it seems to us a proof of greater piety to believe that it is a real history, like many we find in the Sacred Scriptures, displaying without figure and type the divine power, and which profane minds are not permitted to explore. Let us consider those only as genuine emblems and allegories, which are indicated to us as such by Holy Scripture itself.

"In the thirteenth year and the fifteenth day of the fourth month, as I was in the midst of the captives on the banks of the river Chobar, the heavens were opened, and I saw the visions of God," etc. "The word of the Lord came to Ezekiel the priest, the son of Buzi, in the land of the Chaldæans by the river Chobar, and the hand of the Lord was upon him."

It is thus that Ezekiel begins his prophecy; and, after having seen a fire and a whirlwind, and in the midst of the fire four living animals resembling a man, having four faces and four wings with feet resembling those of calves, and a wheel which was upon the earth, and which had four parts, the four parts of the wheel going at the same time, etc.

He goes on to say, "The spirit entered into me, and placed me firm upon my feet.... Then the Lord said unto me: 'Son of man, eat that thou findest; eat this book, and go and speak to the children of Israel.' So I opened my mouth, and He caused me to eat that book. And the spirit entered into me and made me stand upon my feet. And he said unto me: 'Go and shut thyself up in the midst of thy house. Son of man, these are the chains with which thou shalt set thy face firm against it; thou shalt be bound,'" etc. "'And thou, son of man, take a tile and place it before thee and portray thereon the city of Jerusalem.'"

"'Take also a pan of iron, and thou shalt place it as a wall of iron between thee and the city; thou shalt be before Jerusalem as if thou didst besiege it; it is a sign to the house of Israel.'"

After this command God orders him to sleep three hundred and ninety days on his left side, on account of the iniquities of the house of Judah.

Before we go further we will transcribe the words of that judicious commentator Calmet, on this part of

Ezekiel's prophecy, which is at once a history and an allegory, a real truth and an emblem. These are the remarks of that learned Benedictine:

"There are some who think that the whole of this occurred merely in vision; that a man cannot continue lying so long on the same side without a miracle; that, as the Scripture gives us no intimation that this is a prodigy, we ought not to multiply miraculous acts without necessity; that, if the prophet continued lying in that manner for three hundred and ninety days, it was only during the nights; in the day he was at liberty to attend to his affairs. But we do not see any necessity for recurring to a miracle, nor for any circuitous explanation of the case here stated. It is by no means impossible for a man to continue chained and lying on his side for three hundred and ninety days. We have every day before us cases which prove the possibility among prisoners, sick persons, and persons deranged and chained in a state of raving madness. Prado testifies that he saw a mad person who continued bound and lying quite naked on his side upwards of fifteen years. If all this had occurred only in vision, how could' the Jews of the captivity have comprehended what Ezekiel meant to say to them? How would that prophet have been able to execute the divine commands? We must in that case admit likewise that he did not prepare the plan of Jerusalem, that he did not represent the siege, that he was not bound, that he did not eat the bread of different kinds of grain in any other than the same way; namely, that of vision, or ideally."

We cannot but adopt the opinion of the learned Calmet, which is that of the most respectable interpreters. It is evident that the Holy Scripture recounts the matter as a real truth, and that such truth is the emblem, type, and figure of another truth.

"Take unto thee wheat and barley, and beans and lentils, and millet and vetches, and make cakes of them for as many days as thou art to sleep on thy side. Thou shalt eat for three hundred and ninety days ... thou shalt eat it as barley cakes, and thou shalt cover it with human ordure. Thus shall the children of Israel eat their bread defiled."

It is evident that the Lord was desirous that the Israelites should eat their bread defiled. It follows therefore that the bread of the prophet must have been defiled also. This defilement was so real that Ezekiel expressed actual horror at it. "Alas!" he exclaimed, "my life (my soul) has not hitherto been polluted," etc. And the Lord says to him, "I allow thee, then, cow's dung instead of man's, and with that shalt thou prepare thy bread."

It appears, therefore, to have been absolutely essential that the food should be defiled in order to its becoming an emblem or type. The prophet in fact put cow-dung with his bread for three hundred and ninety days, and the case includes at once a fact and a symbol.

Of the Emblem of Aholah and Aholibah.

The Holy Scripture expressly declares that Aholah is the emblem of Jerusalem. "Son of man, cause Jerusalem to know her abominations; thy father was an Amorite, and thy mother was a Hittite." The prophet then, without any apprehension of malignant interpretations or wanton railleries, addresses the young Aholah in the following words:

"*Ubera tua intumuerunt, et pilus tuus germinavit; et eras nuda et confusione plena.*"—"Thy breasts were fashioned, and thy hair was grown, and thou wast naked and confused."

"*Et transivi per te; et ecce tempus tuum, tempus amantium; et expandi amictum meum super te et operui ignominiam tuam. Et juravi tibi, et ingressus sum pactum tecum (ait Dominus Deus), et facta es mihi.*"—"I passed by and saw thee; and saw thy time was come, thy time for lovers; and I spread my mantle over thee and concealed thy shame. And I swore to thee, and entered into a contract with thee, and thou becamest mine."

"*Et habens fiduciam in pulchritudine tua fornicata es in nomine tuo; et exposuisti fornicationem tuam omni transeunti, at ejus fieres.*"—"And, proud of thy beauty, thou didst commit fornication without disguise, and hast exposed thy fornication to every passerby, to become his."

"*Et ædificavisti tibi lupanar, et fecisti tibi prostibulum in cunctis plateis.*"—"And thou hast built a high place for thyself, and a place of eminence in every public way."

"*Et divisisti pedes tuos omni transeunti, et multiplicasti fornicationes tuas.*"—"And thou hast opened thy feet to every passerby, and hast multiplied thy fornications."

"*Et fornicata es cum filiis Egypti vicinis tuis, magnarum carnium; et multiplicasti fornicationem tuam ad irritandum me.*"—"And thou hast committed fornication with the Egyptians thy neighbors, powerful in the flesh; and thou hast multiplied thy fornication to provoke me."

The article of Aholibah, which signifies Samaria, is much stronger and still further removed from the propriety and decorum of modern manners and language.

"*Denudavit quoque fornicationes suas, discooperuit ignominiam suam.*"—"And she has made bare her fornications and discovered her shame."

"*Multiplicavit enim fornicationes suas, recordans dies adolescentiæ suæ.*"—"For she has multiplied her fornications, remembering the days of her youth."

"*Et insanivit libidine super concubitum eorum carnes sunt ut carnes asinorum, et sicut fluxus equorum, fluxus eorum.*"—"And she has maddened for the embraces of those whose flesh is as the flesh of asses, and whose issue is as the issue of horses."

These images strike us as licentious and revolting. They were at that time simply plain and ingenuous.

There are numerous instances of the like in the "Song of Songs," intended to celebrate the purest of all possible unions. It must be attentively considered that these expressions and images are always delivered with seriousness and gravity, and that in no book of equally high antiquity is the slightest jeering or raillery ever applied to the great subject of human production. When dissoluteness is condemned, it is so in natural and undisguised terms, but such are never used to stimulate voluptuousness or pleasantry.

This high antiquity has not the slightest touch of similarity to the licentiousness of Martial, Catullus, or Petronius.

Of Hosea, and Some Other Emblems.

We cannot regard as a mere vision, as simply a figure, the positive command given by the Lord to Hosea to take to himself a wife of whoredoms and have by her three children. Children are not produced in a dream. It is not in a vision that he made a contract with Gomer, the daughter of Diblaim, by whom he had two boys and a girl. It was not in a vision that he afterwards took to himself an adulteress by the express order of the Lord, giving her fifteen pieces of silver and a measure and a half of barley.

The first of these disgraced women signified Jerusalem and the second Samaria. But the two unions with these worthless persons, the three children, the fifteen pieces of silver, and the bushel and a half of barley, were not the less real for having included or been intended as an emblem.

It was not in a vision that the patriarch Salmon married the harlot Rahab, the grandmother of David. It was not in a vision that Judah committed incest with his daughter-in-law Thamar, from which incest sprang David. It was not in a vision that Ruth, David's other grandmother, placed herself in the bed with Boaz. It was not in a vision that David murdered Uriah and committed adultery with Bathsheba, of whom was born King Solomon. But, subsequently, all these events became emblems and figures, after the things which they typified were accomplished.

It is perfectly clear, from Ezekiel, Hosea, Jeremiah, and all the Jewish prophets, and all the Jewish books, as well as from all other books which give us any information concerning the usages of the Chaldæans, Persians, Phœnicians, Syrians, Indians, and Egyptians; it is, I say, perfectly clear that their manners were very different from ours, and that the ancient world was scarcely in a single point similar to the modern one.

Pass from Gibraltar to Mequinez, and the decencies and decorums of life are no longer the same; you no longer find the same ideas. Two sea leagues have changed everything.

ENCHANTMENT.

MAGIC, CONJURATION, SORCERY, ETC.

It is not in the smallest degree probable that all those abominable absurdities are owing, as Pluche would have us believe, to the foliage with which the heads of Isis and Osiris were formerly crowned. What connection can this foliage have with the art of charming serpents, with that of resuscitating the dead, killing men by mere words, inspiring persons with love, or changing men into beasts?

Enchantment *(incantatio)* comes, say some, from a Chaldee word, which the Greeks translate "productive song." *Incantatio* comes from the Chaldee. Truly, the Bocharts are great travellers and proceed from Italy to Mesopotamia in a twinkling! The great and learned Hebrew nation is rapidly explored, and all sorts of books, and all sorts of usages, are the fruits of the journey; the Bocharts are certainly not charlatans.

Is not a large portion of the absurd superstitions which have prevailed to be ascribed to very natural causes? There are scarcely any animals that may not be accustomed to approach at the sound of a bagpipe, or a single horn, to take their food. Orpheus, or some one of his predecessors, played the bagpipe better than other shepherds, or employed singing. All the domestic animals flocked together at the sound of his voice. It was soon supposed that bears and tigers were among the number collected; this first step accomplished, there was no difficulty in believing that Orpheus made stones and trees dance.

If rocks and pine-trees can be thus made to dance a ballet, it will cost little more to build cities by harmony, and the stones will easily arrange themselves at Amphion's song. A violin only will be wanted to build a city, and a ram's horn to destroy it.

The charming of serpents may be attributed to a still more plausible cause. The serpent is neither a voracious nor a ferocious animal. Every reptile is timid. The first thing a reptile does, at least in Europe, on seeing a man, is to hide itself in a hole, like a rabbit or a lizard. The instinct of a man is to pursue everything that flies from him, and to fly from all that pursue him, except when he is armed, when he feels his strength, and, above all, when he is in the presence of many observers.

The serpent, far from being greedy of blood and flesh, feeds only upon herbs, and passes a considerable time without eating at all; if he swallows a few insects, as lizards and chameleons do, he does us a service.

All travellers relate that there are some very large and long ones; although we know of none such in Europe. No man or child was ever attacked there by a large serpent or a small one. Animals attack only what they want to eat; and dogs never bite passengers but in defence of their masters. What could a serpent do with a little infant? What pleasure could it derive from biting it? It could not swallow even the fingers.

Serpents do certainly bite, and squirrels also, but only when they are injured, or are fearful of being so.

I am not unwilling to believe that there have been monsters among serpents as well as among men. I will admit that the army of Regulus was put under arms in Africa against a dragon; and that there has since been a Norman there who fought against the waterspout. But it will be granted, on the other hand, that such cases are exceedingly rare.

The two serpents that came from Tenedos for the express purpose of devouring Laocoon, and two great lads twenty years of age, in the presence of the whole Trojan army, form a very fine prodigy, and one worthy of being transmitted to posterity by hexameter verses, and by statues which represent Laocoon like a giant, and his stout boys as pygmies.

I conceive this event to have happened in those times when a prodigious wooden horse took cities which had been built by the gods, when rivers flowed backward to their fountains, when waters were changed to blood, and both sun and moon stood still on the slightest possible occasion.

Everything that has been related about serpents was considered probable in countries in which Apollo came down from heaven to slay the serpent Python.

Serpents were also supposed to be exceedingly sensible animals. Their sense consists in not running so fast as we do, and in suffering themselves to be cut in pieces.

The bite of serpents, and particularly of vipers, is not dangerous, except when irritation has produced the fermentation of a small reservoir of very acid humor which they have under their gums. With this exception, a serpent is no more dangerous than an eel.

Many ladies have tamed and fed serpents, placed them on their toilets, and wreathed them about their arms. The negroes of Guinea worship a serpent which never injures any one.

There are many species of those reptiles, and some are more dangerous than others in hot countries; but in general, serpents are timid and mild animals; it is not uncommon to see them sucking the udder of a cow.

Those who first saw men more daring than themselves domesticate and feed serpents, inducing them to come to them by a hissing sound in a similar way to that by which we induce the approach of bees, considered them as possessing the power of enchantment. The Psilli and Marsæ, who familiarly handled and fondled serpents, had a similar reputation. The apothecaries of Poitou, who take up vipers by the tail, might also, if they chose, be respected as magicians of the first order.

The charming of serpents was considered as a thing regular and constant. The Sacred Scripture itself, which always enters into our weaknesses, deigned to conform itself to this vulgar idea.

"The deaf adder, which shuts its ears that it may not hear the voice of the charmer."

"I will send among you serpents which will resist enchantments."

"The slanderer is like the serpent, which yields not to the enchanter."

The enchantment was sometimes so powerful as to make serpents burst asunder. The natural philosophy of antiquity made this animal immortal. If any rustic found a dead serpent in his road, some enchanter must inevitably have deprived it of its right to immortality:

> *Frigidus in pratis cantando rumpitur anguis.*
> —VIRG. *Eclogue* viii. 71.
> Verse breaks the ground, and penetrates the brake,
> And in the winding cavern splits the snake.
> —DRYDEN.

Enchantment of the Dead, or Evocation.

To enchant a dead person, to resuscitate him, or barely to evoke his shade to speak to him, was the most simple thing in the world. It is very common to see the dead in dreams, in which they are spoken to and return answers. If any one has seen them during sleep, why may he not see them when he is awake? It is only necessary to have a spirit like the pythoness; and, to bring this spirit of python-ism into successful operation it is only necessary that one party should be a knave and the other a fool; and no one can deny that such *rencontres* very frequently occur.

The evocation of the dead was one of the sublimest mysteries of magic. Sometimes there was made to pass before the eyes of the inquiring devotee a large, black figure, moved by secret springs in dimness and obscurity. Sometimes the performers, whether sorcerers or witches, limited themselves to declaring that *they* saw the shade which was desired to be evoked, and their word was sufficient; this was called necromancy. The famous witch of Endor has always been a subject of great dispute among the fathers of the Church. The sage Theodoret, in his sixty-second question on the Book of Kings, asserts that it is universally the practice for the dead to appear with the head downwards, and that what terrified the witch was Samuel's being upon his legs.

St. Augustine, when interrogated by Simplicion, replies, in the second book of his "Questions," that there is nothing more extraordinary in a witch's invoking a shade than in the devil's transporting Jesus Christ through the air to the pinnacle of the temple on the top of a mountain.

Some learned men, observing that there were oracular spirits among the Jews, have ventured to conclude that the Jews began to write only at a late period, and that they built almost everything upon Greek fable; but this opinion cannot be maintained.

Of Other Sorceries.

When a man is sufficiently expert to evoke the dead by words, he may yet more easily destroy the living, or at least threaten them with doing so, as the physician, *malgré lui*, told Lucas that he would give him a fever. At all events, it was not in the slightest degree doubtful that sorcerers had the power of killing beasts; and, to insure the stock of cattle, it was necessary to oppose sorcery to sorcery. But the ancients can with little propriety be laughed at by us, who are ourselves scarcely even yet extricated from the same barbarism. A hundred years have not yet expired since sorcerers were burned all over Europe; and even as recently as 1750, a sorceress, or witch, was burned at Wurzburg. It is unquestionable that certain words and ceremonies will effectually destroy a flock of sheep, if administered with a sufficient portion of arsenic.

The "Critical, History of Superstitious Ceremonies," by Lebrun of the Oratory, is a singular work. His object is to oppose the ridiculous doctrine of witchcraft, and yet he is himself so ridiculous as to believe in its reality. He pretends that Mary Bucaille, the witch, while in prison at Valognes, *appeared* at some leagues distance, according to the evidence given on oath to the judge of Valognes. He relates the famous prosecution of the shepherds of Brie, condemned in 1691, by the Parliament of Paris, to be hanged and burned. These shepherds had been fools enough to think themselves sorcerers, and villains enough to mix real poisons with their imaginary sorceries.

Father Lebrun solemnly asserts that there was much of what was "supernatural" in what they did, and that they were hanged in consequence. The sentence of the parliament is in direct opposition to this author's statement. "The court declares the accused duly attainted and convicted of superstitions, impieties, sacrileges, profanations, and poisonings."

The sentence does not state that the death of the cattle was caused by profanations, but by poison. A man may commit sacrilege without as well as with poison, without being a sorcerer.

Other judges, I acknowledge, sentenced the priest Ganfredi to be burned, in the firm belief that, by the influence of the devil, he had an illicit commerce with all his female penitents. Ganfredi himself imagined that he was under that influence; but that was in 1611, a period when the majority of our provincial population was very little raised above the Caribs and negroes. Some of this description have existed even in our own times; as, for example, the Jesuit Girard, the ex-Jesuit Nonnotte, the Jesuit Duplessis, and the ex-Jesuit Malagrida; but this race of imbeciles is daily hastening to extinction.

With respect to lycanthropy, that is, the transformation of men into wolves by the power of enchantment, we may observe that a young shepherd's having killed a wolf, and clothed himself with its skin, was enough to excite the terror of all the old women of the district, and to spread throughout the province, and thence through other provinces, the notion of a man's having been changed into a wolf. Some Virgil will soon be found to say:

His ego sæpe lupum fieri, et se condere silvis Moerim sæpe animas imis exire sepulchris.

Smeared with these powerful juices on the plain.

He howls a wolf among the hungry train,
And oft the mighty necromancer boasts
With these to call from tombs the stalking ghosts.
—DRYDEN.

To see a man-wolf must certainly be a great curiosity; but to see human souls must be more curious still; and did not the monks of Monte Cassino see the soul of the holy Benedict, or Bennet? Did not the monks of Tours see St. Martin's? and the monks of St. Denis that of Charles Martel?

Enchantments to Kindle Love.

These were for the young. They were vended by the Jews at Rome and Alexandria, and are at the present day sold in Asia. You will find some of these secrets in the "*Petit Albert*"; and will become further initiated by reading the pleading composed by Apuleius on his being accused by a Christian, whose daughter he had married, of having bewitched her by philtres. Emilian, his father-in-law, alleged that he had made use of certain fishes, since, Venus having been born of the sea, fishes must necessarily have prodigious influence in exciting women to love.

What was generally made use of consisted of vervain, tenia, and hippomanes; or a small portion of the secundine of a mare that had just foaled, together with a little bird called wagtail; in Latin *motacilla*.

But Apuleius was chiefly accused of having employed shell-fish, lobster patties, she-hedgehogs, spiced oysters, and cuttle-fish, which was celebrated for its productiveness.

Apuleius clearly explains the real philtre, or charm, which had excited Pudentilla's affection for him. He undoubtedly admits, in his defence, that his wife had called him a magician. "But what," says he, "if she had called me a consul, would that have made me one?"

The plant satyrion was considered both among the Greeks and Romans as the most powerful of philtres. It was called *planto aphrodisia*, the plant of Venus. That called by the Latins *eruca* is now often added to the former.—*Et venerem revocans eruca morantem.*

A little essence of amber is frequently used. Mandragora has gone out of fashion. Some exhausted debauchees have employed cantharides, which strongly affect the susceptible parts of the frame, and often produce severe and painful consequences.

Youth and health are the only genuine philtres. Chocolate was for a long time in great celebrity with our debilitated *petits-maîtres*. But a man may take twenty cups of chocolate without inspiring any attachment to his person.—"... *ut amoris amabilis esto.*" (Ovid, A. A. ii., 107.)—"Wouldst thou be loved, be amiable."

END OF THE WORLD.

The greater part of the Greek philosophers held the universe to be eternal both with respect to commencement and duration. But as to this petty portion of the world or universe, this globe of stone and earth and water, of minerals and vapors, which we inhabit, it was somewhat difficult to form an opinion; it was, however, deemed very destructible. It was even said that it had been destroyed more than once, and would be destroyed again. Every one judged of the whole world from his own particular country, as an old woman judges of all mankind from those in her own nook and neighborhood.

This idea of the end of our little world and its renovation strongly possessed the imagination of the nations under subjection to the Roman Empire, amidst the horrors of the civil wars between Cæsar and Pompey. Virgil, in his "Georgics" (i., 468), alludes to the general apprehension which rilled the minds of the common people from this cause: *"Impiaque eternam timuerunt secula noctem."*— "And impious men now dread eternal night."

Lucan, in the following lines, expresses himself much more explicitly:

> *Hos Cæsar populos, si nunc non usserit ignis*
> *Uret cum terris, uret cum gurgite ponti.*
> *Communis mundo superest rogus....*
> —PHARS. vii. v. 812, 14.

Though now thy cruelty denies a grave,

These and the world one common lot shall have;
One last appointed flame, by fate's decree,
Shall waste yon azure heavens, the earth, and sea.
—ROWE.

And Ovid, following up the observations of Lucan, says:

Esse quoque in fatis reminiscitur affore tempus,
Quo mare, quo tellus, correptaque regia cœli,
Ardent et mundi moles operosa laboret.
—MET. i. v. 256, 58.

For thus the stern, unyielding fates decree,
That earth, air, heaven, with the capacious sea,
All shall fall victims to consuming fire,
And in fierce flames the blazing world expire.

Consult Cicero himself, the philosophic Cicero. He tells us, in his book concerning the "Nature of the Gods," the best work perhaps of all antiquity, unless we make an exception in favor of his treatise on human duties, called "The Offices"; in that book, I say, he remarks:

"Ex quo eventurum nostri putant id, de quo Panœtium addubitare dicebant; ut ad extremum omnis mundus ignosceret, cum, humore consumpto, neque terra ali posset, neque remearet, aer cujus ortus, aqua omni exhausta, esse non posset; ita relinqui nihil prœter ignem, a quo rursum animante ac Deo renovatio mundi fieret; atque idem ornatus oriretur."

"According to the Stoics, the whole world will eventually consist only of fire; the water being then exhausted, will leave no nourishment for the earth; and the air, which derives its existence from water, can of course no longer be supplied. Thus fire alone will remain, and this fire, reanimating everything with, as it were, god-like power and energy, will restore the world with improved beauty."

This natural philosophy of the Stoics, like that indeed of all antiquity, is not a little absurd; it shows, however, that the expectation of a general conflagration was universal.

Prepare, however, for greater astonishment than the errors of antiquity can excite. The great Newton held the same opinion as Cicero. Deceived by an incorrect experiment of Boyle, he thought that the moisture of the globe would at length be dried up, and that it would be necessary for God to apply His reforming hand "*manum emendatricem.*" Thus we have the two greatest men of ancient Rome and modern England precisely of the same opinion, that at some future period fire will completely prevail over water.

This idea of a perishing and subsequently to be renewed world was deeply rooted in the minds of the inhabitants of Asia Minor, Syria, and Egypt, from the time of the civil wars of the successors of Alexander. Those of the Romans augmented the terror, upon this subject, of the various nations which became the victims of them. They expected the destruction of the world and hoped for a new one. The Jews, who are slaves in Syria and scattered through every other land, partook of this universal terror.

Accordingly, it does not appear that the Jews were at all astonished when Jesus said to them, according to St. Matthew and St. Luke: "Heaven and earth shall pass away." He often said to them: "The kingdom of God is at hand." He preached the gospel of the kingdom of God.

St. Peter announces that the gospel was preached to them that were dead, and that the end of the world drew near. "We expect," says he, "new heavens and a new earth."

St. John, in his first Epistle, says: "There are at present many antichrists, which shows that the last hour draws near."

St. Luke, in much greater detail, predicts the end of the world and the last judgment. These are his words:

"There shall be signs in the moon and in the stars, roarings of the sea and the waves; men's hearts failing them for fear shall look with trembling to the events about to happen. The powers of heaven shall be shaken; and then shall they see the Son of Man coming in a cloud, with great power and majesty. Verily I say unto you, the present generation shall not pass away till all this be fulfilled."

We do not dissemble that unbelievers upbraid us with this very prediction; they want to make us blush for our faith, when we consider that the world is still in existence. The generation, they say, is passed away, and yet nothing at all of this is fulfilled. Luke, therefore, ascribes language to our Saviour which he never uttered, or we must conclude that Jesus Christ Himself was mistaken, which would be blasphemy. But we close the mouth of these impious cavillers by observing that this prediction, which appears so false in its literal meaning, is true in its spirit; that the whole world meant Judæa, and that the end of the world signified the reign of Titus and his successors.

St. Paul expresses himself very strongly on the subject of the end of the world in his Epistle to the Thessalonians: "We who survive, and who now address you, shall be taken up into the clouds to meet the Lord in the air."

According to these very words of Jesus and St. Paul, the whole world was to have an end under Tiberius, or at latest under Nero. St. Paul's prediction was fulfilled no more than St. Luke's.

These allegorical predictions were undoubtedly not meant to apply to the times of the evangelists and apostles, but to some future time, which God conceals from all mankind.

Tu ne quaesieris (scire nefas) quem mihi, quem
tibi
Finem Dii dederint, Leuconoe, nec Babylonios
Tentaris numeros. Ut melius, quicquid erit, pati!
—HORACE i. ode xl.

Strive not Leuconoe, to pry
Into the secret will of fate,

243

Nor impious magic vainly try
To know our lives' uncertain date.
—FRANCIS.

It is still perfectly certain that all nations then known entertained the expectation of the end of the world, of a new earth and a new heaven. For more than sixteen centuries we see that donations to monkish institutions have commenced with these words: "*Adventante mundi vespere*," etc.—"The end of the world being at hand, I, for the good of my soul, and to avoid being one of the number of the goats on the left hand.... leave such and such lands to such a convent." Fear influenced the weak to enrich the cunning.

The Egyptians fixed this grand epoch at the end of thirty-six thousand five hundred years; Orpheus is stated to have fixed it at the distance of a hundred and twenty thousand years.

The historian Flavius Josephus asserts that Adam, having predicted that the world would be twice destroyed, once by water and next by fire, the children of Seth were desirous of announcing to the future race of men the disastrous catastrophe. They engraved astronomical observations on two columns, one made of bricks, which should resist the fire that was to consume the world; the other of stones, which would remain uninjured by the water that was to drown it. But what thought the Romans, when a few slaves talked to them about an Adam and a Seth unknown to all the world besides? They smiled.

Josephus adds that the column of stones was to be seen in his own time in Syria.

From all that has been said, we may conclude that we know exceedingly little of past events—that we are but ill acquainted with those present—that we know nothing at all about the future—and that we ought to refer everything relating to them to God, the master of those three divisions of time and of eternity.

ENTHUSIASM.

This Greek word signifies "emotion of the bowels, internal agitation." Was the word invented by the Greeks to express the vibrations experienced by the nerves, the dilation and shrinking of the intestines, the violent contractions of the heart, the precipitous course of those fiery spirits which mount from the viscera to the brain whenever we are strongly and vividly affected?

Or was the term "enthusiasm," after painful affection of the bowels, first applied to the contortions of the Pythia, who, on the Delphian tripod, admitted the inspiration of Apollo in a place apparently intended for the receptacle of body rather than of spirit?

What do we understand by enthusiasm? How many shades are there in our affections! Approbation, sensibility, emotion, distress, impulse, passion, transport, insanity, rage, fury. Such are the stages through which the miserable soul of man is liable to pass.

A geometrician attends at the representation of an affecting tragedy. He merely remarks that it is a judicious, well-written performance. A young man who sits next to him is so interested by the performance that he makes no remark at all; a lady sheds tears over it; another young man is so transported by the exhibition that to his great misfortune he goes home determined to compose a tragedy himself. He has caught the disease of enthusiasm.

The centurion or military tribune who considers war simply as a profession by which he is to make his fortune, goes to battle coolly, like a tiler ascending the roof of a house. Cæsar wept at seeing the statue of Alexander.

Ovid speaks of love only like one who understood it. Sappho expressed the genuine enthusiasm of the passion, and if it be true that she sacrificed her life to it, her enthusiasm must have advanced to madness.

The spirit of party tends astonishingly to excite enthusiasm; there is no faction that has not its "*energumens*" its devoted and possessed partisans. An animated speaker who employs gesture in his addresses, has in his eyes, his voice, his movements, a subtle poison which passes with an arrow's speed into the ears and hearts of his partial hearers. It was on this ground that Queen Elizabeth forbade any one to preach, during six months, without an express licence under her sign manual, that the peace of her kingdom might be undisturbed.

St. Ignatius, who possessed very warm and susceptible feelings, read the lives of the fathers of the desert after being deeply read in romances. He becomes, in consequence, actuated by a double enthusiasm. He constitutes himself knight to the Virgin Mary, he performed the vigil of arms; he is eager to fight for his lady patroness; he is favored— with visions; the virgin appears and recommends to him her son, and she enjoins him to give no other name to his society than that of the "Society of Jesus."

Ignatius communicates his enthusiasm to another Spaniard of the name of Xavier. Xavier hastens away to the Indies, of the language of which he is utterly ignorant, thence to Japan, without knowing a word of Japanese. That, however, is of no consequence; the flame of his enthusiasm catches the imagination of some young Jesuits, who, at length, make themselves masters of that language. These disciples, after Xavier's death, entertain not the shadow of a doubt that he performed more miracles than ever the apostles did, and that he resuscitated seven or eight persons at the very least. In short, so epidemic and powerful becomes the enthusiasm that they form in Japan what they denominate a Christendom (*une Chrétienté*). This Christendom ends in a civil war, in which a hundred thousand persons are slaughtered: the enthusiasm then is at its highest point, fanaticism; and fanaticism has become madness.

The young fakir who fixes his eye on the tip of his nose when saying his prayers, gradually kindles in devotional ardor until he at length believes that if he burdens himself with chains of fifty pounds weight the Supreme Being will be obliged and grateful to him. He goes to sleep with an imagination totally absorbed by Brahma, and is sure to have a sight of him in a dream. Occasionally even in the intermediate state between sleeping and waking, sparks radiate from his eyes; he beholds Brahma resplendent with light; he falls into ecstasies, and the disease frequently becomes incurable.

What is most rarely to be met with is the combination of reason with enthusiasm. Reason consists in constantly perceiving things as they really are. He, who, under the influence of intoxication, sees objects double is at the time deprived of reason.

Enthusiasm is precisely like wine, it has the power to excite such a ferment in the blood-vessels, and such strong vibrations in the nerves, that reason is completely destroyed by it. But it may also occasion only slight agitations so as not to convulse the brain, but merely to render it more active, as is the case in grand bursts of eloquence and more especially in sublime poetry. Reasonable enthusiasm is the patrimony of great poets.

This reasonable enthusiasm is the perfection of their art. It is this which formerly occasioned the belief that poets were inspired by the gods, a notion which was never applied to other artists.

How is reasoning to control enthusiasm? A poet should, in the first instance, make a sketch of his design. Reason then holds the crayon. But when he is desirous of animating his characters, to communicate to them the different and just expressions of the passions, then his imagination kindles, enthusiasm is in full operation and urges him on like a fiery courser in his career. But his course has been previously traced with coolness and judgment.

Enthusiasm is admissible into every species of poetry which admits of sentiment; we occasionally find it even in the eclogue; witness the following lines of Virgil (Eclogue x. v. 58):

Jam mihi per rupes videor lucosque sonantes
Ire; libet Partho torquere cydonia cornu
Spicula; tanquam haec sint nostri medicina furoris,
Aut deus ille malis hominum mitescere discat!

Nor cold shall hinder me, with horns and hounds
To thrid the thickets, or to leap the mounds.
And now, methinks, through steepy rocks I go,
And rush through sounding woods and bend the Parthian
bow:
As if with sports my sufferings I could ease,
Or by my pains the god of Love appease.

The style of epistles and satires represses enthusiasm, we accordingly see little or nothing of it in the works of Boileau and Pope.

Our odes, it is said by some, are genuine lyrical enthusiasm, but as they are not sung with us, they are, in fact, rather collections of verses, adorned with ingenious reflections, than odes.

Of all modern odes that which abounds with the noblest enthusiasm, an enthusiasm that never abates, that never falls into the bombastic or the ridiculous, is "Timotheus, or Alexander's Feast," by Dryden. It is still considered in England as an inimitable masterpiece, which Pope, when attempting the same style and the same subject, could not even approach. This ode was sung, set to music, and if the musician had been worthy of the poet it would have been the masterpiece of lyric poesy.

The most dangerous tendency of enthusiasm in this occurs in an ode on the birth of a prince of the bast, rant, and burlesque. A striking example of this occurs in an ode on the birth of a prince of the blood royal:

> *Où suis-je? quel nouveau miracle*
> *Tient encore mes sens enchantés*
> *Quel vaste, quel pompeux spectacle*
> *Frappe mes yeux épouvantés?*
> *Un nouveau monde vient d'éclore*
> *L'univers se reforme encore*
> *Dans les abîmes du chaos;*
> *Et, pour réparer ses ruines*
> *Je vois des demeures divines*
> *Descendre un peuple de héros.*
> —J.B. ROUSSEAU.
> "Ode on the Birth of the Duke of Brittany."

Here we find the poet's senses enchanted and alarmed at the appearance of a prodigy—a vast and magnificent spectacle—a new birth which is to reform the universe and redeem it from a state of chaos, all which means simply that a male child is born to the house of Bourbon. This is as bad as "*Je chante les vainqueurs, des vainqueurs de la terre.*"

We will avail ourselves of the present opportunity to observe that there is a very small portion of enthusiasm in the "Ode on the Taking of Namur."

ENVY.

We all know what the ancients said of this disgraceful passion and what the moderns have repeated. Hesiod is the first classic author who has spoken of it.

"The potter envies the potter, the artisan the artisan, the poor even the poor, the musician the musician—or, if any one chooses to give a different meaning to the word *avidos*—the poet the poet."

Long before Hesiod, Job had remarked, "Envy destroys the little-minded."

I believe Mandeville, the author of the "Fable of the Bees," is the first who has endeavored to prove that envy is a good thing, a very useful passion. His first reason is that envy was as natural to man as hunger and thirst; that it may be observed in all children, as well as in horses and dogs. If you wish your children to hate one another, caress one more than the other; the prescription is infallible.

He asserts that the first thing two young women do when they meet together is to discover matter for ridicule, and the second to flatter each other.

He thinks that without envy the arts would be only moderately cultivated, and that Raphael would never have been a great painter if he had not been jealous of Michael Angelo.

Mandeville, perhaps, mistook emulation for envy; perhaps, also, emulation is nothing but envy restricted within the bounds of decency.

Michael Angelo might say to Raphael, your envy has only induced you to study and execute still better than I do; you have not depreciated me, you have not caballed against me before the pope, you have not endeavored to get me excommunicated for placing in my picture of the Last Judgment one-eyed and lame persons in paradise, and pampered cardinals with beautiful women perfectly naked in hell! No! your envy is a laudable feeling; you are brave as well as envious; let us be good friends.

But if the envious person is an unhappy being without talents, jealous of merit as the poor are of the rich; if under the pressure at once of indigence and baseness he writes "News from Parnassus," "Letters from a Celebrated Countess," or "Literary Annals," the creature displays an envy which is in fact absolutely good for nothing, and for which even Mandeville could make no apology.

Descartes said: "Envy forces up the yellow bile from the lower part of the liver, and the black bile that comes from the spleen, which diffuses itself from the heart by the arteries." But as no sort of bile is formed in the spleen, Descartes, when he spoke thus, deserved not to be envied for his physiology.

A person of the name of Poet or Poetius, a theological blackguard, who accused Descartes of atheism, was exceedingly affected by the black bile.

But he knew still less than Descartes how his detestable bile circulated through his blood.

Madame Pernelle is perfectly right: "*Les envieux mourront, mais non jamais l'envie.*"—The envious will die, but envy never. ("*Tartuffe*," Act V, Scene 3.)

That it is better to excite envy than pity is a good proverb. Let us, then, make men envy us as much as we are able.

EPIC POETRY.

Since the word *"epos,"* among the Greeks, signified a discourse, an epic poem must have been a discourse, and it was in verse because it was not then the custom to write in prose. This appears strange, but it is no less true. One Pherecydes is supposed to have been the first Greek who made exclusive use of prose to compose one of those half-true, half-false histories so common to antiquity.

Orpheus, Linus, Thamyris, and Musæus, the predecessors of Homer, wrote in verse only. Hesiod, who was certainly contemporary with Homer, wrote his "Theogony" and his poem of "Works and Days" entirely in verse. The harmony of the Greek language so invited men to poetry, a maxim turned into verse was so easily engraved on the memory that the laws, oracles, morals, and theology were all composed in verse.

Of Hesiod.

He made use of fables which had for a long time been received in Greece. It is clearly seen by the succinct manner in which he speaks of Prometheus and Epimetheus that he supposes these notions already familiar to all the Greeks. He only mentions them to show that it is necessary to labor, and that an indolent repose, in which other mythologists have made the felicity of man to consist, is a violation of the orders of the Supreme Being.

Hesiod afterwards describes the four famous ages, of which he is the first who has spoken, at least among the ancient authors who remain to us. The first age is that which preceded Pandora—the time in which men lived with the gods. The iron age is that of the siege of Thebes and Troy. "I live in the fifth," says he, "and I would I had never been born." How many men, oppressed by envy, fanaticism, and tyranny, since Hesiod, have said the same!

It is in this poem of "Works and Days" that those proverbs are found which have been perpetuated, as—"the potter is jealous of the potter," and he adds, "the musician of the musician, and the poor even of the poor." We there find the original of our fable of the nightingale fallen into the claws of the vulture. The nightingale sings in vain to soften him; the vulture devours her. Hesiod does not conclude that a hungry belly has no ears, but that tyrants are not to be mollified by genius.

A hundred maxims worthy of Xenophon and Cato are to be found in this poem.

Men are ignorant of the advantage of society: they know not that the half is more valuable than the whole.

Iniquity is pernicious only to the powerless.

Equity alone causes cities to flourish.

One unjust man is often sufficient to ruin his country.

The wretch who plots the destruction of his neighbor often prepares the way to his own.

The road to crime is short and easy. That of virtue is long and difficult, but towards the end it is delightful.

God has placed labor as a sentinel over virtue.

Lastly, the precepts on agriculture were worthy to be imitated by Virgil. There are, also, very fine passages in his "Theogony." Love, who disentangles chaos; Venus, born of the sea from the genital parts of a god nourished on earth, always followed by Love, and uniting heaven, earth, and sea, are admirable emblems.

Why, then, has Hesiod had less reputation than Homer? They seem to me of equal merit, but Homer has been preferred by the Greeks because he sang their exploits and victories over the Asiatics, their eternal enemies. He celebrated all the families which in his time reigned in Achaia and Peloponnesus; he wrote the most memorable war of the first people in Europe against the most flourishing nation which was then known in Asia. His poem was almost the only monument of that great epoch. There was no town nor family which did not think itself honored by having its name mentioned in these records of valor. We are even assured that a long time after him some differences between the Greek towns on the subject of adjacent lands were decided by the verses of Homer. He became, after his death, the judge of cities in which it is pretended that he asked alms during his life, which proves, also, that the Greeks had poets long before they had geographers.

It is astonishing that the Greeks, so disposed to honor epic poems which immortalized the combats of their ancestors, produced no one to sing the battles of Marathon, Thermopylæ, Platæa, and Salamis. The heroes of these times were much greater men than Agamemnon, Achilles, and Ajax.

Tyrtæus, a captain, poet, and musician, like the king of Prussia in our days, made war and sang it. He animated the Spartans against the Messenians by his verses, and gained the victory. But his works are lost. It does not appear that any epic poem was written-in the time of Pericles. The attention of genius was turned towards tragedy, so that Homer stood alone, and his glory increased daily. We now come to his "Iliad."

Of the Iliad.

What confirms me in the opinion that Homer was of the Greek colony established at Smyrna is the oriental style of all his metaphors and pictures: The earth which shook under the feet of the army when it marched like the thunderbolts of Jupiter on the hills which overwhelmed the giant Typhon; a wind blacker than night winged with tempests; Mars and Minerva followed by Terror, Flight, and insatiable Discord, the sister and companion of Homicide, the goddess of battles, who raises tumults wherever she appears, and who, not content with setting the world by the ears, even exalts her proud head into heaven. The "Iliad" is full of these images, which caused the sculptor Bouchardon to say, "When I read Homer I believe myself twenty feet high."

His poem, which is not at all interesting to us, was very precious to the Greeks. His gods are ridiculous to reasonable but they were not so to partial eyes, and it was for partial eyes that he wrote.

We laugh and shrug our shoulders at these gods, who abused one another, fought one another, and combated with men—who were wounded and whose blood flowed, but such was the ancient theology of Greece and of almost all the Asiatic people. Every nation, every little village had its particular god, which conducted it to battle.

The inhabitants of the clouds and of the stars which were supposed in the clouds, had a cruel war. The combat of the angels against one another was from time immemorial the foundation of the religion of the Brahmins. The battle of the Titans, the children of heaven and earth, against the chief gods of Olympus, was also the leading mystery of the Greek religion. Typhon, according to the Egyptians, had fought against Oshiret, whom we call Osiris, and cut him to pieces.

Madame Dacier, in her preface to the "Iliad," remarks very sensibly, after Eustathius, bishop of Thessalonica, and Huet, bishop of Avranches, that every neighboring nation of the Hebrews had its god of war. Indeed, does not Jephthah say to the Ammonites, "Wilt not thou possess that which Chemosh thy god giveth thee to possess? So, whomsoever the Lord our God shall drive out from before us, from them will we possess."

Do we not see the God of Judah a conqueror in the mountains and repulsed in the valleys?

As to men wrestling against divinities, that is a received idea. Jacob wrestled one whole night with an angel. If Jupiter sent a deceiving dream to the chief of the Greeks, the Lord also sent a deceiving spirit to King Ahab. These emblems were frequent and astonished nobody. Homer has then painted the ideas of his own age; he could not paint those of the generations which succeeded him.

Homer has great faults. Horace confesses it, and all men of taste agree to it; there is only one commentator who is blind enough not to see them. Pope, who was himself a translator of the Greek poet, says: "It is a vast but uncultivated country where we meet with all kinds of natural beauties, but which do not present themselves as regularly as in a garden; it is an abundant nursery which contains the seeds of all fruits; a great tree that extends superfluous branches which it is necessary to prune."

Madame Dacier sides with the vast country, the nursery and the tree, and would have nothing curtailed. She was no doubt a woman superior to her sex, and has done great service to letters, as well as her husband, but when she became masculine and turned commentator, she so overacted her part that she piqued people into finding fault with Homer. She was so obstinate as to quarrel even with Monsieur de La Motte. She wrote against him like the head of a college, and La Motte answered like a polite and witty woman. He translated the "Iliad" very badly, but he attacked Madame Dacier very well.

We will not speak of the "Odyssey" here; we shall say something of that poem while treating of Ariosto.

Of Virgil.

It appears to me that the second, fourth, and sixth book of the "Æneid" are as much above all Greek and Latin poets, without exception, as the statues of Girardon are superior to all those which preceded them in France.

It is often said that Virgil has borrowed many of the figures of Homer, and that he is even inferior to him in his imitations, but he has not imitated him at all in the three books of which I am speaking; he is there himself touching and appalling to the heart. Perhaps he was not suited for terrific detail, but there had been battles enough. Horace had said of him, before he attempted the "Æneid:"

Molle atque facetum
Virgilio annuerunt gaudentes rure camoenæ.

Smooth flow his lines, and elegant his style,
On Virgil all the rural muses smile.
—FRANCIS.

"*Facetum*" does not here signify facetious but agreeable. I do not know whether we shall not find a little of this happy and affecting softness in the fatal passion of Dido. I think at least that we shall there recognize the author of those admirable verses which we meet with in his Eclogues: "*Ut vidi, ut perii, ut me malus abstulit error!*"—I saw, I perished, yet indulged my pain.—(Dryden.)

Certainly the description of the descent into hell would not be badly matched with these lines from the fourth Eclogue:

Ille Deum vitam accipiet, divisque videbit Permistos heroas, et ipse videbitur illis— Pacatumque reget patriis virtutibus orbem.

The sons shall lead the lives of gods, and be
By gods and heroes seen, and gods and heroes see.
The jarring nations he in peace shall bind,
And with paternal virtues rule mankind.
—DRYDEN.

I meet with many of these simple, elegant, and affecting passages in the three beautiful books of the "Æneid."

All the fourth book is filled with touching verses, which move those who have any ear or sentiment at all, even to tears, and to point out all the beauties of this book it would be necessary to transcribe the whole of it. And in the sombre picture of hell, how this noble and affecting tenderness breathes through every line.

It is well known how many tears were shed by the emperor Augustus, by Livia, and all the palace, at hearing this half line alone: "*Tu Marcellus eris.*"—A new Marcellus will in thee arise.

Homer never produces tears. The true poet, according to my idea, is he who touches the soul and softens it, others are only fine speakers. I am far from proposing this opinion as a rule. "I give my opinion," says Montaigne, "not as being good, but as being my own."

Of Lucan.

If you look for unity of time and action in Lucan you will lose your labor, but where else will you find it? If you expect to feel any emotion or any interest you will not experience it in the long details of a war, the subject of which is very dry and the expressions bombastic, but if you would have bold ideas, an eloquent expatiation on sublime and philosophical courage, Lucan is the only one among the ancients in whom you will meet with it. There is nothing finer than the speech of Labienus to Cato at the gates of the temple of Jupiter Ammon, if we except the answer of Cato itself:

> *Hæremus cuncti superis? temploque tacente*
> *Nil facimus non sponte Dei*
> *.... Steriles num legit arenas.*
> *Ut caneret paucis; mersit ne hoc pulvere verum!*
> *Estne Dei sedes nisi terra et pontus et aer,*
> *Et cœlum et virtus? Superos quid quærimus ultra?*
> *Jupiter est quodcumque vides quocumque moveris.*

> And though our priests are mutes, and temples still,
> We act the dictates of his mighty will;
> Canst thou believe, the vast eternal mind,
> Was e'er to Syrts and Libyan sands confined?

That he would choose this waste, this barren
ground,
To teach the thin inhabitants around?
Is there a place that God would choose to love
Beyond this earth, the seas, yon heaven above,
And virtuous minds, the noblest throne of Jove?
Why seek we farther, then? Behold around;
How all thou seest doth with the God abound,
Jove is seen everywhere, and always to be found.
—ROWE.

Put together all that the ancients poets have said
of the gods and it is childish in comparison with this
passage of Lucan, but in a vast picture, in which there
are a hundred figures, it is not sufficient that one or
two of them are finely designed.

Of Tasso.

Boileau has exposed the tinsel of Tasso, but if
there be a hundred spangles of false gold in a piece
of gold cloth, it is pardonable. There are many rough
stones in the great marble building raised by Homer.
Boileau knew it, felt it, and said nothing about it. We
should be just.

We recall the reader's memory to what has been
said of Tasso in the "Essay on Epic Poetry," but we
must here observe that his verses are known by heart
all over Italy. If at Venice any one in a boat sings a
stanza of the "Jerusalem Delivered," he is answered
from a neighboring bark with the following one.

If Boileau had listened to these concerts he could
have said nothing in reply. As enough is known of

Tasso, I will not repeat here either eulogies or criticisms. I will speak more at length of Ariosto.

Of Ariosto.

Homer's "Odyssey" seems to have been the first model of the *"Morgante,"* of the *"Orlando Innamorato,"* and the *"Orlando Furioso,"* and, what very seldom happens, the last of the poems is without dispute the best.

The companions of Ulysses changed into swine; the winds shut up in goats' skins; the musicians with fishes' tails, who ate all those who approached them; Ulysses, who followed the chariot of a beautiful princess who went to bathe quite naked; Ulysses, disguised as a beggar, who asked alms, and afterwards killed all the lovers of his aged wife, assisted only by his son and two servants—are imaginations which have given birth to all the poetical romances which have since been written in the same style.

But the romance of Ariosto is so full of variety and so fertile in beauties of all kinds that after having read it once quite through I only wish to begin it again. How great the charm of natural poetry! I never could read a single canto of this poem in a prose translation.

That which above all charms me in this wonderful work is that the author is always above his subject, and treats it playfully. He says the most sublime things without effort and he often finishes them by a turn of pleasantry which is neither misplaced nor far-fetched. It is at once the "Iliad," the "Odyssey," and "Don Quixote," for his principal knight-errant becomes mad like the Spanish hero, and is infinitely more pleasant.

The subject of the poem, which consists of so many things, is precisely that of the romance of "Cassandra," which was formerly so much in fashion with us, and which has entirely lost its celebrity because it had only the length of the *"Orlando Furioso,"* and few of its beauties, and even the few being in French prose, five or six stanzas of Ariosto will eclipse them all. His poem closes with the greater part of the heroes and princesses who have not perished during the war all meeting in Paris, after a thousand adventures, just as the personages in the romance of "Cassandra" all finally meet again in the house of Palemon.

The *"Orlando Furioso"* possesses a merit unknown to the ancients—it is that of its exordiums.

Every canto is like an enchanted palace, the vestibule of which is always in a different taste—sometimes majestic, sometimes simple, and even grotesque. It is moral, lively, or gallant, and always natural and true.

EPIPHANY.

The Manifestation, the Appearance, the Illustration, the Radiance.

It is not easy to perceive what relation this word can have to the three kings or magi, who came from the east under the guidance of a star. That brilliant star was evidently the cause of bestowing on the day of its appearance the denomination of the Epiphany.

It is asked whence came these three kings? What place had they appointed for their rendezvous? One of them, it is said, came from Africa; he did not, then, come from the East. It is said they were three magi, but the common people have always preferred the interpretation of three kings. The feast of the kings is everywhere celebrated, but that of the magi nowhere; people eat king's-cake and not magi-cake, and exclaim "the king drinks"—not "the magi drink."

Moreover, as they brought with them much gold, incense, and myrrh, they must necessarily have been persons of great wealth and consequence. The magi of that day were by no means very rich. It was not then as in the times of the false Smerdis.

Tertullian is the first who asserted that these three travellers were kings. St. Ambrose, and St. Cæsar of Arles, suppose them to be kings, and the following passages of Psalm lxxi. are quoted in proof of it: "The kings of Tarshish and of the isles shall offer him gifts. The kings of Arabia and of Saba shall bring him presents." Some have called these three kings Magalat, Galgalat, and Saraim, others Athos, Satos, and Paratoras. The Catholics knew them under the names of Gaspard, Melchior, and Balthazar. Bishop Osorio relates that it was a king of Cranganore, in the kingdom of Calicut, who undertook this journey with two magi, and that this king on his return to his own country built a chapel to the Holy Virgin.

It has been inquired how much gold they gave Joseph and Mary. Many commentators declare that they made them the richest presents; they built on the authority of the "Gospel of the Infancy," which states that Joseph and Mary were robbed in Egypt by Titus and Dumachus, "but," say they, "these men would never have robbed them if they had not had a great deal of money." These two robbers were afterwards hanged; one was the good thief and the other the bad one. But the "Gospel of Nicodemus" gives them other names; it calls them Dimas and Gestas.

The same "Gospel of the Infancy" says that they were magi and not kings who came to Bethlehem; that they had in reality been guided by a star, but that the star having ceased to appear while they were in the stable, an angel made its appearance in the form of a star to act in its stead. This gospel asserts that the visit of the three magi had been predicted by Zerdusht, whom we call Zoroaster.

Suarez has investigated what became of the gold which the three kings or magi presented; he maintains that the amount must have been very large, and that three kings could never make a small or moderate present. He says that the whole sum was afterwards given to Judas, who, acting as steward, turned out a rogue and stole the whole amount.

All these puerilities can do no harm to the Feast of the Epiphany, which was first instituted by the Greek Church, as the term implies, and was afterwards celebrated by the Latin Church.

EQUALITY.

Nothing can be clearer than that men, enjoying the faculties of their common nature, are in a state of equality; they are equal when they perform their animal functions, and exercise their understandings. The king of China, the great mogul, or the Turkish pasha cannot say to the lowest of his species, "I forbid you to digest your food, to discharge your fæces, or to think." All animals of every species are on an equality with one another, and animals have by nature beyond ourselves the advantages of independence. If a bull, while paying his attentions to a heifer, is driven away by the horns of another bull stronger than himself, he goes to seek a new mistress in another meadow, and lives in freedom. A cock, after being defeated, finds consolation in another hen-roost. It is not so with us. A petty vizier banishes a bostangi to Lemnos; the vizier Azem banishes the petty vizier to Tenedos; the pasha banishes the vizier Azem to Rhodes; the janissaries imprison the pasha and elect another who will banish the worthy Mussulmans just when and where he pleases, while they will feel inexpressibly obliged to him for so gentle a display of his authority.

If the earth were in fact what it might be supposed it should be—if men found upon it everywhere an easy and certain subsistence, and a climate congenial to their nature, it would be evidently impossible for one man to subjugate another. Let the globe be covered with wholesome fruits; let the air on which we depend for life convey to us no diseases and premature death; let man require no other lodging than the deer or roebuck, in that case the Genghis Khans and Tamerlanes will have no other attendants than their own children, who will be very worthy persons, and assist them affectionately in their old age.

In that state of nature enjoyed by all undomesticated quadrupeds, and by birds and reptiles, men would be just as happy as they are. Domination would be a mere chimera—an absurdity which no one would think of, for why should servants be sought for when no service is required?

If it should enter the mind of any individual of a tyrannical disposition and nervous arm to subjugate his less powerful neighbor, his success would be impossible; the oppressed would be on the Danube before the oppressor had completed his preparations on the Volga.

All men, then, would necessarily have been equal had they been without wants; it is the misery attached to our species which places one man in subjection to another; inequality is not the real grievance, but dependence. It is of little consequence for one man to be called his highness and another his holiness, but it is hard for me to be the servant of another.

A numerous family has cultivated a good soil, two small neighboring families live on lands unproductive and barren. It will therefore be necessary for the two poor families to serve the rich one, or to destroy it. This is easily accomplished. One of the two indigent families goes and offers its services to the rich one in exchange for bread, the other makes an attack upon it and is conquered. The serving family is the origin of domestics and laborers, the one conquered is the origin of slaves.

It is impossible in our melancholy world to prevent men living in society from being divided into two classes, one of the rich who command, the other of the poor who obey, and these two are subdivided into various others, which have also their respective shades of difference.

You come and say, after the lots are drawn, I am a man as well as you; I have two hands and two feet; as much pride as yourself, or more; a mind as irregular, inconsequent, and contradictory as your own. I am a citizen of San Marino, or Ragusa, or Vaugirard; give me my portion of land. In our known hemisphere are about fifty thousand millions of acres of cultivable land, good and bad. The number of our two-footed, featherless race within these bounds is a thousand millions; that is just fifty acres for each: do me justice; give me my fifty acres.

The reply is: go and take them among the Kaffirs, the Hottentots, and the Samoyeds; arrange the matter amicably with them; here all the shares are filled up. If you wish to have food, clothing, lodging, and warmth among us, work for us as your father did— serve us or amuse us, and you shall be paid; if not, you will be obliged to turn beggar, which would be highly degrading to your sublime nature, and certainly preclude that actual equality with kings, or even village curates, to which you so nobly pretend.

All the poor are not unhappy. The greater number are born in that state, and constant labor prevents them from too sensibly feeling their situation; but when they do strongly feel it, then follow wars such as those of the popular party against the senate at Rome, and those of the peasantry in Germany, England, and France. All these wars ended sooner or later in the subjection of the people, because the great have money, and money in a state commands everything; I say in a state, for the case is different between nation and nation. That nation which makes the best use of iron will always subjugate another that has more gold but less courage.

Every man is born with an eager inclination for power, wealth, and pleasure, and also with a great taste for indolence. Every man, consequently, would wish to possess the fortunes and the wives or daughters of others, to be their master, to retain them in subjection to his caprices, and to do nothing, or at least nothing but what is perfectly agreeable. You clearly perceive that with such amiable dispositions, it is as impossible for men to be equal as for two preachers or divinity professors not to be jealous of each other.

The human race, constituted as it is, cannot exist unless there be an infinite number of useful individuals possessed of no property at all, for most certainly a man in easy circumstances will not leave his own land to come and cultivate yours; and if you want a pair of shoes you will not get a lawyer to make them for you. Equality, then, is at the same time the most natural and the most chimerical thing possible.

As men carry everything to excess if they have it in their power to do so, this inequality has been pushed too far; it has been maintained in many countries that no citizen has a right to quit that in which he was born. The meaning of such a law must evidently be: "This country is so wretched and ill-governed we prohibit every man from quitting it, under an apprehension that otherwise all would leave it." Do better; excite in all your subjects a desire to stay with you, and in foreigners a desire to come and settle among you.

Every man has a right to entertain a private opinion of his own equality to other men, but it follows not that a cardinal's cook should take it upon him to order his master to prepare his dinner. The cook, however, may say: "I am a man as well as my master; I was born like him in tears, and shall like him die in anguish, attended by the same common ceremonies. We both perform the same animal functions. If the Turks get possession of Rome, and I then become a cardinal and my master a cook, I will take him into my service." This language is perfectly reasonable and just, but, while waiting for the Grand Turk to get possession of Rome, the cook is bound to do his duty, or all human society is subverted.

With respect to a man who is neither a cardinal's cook nor invested with any office whatever in the state—with respect to an individual who has no connections, and is disgusted at being everywhere received with an air of protection or contempt, who sees quite clearly that many men of quality and title have not more knowledge, wit, or virtue than himself, and is wearied by being occasionally in their antechambers—what ought such a man to do? He ought to stay away.

ESSENIANS.

The more superstitious and barbarous any nation is, the more obstinately bent on war, notwithstanding its defeats; the more divided into factions, floating between royal and priestly claims; and the more intoxicated it may be by fanaticism, the more certainly will be found among that nation a number of citizens associated together in order to live in peace.

It happens during a season of pestilence that a small canton forbids all communication with large cities. It preserves itself from the prevailing contagion, but remains a prey to other maladies.

Of this description of persons were the Gymnosophists in India, and certain sects of philosophers among the Greeks. Such also were the Pythagoreans in Italy and Greece, and the Therapeutæ in Egypt. Such at the present day are those primitive people called Quakers and Dunkards, in Pennsylvania, and very nearly such were the first Christians who lived together remote from cities.

Not one of these societies was acquainted with the dreadful custom of binding themselves by oath to the mode of life which they adopted, of involving themselves in perpetual chains, of depriving themselves, on a principle of religion, of the grand right and first principle of human nature, which is liberty; in short, of entering into what we call vows. St. Basil was the first who conceived the idea of those vows, of this oath of slavery. He introduced a new plague into the world, and converted into a poison that which had been invented as a remedy.

There were in Syria societies precisely similar to those of the Essenians. This we learn from the Jew Philo, in his treatise on the "Freedom of the Good." Syria was always superstitious and factious, and always under the yoke of tyrants. The successors of Alexander made it a theatre of horrors. It is by no means extraordinary that among such numbers of oppressed and persecuted beings, some, more humane and judicious than the rest, should withdraw from all intercourse with great cities, in order to live in common, in honest poverty, far from the blasting eyes of tyranny.

During the civil wars of the latter Ptolemies, similar asylums were formed in Egypt, and when that country was subjugated by the Roman arms, the Therapeutæ established themselves in a sequestered spot in the neighborhood of Lake Mœris.

It appears highly probable that there were Greek, Egyptian, and Jewish Therapeutæ. Philo, after eulogizing Anaxagoras, Democritus, and other philosophers, who embraced their way of life, thus expresses himself:

"Similar societies are found in many countries; Greece and other regions enjoy institutions of this consoling character. They are common in Egypt in every district, and particularly in that of Alexandria. The most worthy and moral of the population have withdrawn beyond Lake Mœris to a secluded but convenient spot, forming a gentle declivity. The air is very salubrious, and the villages in the neighborhood sufficiently numerous," etc.

Thus we perceive that there have everywhere existed societies of men who have endeavored to find a refuge from disturbances and factions, from the insolence and rapacity of oppressors. All, without exception, entertained a perfect horror of war, considering it precisely in the same light in which we contemplate highway robbery and murder.

Such, nearly, were the men of letters who united, in France and founded the Academy. They quietly withdrew from the factious and cruel scenes which desolated the country in the reign of Louis XIII. Such also were the men who founded the Royal Society at London, while the barbarous idiots called Puritans and Episcopalians were cutting one another's throats about the interpretation of a few passages from three or four old and unintelligible books.

Some learned men have been of opinion that Jesus Christ, who condescended to make his appearance for some time in the small district of Capernaum, in Nazareth, and some other small towns of Palestine, was one of those Essenians who fled from the tumult of affairs and cultivated virtue in peace. But the name "Essenian," never even once occurs in the four Gospels, in the Apocrypha, or in the Acts, or the Epistles of the apostles.

Although, however, the name is not to be found, a resemblance is in various points observable— confraternity, community of property, strictness of moral conduct, manual labor, detachment from wealth and honors; and, above all, detestation of war. So great is this detestation, that Jesus Christ commands his disciples when struck upon one cheek to offer the other also, and when robbed of a cloak to deliver up the coat likewise. Upon this principle the Christians conducted themselves, during the two first centuries, without altars, temples, or magistracies— all employed in their respective trades or occupations, all leading secluded and quiet lives.

Their early writings attest that they were not permitted to carry arms. In this they perfectly resembled our Quakers, Anabaptists, and Mennonites of the present day, who take a pride in following the literal meaning of the gospel. For although there are in the gospel many passages which, when incorrectly understood, might breed violence—as the case of the merchants scourged out of the temple avenues, the phrase "compel them to come in," the dangers into which they were thrown who had not converted their master's one talent into five talents, and the treatment of those who came to the wedding without the wedding garment— although, I say, all these may seem contrary to the pacific spirit of the gospel, yet there are so many other passages which enjoin sufferance instead of contest, that it is by no means astonishing that, for a period of two hundred years, Christians held war in absolute execration.

Upon this foundation was the numerous and respectable society of Pennsylvanians established, as were also the minor sects which have imitated them. When I denominate them respectable, it is by no means in consequence of their aversion to the splendor of the Catholic church. I lament, undoubtedly, as I ought to do, their errors. It is their virtue, their modesty, and their spirit of peace, that I respect.

Was not the great philosopher Bayle right, then, when he remarked that a Christian of the earliest times of our religion would be a very bad soldier, or that a soldier would be a very bad Christian?

This dilemma appears to be unanswerable; and in this point, in my opinion, consists the great difference between ancient Christianity and ancient Judaism.

The law of the first Jews expressly says, "As soon as you enter any country with a view to possess it, destroy everything by fire and sword; slay, without mercy, aged men, women, and children at the breast; kill even all the animals; sack everything and burn everything. It is your God who commands you so to do." This injunction is not given in a single instance, but on twenty different occasions, and is always followed.

Mahomet, persecuted by the people of Mecca, defends himself like a brave man. He compels his vanquished persecutors to humble themselves at his feet, and become his disciples. He establishes his religion by proselytism and the sword.

Jesus, appearing between the times of Moses and Mahomet, in a corner of Galilee, preaches forgiveness of injuries, patience, mildness, and forbearance, dies himself under the infliction of capital punishment, and is desirous of the same fate for His first disciples.

I ask candidly, whether St. Bartholomew, St. Andrew, St. Matthew, and St. Barnabas, would have been received among the cuirassiers of the emperor, or among the royal guards of Charles XII.?

Would St. Peter himself, though he cut off Malchus' ear, have made a good officer? Perhaps St. Paul, accustomed at first to carnage, and having had the misfortune to be a bloody persecutor, is the only one who could have been made a warrior. The impetuosity of his temperament and the fire of his imagination would have made him a formidable commander. But, notwithstanding these qualities, he made no effort to revenge himself on Gamaliel by arms. He did not act like the Judases, the Theudases, and the Barchochebases, who levied troops: he followed the precepts of Jesus Christ; he suffered; and, according to an account we have of his death, he was beheaded.

To compose an army of Christians, therefore, in the early period of Christianity, was a contradiction in terms.

It is certain that Christians were not enlisted among the troops of the empire till the spirit by which they were animated was changed. In the first two centuries they entertained a horror for temples, altars, tapers, incense, and lustral water. Porphyry compares them to the foxes who said "the grapes are sour." "If," said he, "you could have had beautiful temples burnished with gold, and large revenues for a clergy, you would then have been passionately fond of temples." They afterwards addicted themselves to all that they had abhorred. Thus, having detested the profession of arms, they at length engaged in war. The Christians in the time of Diocletian were as different from those of the time of the apostles, as we are from the Christians of the third century.

I cannot conceive how a mind so enlightened and bold as Montesquieu's could severely censure another genius much more accurate than his own, and oppose the following just remark made by Bayle: "a society of real Christians might live happily together, but they would make a bad defence on being attacked by an enemy."

"They would," says Montesquieu, "be citizens infinitely enlightened on the subject of their duties, and ardently zealous to discharge them. They would be fully sensible of the rights of natural defence. The more they thought they owed religion, the more they would think they owed their country. The principles of Christianity deeply engraved on their hearts would be infinitely more powerful than the false honor of monarchies, the human virtues of republics, or the servile fear which operates under despotism."

Surely the author of the "Spirit of Laws" did not reflect upon the words of the gospel, when saying that real Christians would be fully sensible of the rights of natural defence. He did not recollect the command to deliver up the coat after the cloak had been taken; and, after having received a blow upon one cheek, to present the other also. Here the principle of natural defence is most decidedly annihilated. Those whom we call Quakers have always refused to fight; but in the war of 1756, if they had not received assistance from the other English, and suffered that assistance to operate, they would have been completely crushed.

Is it not unquestionable that men who thought and felt as martyrs would fight very ill as grenadiers? Every sentence of that chapter of the "Spirit of Laws" appears to me false. "The principles of Christianity deeply engraved on their hearts, would be infinitely more powerful," etc. Yes, more powerful to prevent their exercise of the sword, to make them tremble at shedding their neighbor's blood, to make them look on life as a burden of which it would be their highest happiness to be relieved.

"If," says Bayle, "they were appointed to drive back veteran corps of infantry, or to charge regiments of cuirassiers, they would be seen like sheep in the midst of wolves."

Bayle was perfectly right. Montesquieu did not perceive that, while attempting to refute him, he contemplated only the mercenary and sanguinary soldiers of the present day, and not the early Christians. It would seem as if he had been desirous of preventing the unjust accusations which he experienced from the fanatics, by sacrificing Bayle to them. But he gained nothing by it. They are two great men, who appear to be of different opinions, but who, if they had been equally free to speak, would have been found to have the same.

"The false honor of monarchies, the human virtues of republics, the servile fear which operates under despotism;" nothing at all of this goes towards the composition of a soldier, as the "Spirit of Laws" pretends. When we levy a regiment, of whom a quarter part will desert in the course of a fortnight, not one of the men enlisted thinks about the honor of the monarchy: they do not even know what it is. The mercenary troops of the republic of Venice know their country; but nothing about republican virtue, which no one ever speaks of in the place of St. Mark. In one word, I do not believe that there is a single man on the face of the earth who has enlisted in his regiment from a principle of virtue.

Neither, again, is it out of a servile fear that Turks and Russians fight with the fierceness and rage of lions and tigers. Fear does not inspire courage. Nor is it by devotion that the Russians have defeated the armies of Mustapha. It would, in my opinion, have been highly desirable that so ingenious a man should have sought for truth rather than display. When we wish to instruct mankind, we ought to forget ourselves, and have nothing in view but truth.

ETERNITY.

In my youth I admired all the reasonings of Samuel Clarke. I loved his person, although he was a determined Arian as well as Newton, and I still revere his memory, because he was a good man; but the impression which his ideas had stamped on my yet tender brain was effaced when that brain became more firm. I found, for example, that he had contested the eternity of the world with as little ability as he had proved the reality of infinite space.

I have so much respect for the Book of Genesis, and for the church which adopts it, that I regard it as the only proof of the creation of the world five thousand seven hundred and eighteen years ago, according to the computation of the Latins, and seven thousand and seventy-eight years, according to the Greeks. All antiquity believed matter, at least, to be eternal; and the greatest philosophers attributed eternity also to the arrangement of the universe.

They are all mistaken, as we well know; but we may believe, without blasphemy, that the eternal Former of all things made other worlds besides ours.

EUCHARIST.

On this delicate subject, we shall not speak as theologians. Submitting in heart and mind to the religion in which we are born, and the laws under which we live, we shall have nothing to do with controversy; it is too hostile to all religions which it boasts of supporting—to all laws which it makes pretensions to explain, and especially to that harmony which in every period it has banished from the world.

One-half of Europe anathematizes the other on the subject of the Eucharist; and blood has flowed in torrents from the Baltic Sea to the foot of the Pyrenees, for nearly two centuries, on account of a single word, which signifies gentle charity.

Various nations in this part of the world view with horror the system of transubstantiation. They exclaim against this dogma as the last effort of human folly. They quote the celebrated passage of Cicero, who says that men, having exhausted all the mad extravagancies they are capable of, have yet never entertained the idea of eating the God whom they adore. They say that as almost all popular opinions are built upon ambiguities and abuse of words, so the system of the Roman Catholics concerning the Eucharist and transubstantiation is founded solely on an ambiguity; that they have interpreted literally what could only have been meant figuratively; and that for the sake of mere verbal contests, for absolute misconceptions, the world has for six hundred years been drenched in blood.

Their preachers in the pulpits, their learned in their publications, and the people in their conversational discussions, incessantly repeat that Jesus Christ did not take His body in His two hands to give His disciples to eat; that a body cannot be in a hundred thousand places at one time, in bread and in wine; that the God who formed the universe cannot consist of bread which is converted into fæces, and of wine which flows off in urine; and that the doctrine may naturally expose Christianity to the derision of the least intelligent, and to the contempt and execration of the rest of mankind.

In this opinion the Tillotsons, the Smallridges, the Claudes, the Daillés, the Amyrauts, the Mestrezats, the Dumoulins, the Blondels, and the numberless multitude of the reformers of the sixteenth century, are all agreed; while the peaceable Mahometan, master of Africa, and of the finest part of Asia, smiles with disdain upon our disputes, and the rest of the world are totally ignorant of them.

Once again I repeat that I have nothing to do with controversy. I believe with a lively faith all that the Catholic apostolic religion teaches on the subject of the Eucharist, without comprehending a single word of it.

The question is, how to put the greatest restraint upon crimes. The Stoics said that they carried God in their hearts. Such is the expression of Marcus Aurelius and Epictetus, the most virtuous of mankind, and who might almost be called gods upon earth. They understood by the words "I carry God within me," that part of the divine universal soul which animates every intelligent being.

The Catholic religion goes further. It says, "You shall have within you physically what the Stoics had metaphysically. Do not set yourselves about inquiring what it is that I give you to eat and drink, or merely to eat. Only believe that what I so give you is God. He is within you. Shall your heart then be defiled by anything unjust or base? Behold then men receiving God within them, in the midst of an august ceremonial, by the light of a hundred tapers, under the influence of the most exquisite and enchanting music, and at the footstool of an altar of burnished gold. The imagination is led captive, the soul is rapt in ecstasy and melted! The votary scarcely breathes; he is detached from every terrestrial object, he is united with God, He is in our flesh, and in our blood! Who will dare, or who even will be able, after this, to commit a single fault, or to entertain even the idea of it? It was clearly impossible to devise a mystery better calculated to retain mankind in virtue."

Yet Louis XI., while receiving God thus within him, poisons his own brother; the archbishop of Florence, while making God, and the Pazzi while receiving Him, assassinate the Medici in the cathedral. Pope Alexander VI., after rising from the bed of his bastard daughter, administers God to Cæsar Borgia, his bastard son, and both destroy by hanging, poison, and the sword, all who are in possession of two acres of land which they find desirable.

Julius II. makes and eats God; but, with his cuirass on his back and his helmet on his head, he imbrues his hands in blood and carnage. Leo X. contains God in his body, his mistress in his arms, and the money extorted by the sale of indulgences, in his own and his sister's coffers.

Trolle, archbishop of Upsala, has the senators of Sweden slaughtered before his face, holding a papal bull in his hand. Von Galen, bishop of Münster, makes war upon all his neighbors, and becomes celebrated for his rapine.

The Abbé N—— is full of God, speaks of nothing but God, imparts God to all the women, or weak and imbecile persons that he can obtain the direction of, and robs his penitents of their property.

What are we to conclude from these contradictions? That all these persons never really believed in God; that they still less, if possible, believed that they had eaten His body and drunk His blood; that they never imagined they had swallowed God; that if they had firmly so believed, they never would have committed any of those deliberate crimes; in a word, that this most miraculous preventive of human atrocities has been most ineffective? The more sublime such an idea, the more decidedly is it secretly rejected by human obstinacy.

The fact is, that all our grand criminals who have been at the head of government, and those also who have subordinately shared in authority, not only never believed that they received God down their throats, but never believed in God at all; at least they had entirely effaced such an idea from their minds. Their contempt for the sacrament which they created or administered was extended at length into a contempt of God Himself. What resource, then, have we remaining against depredation, insolence, outrage, calumny, and persecution? That of persuading the strong man who oppresses the weak that God really exists. He will, at least, not laugh at this opinion; and, although he may not believe that God is within him, he yet may believe that God pervades all nature. An incomprehensible mystery has shocked him. But would he be able to say that the existence of a remunerating and avenging God is an incomprehensible mystery? Finally, although he does not yield his belief to a Catholic bishop who says to him, "Behold, that is your God, whom a man consecrated by myself has put into your mouth;" he may believe the language of all the stars and of all animated beings, at once exclaiming: "God is our creator!"

EXECUTION.

SECTION I.

Yes, we here repeat the observation, a man that is hanged is good for nothing; although some executioner, as much addicted to quackery as cruelty, may have persuaded the wretched simpletons in his neighborhood that the fat of a person hanged is a cure for the epilepsy.

Cardinal Richelieu, when going to Lyons to enjoy the spectacle of the execution of Cinq-Mars and de Thou, was informed that the executioner had broken his leg. "What a dreadful thing it is," says he to the chancellor Séguier, "we have no executioner!" I certainly admit that it must have been a terrible disaster. It was a jewel wanting in his crown. At last, however, an old worthy was found, who, after twelve strokes of the sabre, brought low the head of the innocent and philosophic de Thou. What necessity required this death? What good could be derived from the judicial assassination of Marshal de Marillac?

I will go farther. If Maximilian, duke of Sully, had not compelled that admirable King Henry IV. to yield to the execution of Marshal Birou, who was covered with wounds which had been received in his service, perhaps Henry would never have suffered assassination himself; perhaps that act of clemency, judiciously interposed after condemnation, would have soothed the still raging spirit of the league; perhaps the outcry would not then have been

incessantly thundered into the ears of the populace—
the king always protects heretics, the king treats good
Catholics shamefully, the king is a miser, the king is
an old debauchée, who, at the age of fifty-seven fell
in love with the young princess of Condé, and forced
her husband to fly the kingdom with her. All these
embers of universal discontent would probably not
have been alone sufficient to inflame the brain of the
fanatical Feuillant, Ravaillac.

With respect to what is ordinarily called justice,
that is, the practice of killing a man because he has
stolen a crown from his master; or burning him, as
was the case with Simon Morin, for having said that
he had had conferences with the Holy Spirit; and as
was the case also with a mad old Jesuit of the name
of Malagrida, for having printed certain
conversations which the holy virgin held with St.
Anne, her mother, while in the womb—this practice,
it must be acknowledged, is neither conformable to
humanity or reason, and cannot possibly be of the
least utility.

We have already inquired what advantage could
ensue to the state from the execution of that poor man
known under the name of the madman; who, while at
supper with some monks, uttered certain nonsensical
words, and who, instead of being purged and bled,
was delivered over to the gallows?

We further ask, whether it was absolutely
necessary that another madman, who was in the
bodyguards, and who gave himself some slight cuts
with a hanger, like many other impostors, to obtain

remuneration, should be also hanged by the sentence of the parliament? Was this a crime of such great enormity? Would there have been any imminent danger to society in saving the life of this man?

What necessity could there be that La Barre should have his hand chopped off and his tongue cut out, that he should be put to the question ordinary and extraordinary, and be burned alive? Such was the sentence pronounced by the Solons and Lycurguses of Abbeville! What had he done? Had he assassinated his father and mother? Had people reason to apprehend that he would burn down the city? He was accused of want of reverence in some secret circumstances, which the sentence itself does not specify. He had, it was said, sung an old song, of which no one could give an account; and had seen a procession of capuchins pass at a distance without saluting it.

It certainly appears as if some people took great delight in what Boileau calls murdering their neighbor in due form and ceremony, and inflicting on him unutterable torments. These people live in the forty-ninth degree of latitude, which is precisely the position of the Iroquois. Let us hope that they may, some time or other, become civilized.

Among this nation of barbarians, there are always to be found two or three thousand persons of great kindness and amiability, possessed of correct taste, and constituting excellent society. These will, at length, polish the others.

I should like to ask those who are so fond of erecting gibbets, piles, and scaffolds, and pouring leaden balls through the human brain, whether they are always laboring under the horrors of famine, and whether they kill their fellow-creatures from any apprehension that there are more of them than can be maintained?

I was once perfectly horror-struck at seeing a list of deserters made out for the short period merely of eight years. They amounted to sixty thousand. Here were sixty thousand co-patriots, who were to be shot through the head at the beat of drum; and with whom, if well maintained and ably commanded, a whole province might have been added to the kingdom.

I would also ask some of these subaltern Dracos, whether there are no such things wanted in their country as highways or crossways, whether there are no uncultivated lands to be broken up, and whether men who are hanged or shot can be of any service?

I will not address them on the score of humanity, but of utility: unfortunately, they will often attend to neither; and, although M. Beccaria met with the applauses of Europe for having proved that punishments ought only to be proportioned to crimes, the Iroquois soon found out an advocate, paid by a priest, who maintained that to torture, hang, rack, and burn in all cases whatsoever, was decidedly the best way.

SECTION II.

But it is England which, more than any other country, has been distinguished for the stern delight of slaughtering men with the pretended sword of the law. Without mentioning the immense number of princes of the blood, peers of the realm, and eminent citizens, who have perished by a public death on the scaffold, it is sufficient to call to mind the execution of Queen Anne Boleyn, Queen Catherine Howard, Lady Jane Grey, Queen Mary Stuart, and King Charles I, in order to justify the sarcasm which has been frequently applied, that the history of England ought to be written by the executioner.

Next to that island, it is alleged that France is the country in which capital punishments have been most common. I shall say nothing of that of Queen Brunehaut, for I do not believe it. I pass by innumerable scaffolds, and stop before that of Count Montecuculi, who was cut into quarters in the presence of Francis I. and his whole court, because Francis, the dauphin, had died of pleurisy.

That event occurred in 1536. Charles V., victorious on all the coasts of Europe and Africa, was then ravaging both Provence and Picardy. During that campaign which commenced advantageously for him, the young dauphin, eighteen years of age, becomes heated at a game of tennis, in the small city of Tournon. When in high perspiration he drinks iced water, and in the course of five days dies of the pleurisy. The whole court and all France exclaim that the Emperor Charles V. had caused the dauphin of France to be poisoned. This accusation, equally horrible and absurd, has been repeated from time to time down to the present. Malherbe, in one of his odes, speaks of Francis, whom Castile, unequal to cope with in arms, bereaved of his son.

We will not stop to examine whether the emperor was unequal to the arms of Francis I., because he left Provence after having completely sacked it, nor whether to poison a dauphin is to steal him; but these bad lines decidedly show that the poisoning of the dauphin Francis by Charles V. was received throughout France as an indisputable truth.

Daniel does not exculpate the emperor. Henault, in his "Chronological Summary," says: "Francis, the dauphin, poisoned." It is thus that all writers copy from one another. At length the author of the "History of Francis I." ventures, like myself, to investigate the fact.

It is certain that Count Montecuculi, who was in the service of the dauphin, was condemned by certain commissioners to be quartered, as guilty of having poisoned that prince.

Historians say that this Montecuculi was his cup-bearer. The dauphins have no such officer: but I will admit that they had. How could that gentleman, just at the instant, have mixed up poison in a glass of fresh water? Did he always carry poison in his pocket, ready whenever his master might call for drink? He was not the only person present with the dauphin, who was, it appears, wiped and rubbed dry by some of his attendants after the game of tennis was finished. The surgeons who opened the body declared, it is said, that the prince had taken arsenic. Had the prince done so, he must have felt intolerable pains about his throat, the water would have been colored, and the case would not have been treated as one of pleurisy. The surgeons were ignorant pretenders, who said just what they were desired to say; a fact which happens every day.

What interest could this officer have in destroying his master? Who was more likely to advance his fortune? But, it is said, it was intended also to poison the king. Here is a new difficulty and a new improbability.

Who was to compensate him for this double crime? Charles V., it is replied—another improbability equally strong. Why begin with a youth only eighteen years and a half old, and who, moreover, had two brothers? How was the king to be got at? Montecuculi did not wait at his table.

Charles V. had nothing to gain by taking away the life of the young dauphin, who had never drawn a sword, and who certainly would have had powerful avengers. It would have been a crime at once base and useless. He did not fear the father, we are to believe, the bravest knight of the French court; yet he was afraid of the son, who had scarcely reached beyond the age of childhood!

But, we are informed, this Montecuculi, on the occasion of a journey to Ferrara, his own country, was presented to the emperor, and that that monarch asked him numerous questions relating to the magnificence of the king's table and the economy of his household. This certainly is decisive evidence that the Italian was engaged by Charles V. to poison the royal family!

Oh! but it was not the emperor himself who urged him to commit this crime: he was impelled to it by Anthony de Leva and the Marquis di Gonzaga. Yes, truly, Anthony de Leva, eighty years of age, and one of the most virtuous knights in Europe! and this noble veteran, moreover, was indiscreet enough to propose executing this scheme of poisoning in conjunction with a prince of Gonzaga. Others mention the Marquis del Vasto, whom we call du Gast. Contemptible impostors! Be at least agreed among yourselves. You say that Montecuculi confessed the fact before his judges. Have you seen the original documents connected with the trial?

You state that the unfortunate man was a chemist. These then are your only proofs, your only reasons, for subjecting him to the most dreadful of executions: he was an Italian, he was a chemist, and Charles V. was hated. His glory then provoked indeed a base revenge. Good God! Your court orders a man of rank to be cut into quarters upon bare suspicion, in the vain hope of disgracing that powerful emperor.

Some time afterwards your suspicions, always light and volatile, charge this poisoning upon Catherine de Medici, wife of Henry II., then dauphin and subsequently king of France. You say that, in order to reign, she destroyed by poison the first dauphin, who stood between her husband and the throne. Miserable impostors! Once again, I say, be consistent! Catherine de Medici was at that time only seventeen years of age.

It has been said that Charles V. himself imputed this murder to Catherine, and the historian Pera is quoted to prove it. This however, is an error. These are the historian's words:

"This year the dauphin of France died at Paris with decided indications of poison. His friends ascribed it to the orders of the Marquis del Vasto and Anthony de Leva, which led to the execution of Count Montecuculi, who was in the habit of corresponding with them: base and absurd suspicion of men so highly honorable, as by destroying the dauphin little or nothing could be gained. He was not yet known by his valor any more than his brothers, who were next in the succession to him.

"To one presumption succeeded another. It was pretended that this murder was committed by order of the duke of Orleans, his brother, at the instigation of his wife, Catherine de Medici, who was ambitious of being a queen, which, in fact, she eventually was. It is well remarked by a certain author, that the dreadful death of the duke of Orleans, afterwards Henry II., was the punishment of heaven upon him for poisoning his brother—at least, if he really did poison him—a practice too common among princes, by which they free themselves at little cost from stumbling-blocks in their career, but frequently and manifestly punished by God."

Signor di Pera, we instantly perceive, is not an absolute Tacitus; besides, he takes Montecuculi, or

Montecuculo, as he calls him, for a Frenchman. He says the dauphin died at Paris, whereas it was at Tournon. He speaks of decided indications of poison from public rumor; but it is clear that he attributes the accusation of Catherine de Medici only to the French. This charge is equally unjust and extravagant with that against Montecuculi.

In fact, this volatile temperament, so characteristic of the French, has in every period of our history led to the most tragical catastrophes. If we go back from the iniquitous execution of Montecuculi to that of the Knights Templars, we shall see a series of the most atrocious punishments, founded upon the most frivolous presumptions. Rivers of blood have flowed in France in consequence of the thoughtless character and precipitate judgment of the French people.

We may just notice the wretched pleasure that some men, and particularly those of weak minds, secretly enjoy in talking or writing of public executions, like that they derive from the subject of miracles and sorceries. In Calmet's "Dictionary of the Bible" you may find a number of fine engravings of the punishments in use among the Hebrews. These prints are absolutely sufficient to strike every person of feeling with horror. We will take this opportunity to observe that neither the Jews nor any other people ever thought of fixing persons to the cross by nails; and that there is not even a single instance of it. It is the fiction of some painter, built upon an opinion completely erroneous.

SECTION III.

Ye sages who are scattered over the world—for some sages there are—join the philosophic Beccaria, and proclaim with all your strength that punishments ought to be proportioned to crimes:

That after shooting through the head a young man of the age of twenty, who has spent six months with his father and mother or his mistress, instead of rejoining his regiment, he can no longer be of any service to his country:

That if you hang on the public gallows the servant girl who stole a dozen napkins from her mistress, she will be unable to add to the number of your citizens a dozen children, whom you may be considered as strangling in embryo with their parent; that there is no proportion between a dozen napkins and human life; and, finally, that you really encourage domestic theft, because no master will be so cruel as to get his coachman hanged for stealing a few of his oats; but every master would prosecute to obtain the infliction of a punishment which should be simply proportioned to the offence:

That all judges and legislators are guilty of the death of all the children which unfortunate, seduced women desert, expose, or even strangle, from a similar weakness to that which gave them birth.

On this subject I shall without scruple relate what has just occurred in the capital of a wise and powerful republic, which however, with all its wisdom, has unhappily retained some barbarous laws from those old, unsocial, and inhuman ages, called by some the ages of purity of manners. Near this capital a new-born infant was found dead; a girl was apprehended on suspicion of being the mother; she was shut up in a dungeon; she was strictly interrogated; she replied that she could not have been the mother of that child, as she was at the present time pregnant. She was ordered to be visited by a certain number of what are called (perfectly malapropos in the present instance) wise women—by a commission of matrons. These poor imbecile creatures declared her not to be with child, and that the appearance of pregnancy was occasioned by improper retention. The unfortunate woman was threatened with the torture; her mind became alarmed and terrified; she confessed that she had killed her supposed child; she was capitally convicted; and during the actual passing of her sentence was seized with the pains of childbirth. Her judges were taught by this most impressive case not lightly to pass sentences of death.

With respect to the numberless executions which weak fanatics have inflicted upon other fanatics equally weak, I will say nothing more about them; although it is impossible to say too much.

There are scarcely any highway robberies committed in Italy without assassinations, because the punishment of death is equally awarded to both crimes.

It cannot be doubted that M. de Beccaria, in his "Treatise on Crimes and Punishments" has noticed this very important fact.

EXECUTIONER.

It may be thought that this word should not be permitted to degrade a dictionary of arts and sciences; it has a connection however with jurisprudence and history. Our great poets have not disdained frequently to avail themselves of this word in tragedy: Clytemnestra, in Iphigenia, calls Agamemnon the executioner of his daughter.

In comedy it is used with great gayety; Mercury in the "Amphitryon" (act i. scene 2), says: *"Comment, bourreau! tu fais des cris*!"—"How, hangman! thou bellowest!"

And even the Romans permitted themselves to say: *"Quorsum vadis, carnifex?"*—"Whither goest thou, hangman?"

The Encyclopædia, under the word "Executioner," details all the privileges of the Parisian executioner; but a recent author has gone farther. In a romance on education, not altogether equal to Xenophon's "Cyropædia" or Fénelon's "Telemachus," he pretends that the monarch of a country ought, without hesitation, to bestow the daughter of an executioner in marriage on the heir apparent of the crown, if she has been well educated, and if she is of a sufficiently congruous disposition with the young prince. It is a pity that he has not mentioned the precise sum she should carry with her as a dower, and the honors that should be conferred upon her father on the day of marriage.

It is scarcely possible, with due *congruity*, to carry further the profound morality, the novel rules of decorum, the exquisite paradoxes, and divine maxims with which the author I speak of has favored and regaled the present age. He would undoubtedly feel the perfect *congruity* of officiating as bridesman at the wedding. He would compose the princess's epithalamium, and not fail to celebrate the grand exploits of her father. The bride may then possibly impart some acrid kisses; for be it known that this same writer, in another romance called "*Héloise*," introduces a young Swiss, who had caught a particular disorder in Paris, saying to his mistress, "Keep your kisses to yourself; they are too acrid."

A time will come when it will scarcely be conceived possible that such works should have obtained a sort of celebrity; had the celebrity continued, it would have done no honor to the age. Fathers of families soon made up their minds that it was not exactly decorous to marry their eldest sons to the daughters of executioners, whatever congruity might appear to exist between the lover and the lady. There is a rule in all things, and certain limits which cannot be rationally passed.

Est modus in rebus, sunt certi denique fines,
Quos ultra citraque nequit consistere rectum.

EXPIATION.

Dieu fit du repentir la vertu des mortels.

The repentance of man is accepted by God as virtue, and perhaps the finest institution of antiquity was that solemn ceremony which repressed crimes by announcing that they would be punished, and at the same time soothed the despair of the guilty by permitting them to redeem their transgressions by appointed modes of penance. Remorse, it is to be remembered, must necessarily have preceded expiation, for diseases are older than medicine, and necessities than relief.

There was, then, previously to all public and legal forms of worship, a natural and instinctive religion which inflicted grief upon the heart of any one who, through ignorance or passion, had committed an inhuman action. A man in a quarrel has killed his friend, or his brother, or a jealous and frantic lover has taken the life of her without whom he felt as if it were impossible to live. The chief of a nation has condemned to death a virtuous man and useful citizen. Such men, if they retain their senses and sensibility, become overwhelmed by despair. Their consciences pursue and haunt them; two courses only are open to them, reparation or to become hardened in guilt. All who have the slightest feeling remaining choose the former; monsters adopt the latter.

As soon as religion was established, expiations were admitted. The ceremonies attending them were, unquestionably, ridiculous; for what connection is there between the water of the Ganges and a murder? How could a man repair homicide by bathing? We have already commented on the excess of absurdity and insanity which can imagine that what washes the body, washes the soul also, and expunges from it the stain of evil actions.

The water of the Nile had afterwards the same virtue as that of the Ganges; other ceremonies were added to these ablutions. The Egyptians took two he-goats and drew lots which of the two should be cast out loaded with the sins of the guilty. This goat was called Hazazel, the expiator. What connection is there, pray, between a goat and the crime of a human being?

It is certainly true that in after times this ceremony was sanctified among our fathers the Jews, who adopted many of the Egyptian rites; but the souls of the Jews were undoubtedly purified, not by the goat but by repentance.

Jason, having killed Absyrtus, his brother-in-law, went, we are told, with Medea, who was more guilty than himself, to be absolved by Circe, the queen and priestess of Æa, who passed in those days for a most powerful sorceress. Circe absolved them with a sucking pig and salt cakes. This might possibly be a very good dish, but it could neither compensate for the blood of Absyrtus, nor make Jason and Medea more worthy people, unless while eating their pig they also manifested the sincerity of their repentance.

The expiation of Orestes, who had avenged his father by the murder of his mother, consisted in going and stealing a statue from the Tartars of the Crimea. The statue was probably extremely ill executed, and there appeared nothing to be gained by such an enterprise. In later times these things were contrived better: mysteries were invented, and the offenders might obtain absolution at these mysteries by submitting to certain painful trials, and swearing to lead a new life. It is from this oath that the persons taking it had attached to them, among all nations, a name corresponding to that of initiated "*qui ineunt vitam novam*,"—who begin a new career, who enter upon the path of virtue.

We have seen under the article on "Baptism" that the Christian catechumens were not called initiated till after they had been baptized.

It is indisputable, that persons had not their sins washed away in these mysteries, but by virtue of their oath to become virtuous: the hierophant in all the Grecian mysteries, when dismissing the assembly, pronounced the two Egyptian words, "*Koth, ompheth*," "watch, be pure"; which at once proves that the mysteries came originally from Egypt, and that they were invented solely for the purpose of making mankind better.

Wise men, we thus see, have, in every age, done all in their power to inspire the love of virtue, and to prevent the weakness of man from sinking under despair; but, at the same time there have existed crimes of such magnitude and horror that no mystery could admit of their expiation. Nero, although an emperor, could not obtain initiation into the mysteries of Ceres. Constantine, according to the narrative of Zosimus, was unable to procure the pardon of his crimes: he was polluted with the blood of his wife, his son, and all his relations. It was necessary, for the protection of the human race, that crimes so flagitious should be deemed incapable of expiation, that the prospect of absolution might not invite to their committal, and that hideous atrocity might be checked by universal horror.

The Roman Catholics have expiations which they call penances. We have seen, under the article on "Austerities," how grossly so salutary an institution has been abused.

According to the laws of the barbarians who subverted the Roman Empire, crimes were expiated by money. This was called compounding: "Let the offender compound by paying ten, twenty, thirty shillings." Two hundred sous constituted the composition price for killing a priest, and four hundred for killing a bishop; so that a bishop was worth exactly two priests.

After having thus compounded with men, God Himself was compounded with, when the practice of confession became generally established. At length Pope John XXII. established a tariff of sins.

The absolution of incest, committed by a layman, cost four livres tournois: "*Ab incestu pro laico in foro conscienticæ turonenses quatuor*." For a man and woman who have committed incest, eighteen livres tournois, four ducats, and nine carlines. This is certainly unjust; if one person pays only four livres tournois, two persons ought not to pay more than eight.

Even crimes against nature have actually their affixed rates, amounting to ninety livres tournois, twelve ducats, and six carlines: "*Cum inhibitione turonenses 90, ducatos 12, carlinos 90*," etc.

It is scarcely credible that Leo X. should have been so imprudent as to print this book of rates or indulgences in 1514, which, however, we are assured he did; at the same time it must be considered that no spark had then appeared of that conflagration, kindled afterwards by the reformers; and that the court of Rome reposed implicitly upon the credulity of the people, and neglected to throw even the slightest veil over its impositions. The public sale of indulgences, which soon followed, shows that that court took no precaution whatever to conceal its gross abominations from the various nations which had been so long accustomed to them. When the complaints against the abuses of the Romish church burst forth, it did all in its power to suppress this publication, but all was in vain.

If I may give my opinion upon this book of rates, I must say that I do not believe the editions of it are genuine; the rates are not in any kind of proportion and do not at all coincide with those stated by d'Aubigné, the grandfather of Madame de

Maintenon, in the confession of de Sancy. Depriving a woman of her virginity is estimated at six gros, and committing incest with a mother or a sister, at five gros. This is evidently ridiculous. I think that there really was a system of rates or taxes established for those who went to Rome to obtain absolution or purchase dispensations, but that the enemies of the Holy See added largely, in order to increase the odium against it. Consult Bayle, under the articles on "Bank," "Dupinet," "Drelincourt."

It is at least positively certain that these rates were never authorized by any council; that they constituted an enormous abuse, invented by avarice, and respected by those who were interested in its not being abolished. The sellers and the purchasers equally found their account in it; and accordingly none opposed it before the breaking out of the disturbances attending the Reformation. It must be acknowledged that an exact list of all these rates or taxes would be eminently useful in the formation of a history of the human mind.

EXTREME.

We will here attempt to draw from the word "extreme" an idea that may be attended with some utility.

It is every day disputed whether in war success is ascribable to conduct or to fortune.

Whether in diseases, nature or medicine is most operative in healing or destroying.

Whether in law it is not judicious for a man to compromise, although he is in the right, and to defend a cause although he is in the wrong.

Whether the fine arts contribute to the glory or to the decline of a state.

Whether it is wise or injudicious to encourage superstition in a people.

Whether there is any truth in metaphysics, history, or morals.

Whether taste is arbitrary, and whether there is in reality a good and a bad taste.

In order to decide at once all these questions, take an advantage of the extreme cases under each, compare these two extremes, and you will immediately discover the truth.

You wish to know whether success in war can be infallibly decided by conduct; consider the most extreme case, the most opposed situations in which conduct alone will infallibly triumph. The hostile army must necessarily pass through a deep mountain gorge; your commander knows this circumstance; he makes a forced march, gets possession of the heights, and completely encloses the enemy in the defile; there they must either perish or surrender. In this extreme case fortune can have no share in the victory. It is demonstrable, therefore, that skill may decide the success of a campaign, and it hence necessarily follows that war is an art.

Afterwards imagine an advantageous but not a decisive position; success is not certain, but it is exceedingly probable. And thus, from one gradation to another, you arrive at what may be considered a perfect equality between the two armies. Who shall then decide? Fortune; that is, some unexpected circumstance or event; the death of a general officer going to execute some important order; the derangement of a division in consequence of a false report, the operation of sudden panic, or various other causes for which prudence can find no remedy; yet it is still always certain that there is an art, that there is a science in war.

The same must be observed concerning medicine; the art of operating with the head or hand to preserve the life which appears likely to be lost.

The first who applied bleeding as speedily as possible to a patient under apoplexy; the first who conceived the idea of plunging a bistoury into the bladder to extract the stone from it, and of closing up the wound; the first who found out the method of stopping gangrene in any part of the human frame, were undoubtedly men, almost divine, and totally unlike the physicians of Molière.

Descend from this strong and decisive example to cases less striking and more equivocal; you perceive fevers and various other maladies cured without its being possible to ascertain whether this is done by the physician or by nature; you perceive diseases, the issue of which cannot be judged; various physicians are mistaken in their opinions of the seat or nature of them; he who has the acutest genius, the keenest eye, develops the character of the complaint. There is then an art in medicine, and the man of superior mind is acquainted with its niceties. Thus it was that La Peyronie discovered that one of the courtiers had swallowed a sharp bone, which had occasioned an ulcer and endangered his life; and thus also did Boerhaave discover the complaint, as unknown as it was dreadful, of a countess of Wassenaer. There is, therefore, it cannot be doubted, an art in medicine, but in every art there are Virgils and Mæviuses.

In jurisprudence, take a case that is clear, in which the law pronounces decisively; a bill of exchange correctly drawn and regularly accepted; the acceptor is bound to pay it in every country in the world. There is, therefore, a useful jurisprudence, although in innumerable cases sentences are arbitrary, because, to the misery of mankind, the laws are ill-framed.

Would you wish to know whether the fine arts are beneficial to a nation? Compare the two extremes:

Cicero and a perfect ignoramus. Decide whether the fall of Rome was owing to Pliny or to Attila.

It is asked whether we should encourage superstition in the people. Consider for a moment what is the greatest extreme on this baleful subject, the massacre of St. Bartholomew, the massacres of Ireland, or the Crusades; and the question is decided.

Is there any truth in metaphysics? Advert to those points which are most striking and true. Something exists; something, therefore, has existed from all eternity. An eternal being exists of himself; this being cannot be either wicked or inconsistent. To these truths we must yield; almost all the rest is open to disputation, and the clearest understanding discovers the truth.

It is in everything else as it is in colors; bad eyes can distinguish between black and white; better eyes, and eyes much exercised, can distinguish every nicer gradation: "*Usque adeo quod tangit idem est, tamen ultima distant.*"

***

EZEKIEL.

Of Some Singular Passages in This Prophet, and of Certain Ancient Usages.

It is well known that we ought not to judge of ancient usages by modern ones; he that would reform the court of Alcinous in the "Odyssey," upon the model of the Grand Turk, or Louis XIV., would not meet with a very gentle reception from the learned; he who is disposed to reprehend Virgil for having described King Evander covered with a bear's skin and accompanied by two dogs at the introduction of ambassadors, is a contemptible critic.

The manners of the ancient Egyptians and Jews are still more different from ours than those of King Alcinous, his daughter Nausicáa, and the worthy Evander. Ezekiel, when in slavery among the Chaldæans, had a vision near the small river Chobar, which falls into the Euphrates.

We ought not to be in the least astonished at his having seen animals with four faces, four wings, and with calves' feet; or wheels revolving without aid and "instinct with life"; these images are pleasing to the imagination; but many critics have been shocked at the order given him by the Lord to eat, for a period of three hundred and ninety days, bread made of barley, wheat, or millet, covered with human ordure.

The prophet exclaimed in strong disgust, "My soul has not hitherto been polluted"; and the Lord replied, "Well, I will allow you instead of man's ordure to use that of the cow, and with the latter you shall knead your bread."

As it is now unusual to eat a preparation of bread of this description, the greater number of men regard the order in question as unworthy of the Divine Majesty. Yet it must be admitted that cow-dung and all the diamonds of the great Mogul are perfectly equal, not only in the eyes of a Divine Being, but in those of a true philosopher; and, with regard to the reasons which God might have for ordering the prophet this repast, we have no right to inquire into them. It is enough for us to see that commands which appear to us very strange, did not appear so to the Jews.

It must be admitted that the synagogue, in the time of St. Jerome, did not suffer "Ezekiel" to be read before the age of thirty; but this was because, in the eighteenth chapter, he says that the son shall not bear the iniquity of his father, and it shall not be any longer said the fathers have eaten sour grapes, and the children's teeth are set on edge.

This expression was considered in direct contradiction to Moses, who, in the twenty-eighth chapter of "Numbers," declares that the children bear the iniquity of the fathers, even to the third and fourth generation.

Ezekiel, again, in the twentieth chapter, makes the Lord say that He has given to the Jews precepts which are not good. Such are the reasons for which the synagogue forbade young people reading an author likely to raise doubts on the irrefragability of the laws of Moses.

The censorious critics of the present day are still more astonished with the sixteenth chapter of Ezekiel. In that chapter he thus takes it upon him to expose the crimes of the city of Jerusalem. He introduces the Lord speaking to a young woman; and the Lord said to her, "When thou wast born, thy navel string was not cut, thou wast not salted, thou wast quite naked, I had pity on thee; thou didst increase in stature, thy breasts were fashioned, thy hair was grown, I passed by thee, I observed thee, I knew that the time of lovers was come, I covered thy shame, I spread my skirt over thee; thou becamest mine; I washed and perfumed thee, and dressed and shod thee well; I gave thee a scarf of linen, and bracelets, and a chain for thy neck; I placed a jewel in thy nose, pendants in thy ears, and a crown upon thy head."

"Then, confiding in thy beauty, thou didst in the height of thy renown, play the harlot with every passer-by.... And thou hast built a high place of profanation ... and thou hast prostituted thyself in public places, and opened thy feet to every one that passed ... and thou hast committed fornication with the Egyptians ... and finally thou hast paid thy lovers and made them presents, that they might lie with thee ... and by hiring them, instead of being hired, thou hast done differently from other harlots.... The proverb is, as is the mother, so is the daughter, and that proverb is used of thee," etc.

Still more are they exasperated on the subject of the twenty-third chapter. A mother had two daughters, who early lost their virginity. The elder was called Ahola, and the younger Aholibah.... "Aholah committed fornication with young lords and captains, and lay with the Egyptians from her early youth.... Aholibah, her sister, committed still greater fornication with officers and rulers and well-made cavaliers; she discovered her shame, she multiplied her fornications, she sought eagerly for the embraces of those whose flesh was as that of asses, and whose issue was as that of horses."

These descriptions, which so madden weak minds, signify, in fact, no more than the iniquities of Jerusalem and Samaria; these expressions, which appear to us licentious, were not so then. The same vivacity is displayed in many other parts of Scripture without the slightest apprehension. Opening the womb is very frequently mentioned. The terms made use of to express the union of Boaz with Ruth, and of Judah with his daughter-in-law, are not indelicate in the Hebrew language, but would be so in our own.

People who are not ashamed of nakedness, never cover it with a veil. In the times under consideration, no blush could have been raised by the mention of particular parts of the frame of man, as they were actually touched by the person who bound himself by any promise to another; it was a mark of respect, a symbol of fidelity, as formerly among ourselves, feudal lords put their hands between those of their sovereign.

We have translated the term adverted to by the word "thigh." Eliezer puts his hand under Abraham's thigh. Joseph puts his hand under the thigh of Jacob. This custom was very ancient in Egypt. The Egyptians were so far from attaching any disgrace to what we are desirous as much as possible to conceal and avoid the mention of, that they bore in procession a large and characteristic image, called Phallus, in order to thank the gods for making the human frame so instrumental in the perpetuation of the human species.

All this affords sufficient proof that our sense of decorum and propriety is different from that of other nations. When do the Romans appear to have been more polished than in the time of Augustus? Yet Horace scruples not to say, in one of his moral pieces: "*Nec metuo, ne dum futuo vir rure recurrat*" (Satire II., book i., v. 127.) Augustus uses the same expression in an epigram on Fulvia.

The man who should among us pronounce the expression in our language corresponding to it, would be regarded as a drunken porter; that word, as well as various others used by Horace and other authors, appears to us even more indecent than the expressions of Ezekiel. Let us then do away with our prejudices when we read ancient authors, or travel among distant nations. Nature is the same everywhere, and usages are everywhere different.

I once met at Amsterdam a rabbi quite brimful of this chapter. "Ah! my friend," says he, "how very much we are obliged to you. You have displayed all the sublimity of the Mosaic law, Ezekiel's breakfast; his delightful left-sided attitudes; Aholah and Aholibah are admirable things; they are types, my brother—types which show that one day the Jewish people will be masters of the whole world; but why did you admit so many others which are nearly of equal strength? Why did not you represent the Lord saying to the sage Hosea, in the second verse of the first chapter, 'Hosea, take to thyself a harlot, and make to her the children of a harlot?' Such are the very words. Hosea takes the young woman and has a son by her, and afterwards a daughter, and then again a son; and it was a type, and that type lasted three years. That is not all; the Lord says in the third chapter, 'Go and take to thyself a woman who is not merely a harlot, but an adulteress.' Hosea obeyed, but it cost him fifteen crowns and eighteen bushels of barley; for, you know, there was very little wheat in the land of promise—but are you aware of the meaning of all this?" "No," said I to him. "Nor I neither," said the rabbi.

A grave person then advanced towards us and said they were ingenious fictions and abounding in exquisite beauty. "Ah, sir," remarked a young man, "if you are inclined for fictions, give the preference to those of Homer, Virgil, and Ovid." He who prefers the prophecies of Ezekiel deserves to breakfast with him.

FABLE.

It is very likely that the more ancient fables, in the style of those attributed to Æsop, were invented by the first subjugated people. Free men would not have had occasion to disguise the truth; a tyrant can scarcely be spoken to except in parables; and at present, even this is a dangerous liberty.

It might also very well happen that men naturally liking images and tales, ingenious persons amused themselves with composing them, without any other motive. However that may be, fable is more ancient than history.

Among the Jews, who are quite a modern people in comparison with the Chaldæans and Tyrians, their neighbors, but very ancient by their own accounts, fables similar to those of Æsop existed in the time of the Judges, 1233 years before our era, if we may depend upon received computations.

It is said in the Book of Judges that Gideon had seventy sons born of his many wives; and that, by a concubine, he had another son named Abimelech.

Now, this Abimelech slew sixty-nine of his brethren upon one stone, according to Jewish custom, and in consequence the Jews, full of respect and admiration, went to crown him king, under an oak near Millo, a city which is but little known in history.

Jotham alone, the youngest of the brothers, escaped the carnage—as it always happens in ancient histories—and harangued the Israelites, telling them that the trees went one day to choose a king; we do not well see how they could march, but if they were able to speak, they might just as well be able to walk. They first addressed themselves to the olive, saying, "Reign thou over us." The olive replied, "I will not quit the care of my oil to be promoted over you." The fig-tree said that he liked his figs better than the trouble of the supreme power. The vine gave the preference to its grapes. At last the trees addressed themselves to the bramble, which answered: "If in truth ye anoint one king over you, then come and put your trust in my shadow; and if not, let fire come out of the bramble and devour the cedars of Lebanon."

It is true that this fable falsifies throughout, because fire cannot come from a bramble, but it shows the antiquity of the use of fables.

That of the belly and the members, which calmed a tumult in Rome about two thousand three hundred years ago, is ingenious and without fault. The more ancient the fables the more allegorical they were.

Is not the ancient fable of Venus, as related by Hesiod, entirely a fable of nature? This Venus is the goddess of beauty. Beauty ceases to be lovely if unaccompanied by the graces. Beauty produces love. Love has features which pierce all hearts; he wears a bandage, which conceals the faults of those beloved. He has wings; he comes quickly and flies away the same.

Wisdom is conceived in the brain of the chief of the gods, under the name of Minerva. The soul of man is a divine fire, which Minerva shows to Prometheus, who makes use of this divine fire to animate mankind.

It is impossible, in these fables, not to recognize a lively picture of pure nature. Most other fables are either corruptions of ancient histories or the caprices of the imagination. It is with ancient fables as with our modern tales; some convey charming morals, and others very insipid ones.

The ingenious fables of the ancients have been grossly imitated by an unenlightened race—witness those of Bacchus, Hercules, Prometheus, Pandora, and many others, which were the amusement of the ancient world. The barbarians, who confusedly heard them spoken of, adopted them into their own savage mythology, and afterwards it is pretended that they invented them. Alas! poor unknown and ignorant people, who knew no art either useful or agreeable— to whom even the name of geometry was unknown— dare you say that you have invented anything? You have not known either how to discover truth, or to lie adroitly.

The most elegant Greek fable was that of Psyche; the most pleasant, that of the Ephesian matron. The prettiest among the moderns is that of Folly, who, having put out Love's eyes, is condemned to be his guide.

The fables attributed to Æsop are all emblems; instructions to the weak, to guard them as much as possible against the snares of the strong. All nations, possessing a little wisdom, have adopted them. La Fontaine has treated them with the most elegance. About eighty of them are masterpieces of simplicity, grace, finesse, and sometimes even of poetry. It is one of the advantages of the age of Louis XIV. to have produced a La Fontaine. He has so well discovered, almost without seeking it, the art of making one read, that he has had a greater reputation in France than genius itself.

Boileau has never reckoned him among those who did honor to the great age of Louis XIV.; his reason or his pretext was that he had never invented anything. What will better bear out Boileau is the great number of errors in language and the incorrectness of style; faults which La Fontaine might have avoided, and which this severe critic could not pardon. His grasshopper, for instance, having sung all the summer, went to beg from the ant, her neighbor, in the winter, telling her, on the word of an animal, that she would pay her principal and interest before midsummer. The ant replies: "You sang, did you? I am glad of it; then now dance."

His astrologer, again, who falling into a ditch while gazing at the stars, was asked: "Poor wretch! do you expect to be able to read things so much above you?" Yet Copernicus, Galileo, Cassini, and Halley have read the heavens very well; and the best astronomer that ever existed might fall into a ditch without being a poor wretch.

Judicial astrology is indeed ridiculous charlatanism, but the ridiculousness does not consist in regarding the heavens; it consists in believing, or in making believe, that you read what is not there. Several of these fables, either ill chosen or badly written, certainly merit the censure of Boileau.

Nothing is more insipid than the fable of the drowned woman, whose corpse was sought contrary to the course of the river, because in her lifetime she had always been contrary.

The tribute sent by the animals to King Alexander is a fable, which is not the better for being ancient. The animals sent no money, neither did the lion advise them to steal it.

The satyr who received a peasant into his hut should not have turned him out on seeing that he blew his fingers because he was cold; and afterwards, on taking the dish between his teeth, that he blew his pottage because it was hot. The man was quite right, and the satyr was a fool. Besides, we do not take hold of dishes with our teeth.

The crab-mother, who reproached her daughter with not walking straight; and the daughter, who answered that her mother walked crooked, is not an agreeable fable.

The bush and the duck, in commercial partnership with the bat, having counters, factors, agents, paying principal and interest, etc., has neither truth, nature, nor any kind of merit.

A bush which goes with a bat into foreign countries to trade is one of those cold and unnatural inventions which La Fontaine should not have adopted. A house full of dogs and cats, living together like cousins and quarrelling for a dish of pottage, seems also very unworthy of a man of taste.

The chattering magpie is still worse. The eagle tells her that he declines her company because she talks too much. On which La Fontaine remarks that it is necessary at court to wear two faces.

Where is the merit of the fable of the kite presented by a bird-catcher to a king, whose nose he had seized with his claws? The ape who married a Parisian girl and beat her is an unfortunate story presented to La Fontaine, and which he has been so unfortunate as to put into verse.

Such fables as these; and some others, may doubtless justify Boileau; it might even happen that La Fontaine could not distinguish the bad fables from the good.

Madame de la Sablière called La Fontaine a fabulist, who bore fables as naturally as a plum-tree bears plums. It is true that he had only one style, and that he wrote an opera in the style of his fables.

Notwithstanding all this, Boileau should have rendered justice to the singular merit of the good man, as he calls him, and to the public, who are right in being enchanted with the style of many of his fables.

La Fontaine was not an original or a sublime writer, a man of established taste, or one of the first geniuses of a brilliant era; and it is a very remarkable fault in him that he speaks not his own language correctly. He is in this respect very inferior to Phaedrus, but he was a man unique in the excellent pieces that he has left us. They are very numerous, and are in the mouths of all those who have been respectably brought up; they contribute even to their education. They will descend to posterity; they are adapted for all men and for all times, while those of Boileau suit only men of letters.

Of Those Fanatics Who Would Suppress the Ancient Fables.

There is among those whom we call Jansenists a little sect of hard and empty heads, who would suppress the beautiful fables of antiquity, to substitute St. Prosper in the place of Ovid, and Santeuil in that of Horace. If they were attended to, our pictures would no longer represent Iris on the rainbow, or Minerva with her aegis; but instead of them, we should have Nicholas and Arnauld fighting against the Jesuits and Protestants; Mademoiselle Perrier cured of sore eyes by a thorn from the crown of Jesus Christ, brought from Jerusalem to Port Royal; Counsellor Carré de Montgeron presenting the account of St. Médard to Louis XV.; and St. Ovid resuscitating little boys.

In the eyes of these austere sages, Fénelon was only an idolater, who, following the example of the impious poem of the "Æneid," introduced the child Cupid with the nymph Eucharis.

Pluche, at the end of his fable of the Heavens, entitled "Their History," writes a long dissertation to prove that it is shameful to have tapestry worked in figures taken from Ovid's "Metamorphoses"; and that Zephyrus and Flora, Vertumnus and Pomona, should be banished from the gardens of Versailles. He exhorts the school of belles-lettres to oppose itself to this bad taste; which reform alone, he says, is capable of re-establishing the belles-lettres.

Other puritans, more severe than sage a little time ago, would have proscribed the ancient mythology as a collection of puerile tales, unworthy the acknowledged gravity of our manners. It would, however, be a pity to burn Ovid, Horace, Hesiod, our fine tapestry pictures and our opera. If we were spared the familiar stories of Æsop, why lay hands on those sublime fables, which have been respected by mankind, whom they have instructed? They are mingled with many insipidities, no doubt, but what good is without an alloy? All ages will adopt Pandora's box, at the bottom of which was found man's only consolation—hope; Jupiter's two vessels, which unceasingly poured forth good and evil; the cloud embraced by Ixion, which is the emblem and punishment of an ambitious man; and the death of Narcissus, which is the punishment of self-love. What is more sublime than the image of Minerva, the goddess of wisdom, formed in the head of the master of the gods? What is more true and agreeable than the goddess of beauty, always accompanied by the graces? The goddesses of the arts, all daughters of memory—do they not teach us, as well as Locke, that without memory we cannot possess either judgment or wit? The arrows of Love, his fillet, and his childhood; Flora, caressed by Zephyrus, etc.—are they not all sensible personifications of pure nature? These fables have survived the religions which consecrated them. The temples of the gods of Egypt, Greece, and Rome are no more, but Ovid still exists. Objects of credulity may be destroyed, but not those of pleasure; we shall forever love these true and lively images. Lucretius did not believe in these fabulous gods, but he celebrated nature under the name of Venus.

Alma Venus cœli subter labentia signa
Quæ mare navigerum, quæ terras frugiferentes
Concelebras, per te quoniam genus omne animantum
Concipitur, visitque exortum lumina solis, etc.

Kind Venus, glory of the blest abodes,
Parent of Rome, and joy of men and gods;
Delight of all, comfort of sea and earth,
To whose kind power all creatures owe their birth,
etc.
—CREECH.

If antiquity in its obscurity was led to acknowledge divinity in its images, how is it to be blamed? The productive soul of the world was adored by the sages; it governed the sea under the name of Neptune, the air under the image of Juno, and the country under that of Pan. It was the divinity of armies under the name of Mars; all these attributes were animated personifications. Jupiter was the only *god*. The golden chain with which he bound the inferior gods and men was a striking image of the unity of a sovereign being. The people were deceived, but what are the people to us?

It is continually asked why the Greek and Roman magistrates permitted the divinities whom they adored in their temples to be ridiculed on their stage? This is a false supposition. The gods were not mocked in their theatres, but the follies attributed to these gods by those who had corrupted the ancient mythology. The consuls and prætors found it good to treat the adventure of the two Sosias wittily, but they would not have suffered the worship of Jupiter and Mercury to be attacked before the people. It is thus that a thousand things which appear contradictory are not so in reality. I have seen, in the theatre of a learned and witty nation, pieces taken from the Golden Legend; will it, on that account, be said that this nation permits its objects of religion to be insulted? It need not be feared we shall become Pagans for having heard the opera of Proserpine at Paris, or for having seen the nuptials of Psyche, painted by Raphael, in the pope's palace at Rome. Fable forms the taste, but renders no person idolatrous.

The beautiful fables of antiquity have also this great advantage over history: they are lessons of virtue, while almost all history narrates the success of vice. Jupiter in the fable descends upon earth to punish Tantalus and Lycaon; but in history our Tantaluses and Lycaons are the gods of the earth.

Baucis and Philemon had their cabin changed into a temple; our Baucises and Philemons are obliged to sell, for the collector of the taxes, those kettles which, in Ovid, the gods changed into vases of gold.

I know how much history can instruct us and how necessary it is to know it; but it requires much ingenuity to be able to draw from it any rules for individual conduct. Those who know politics only through books will be often reminded of those lines of Corneille, which observe that examples will seldom suffice for our guidance, as it often happens that one person perishes by the very expedient which has proved the salvation of another.

Les exemples recens suffiraient pour m'instruire
Si par l'exemple seul on devait se conduire;
Mais souvent l'un se perd où l'autre s'est sauvé,
Et par où l'un périt, un autre est conservé.

Henry VIII., the tyrant of his parliament, his ministers and his wives, of consciences and purses, lived and died peaceably. Charles I. perished on the scaffold. Margaret of Anjou in vain waged war in person a dozen times with the English, the subjects of her husband, while William III. drove James II. from England without a battle. In our days we have seen the royal family of Persia murdered, and strangers upon the throne.

To look at events only, history seems to accuse Providence, and fine moral fables justify it. It is clear that both the useful and agreeable may be discovered in them, however exclaimed against by those who are neither the one nor the other. Let them talk on, and let us read Homer and Ovid, as well as Titus Livius and Rapin de Thoyras. Taste induces preferences and fanaticism exclusions. The arts are united, and those who would separate them know nothing about them. History teaches us what we are—fable what we ought to be.

> *Tous les arts sont amis, ainsi qu ils sont divins;*
> *Qui veut les séparer est loin de les connaître.*
> *L'histoire nous apprend ce que sont les humains,*
> *La fable ce qu ils doivent être.*

FACTION.

On the Meaning of the Word.

The word "faction" comes from the Latin "*facere*"; it is employed to signify the state of a soldier at his post, on duty (*en faction*), squadrons or troops of combatants in the circus; green, blue, red, and white factions.

The acceptation in which the term is generally used is that of a seditious party in the state. The term "party" in itself implies nothing that is odious, that of faction is always odious.

A great man, and even a man possessing only mediocrity of talent, may easily have a party at court, in the army, in the city, or in literature. A man may have a party in consequence of his merit, in consequence of the zeal and number of his friends, without being the head of a party. Marshal Catinat, although little regarded at court, had a large party in the army without making any effort to obtain it.

A head of a party is always a head of a faction; such were Cardinal Retz, Henry, duke of Guise, and various others. A seditious party, while it is yet weak and has no influence in the government, is only a faction.

Cæsar's faction speedily became a dominant party, which swallowed up the republic. When the emperor Charles VI. disputed the throne of Spain with Philip V. he had a party in that kingdom, and at length he had no more than a faction in it. Yet we may always be allowed to talk of the "party" of Charles VI.

It is different with respect to private persons. Descartes for a long time had a party in France; it would be incorrect to say he had a faction. Thus we perceive that words in many cases synonymous cease to be so in others.

FACULTY.

All the powers of matter and mind are faculties; and, what is still worse, faculties of which we know nothing, perfectly occult qualities; to begin with motion, of which no one has discovered the origin.

When the president of the faculty of medicine in the "*Malade Imaginaire*," asks Thomas Diafoirus: "*Quare opium facit dormire?*"—Why does opium cause sleep? Thomas very pertinently replies, "*Quia est in eo virtus dormitiva quæ facit sopire.*"—Because it possesses a dormitive power producing sleep. The greatest philosophers cannot speak more to the purpose.

The honest chevalier de Jaucourt acknowledges, under the article on "Sleep," that it is impossible to go beyond conjecture with respect to the cause of it. Another Thomas, and in much higher reverence than his bachelor namesake in the comedy, has, in fact, made no other reply to all the questions which are started throughout his immense volumes.

It is said, under the article on "Faculty," in the grand "Encyclopædia," "that the vital faculty once established in the intelligent principle by which we are animated, it may be easily conceived that the faculty, stimulated by the expressions which the vital *sensorium* transmits to part of the common *sensorium,* determines the alternate influx of the nervous fluid into the fibres which move the vital organs in order to produce the alternate contradiction of those organs."

This amounts precisely to the answer of the young physician Thomas: "*Quia est in eo virtus alterniva quæ facit alternare.*" And Thomas Diafoirus has at least the merit of being shortest.

The faculty of moving the foot when we wish to do so, of recalling to mind past events, or of exercising our five senses; in short, any and all of our faculties will admit of no further or better explanation than that of Diafoirus.

But consider thought! say those who understand the whole secret. Thought, which distinguishes man from all animals besides: "*Sanctius his animal, mentisque capacius altæ.*" (Ovid's Metamorph. i. 76.)—More holy man, of more exalted mind!

As holy as you like; it is on this subject, that of thought or mind, that Diafoirus is more triumphant than ever. All would reply in accordance with him: "*Quia est in eo virtus pensativa quæ facit pensare.*" No one will ever develop the mysterious process by which he thinks.

The case we are considering then might be extended to everything in nature. I know not whether there may not be found in this profound and unfathomable gulf of mystery an evidence of the existence of a Supreme Being. There is a secret in the originating or conservatory principles of all beings, from a pebble on the seashore to Saturn's Ring and the Milky Way. But how can there be a secret which no one knows? It would seem that some being must exist who can develop all.

Some learned men, with a view to enlighten our ignorance, tell us that we must form systems; that we shall at last find the secret out. But we have so long sought without obtaining any explanation that disgust against further search has very naturally succeeded. That, say they, is the mere indolence of philosophy; no, it is the rational repose of men who have exerted themselves and run an active race in vain. And after all, it must be admitted that indolent philosophy is far preferable to turbulent divinity and metaphysical delusion.

FAITH.

SECTION I.

What is faith? Is it to believe that which is evident? No. It is perfectly evident to my mind that there exists a necessary, eternal, supreme, and intelligent being. This is no matter of faith, but of reason. I have no merit in thinking that this eternal and infinite being, whom I consider as virtue, as goodness itself, is desirous that I should be good and virtuous. Faith consists in believing not what seems true, but what seems false to our understanding. The Asiatics can only by faith believe the journey of Mahomet to the seven planets, and the incarnations of the god Fo, of Vishnu, Xaca, Brahma, and Sommonocodom. They submit their understandings; they tremble to examine: wishing to avoid being either impaled or burned, they say: "I believe."

We do not here intend the slightest allusion to the Catholic faith. Not only do we revere it, but we possess it. We speak of the false, lying faith of other nations of the world, of that faith which is not faith, and which consists only in words.

There is a faith for things that are merely astonishing and prodigious, and a faith for things contradictory and impossible.

Vishnu became incarnate five hundred times; this is extremely astonishing, but it is not, however, physically impossible; for if Vishnu possessed a soul, he may have transferred that soul into five hundred different bodies, with a view to his own felicity. The Indian, indeed, has not a very lively faith; he is not intimately and decidedly persuaded of these metamorphoses; but he will nevertheless say to his bonze, "I have faith; it is your will and pleasure that Vishnu has undergone five hundred incarnations, which is worth to you an income of five hundred rupees: very well; you will inveigh against me, and denounce me, and ruin my trade if I have not faith; but I have faith, and here are ten rupees over and above for you." The Indian may swear to the bonze that he believes without taking a false oath, for, after all, there is no demonstration that Vishnu has not actually made five hundred visits to India.

But if the bonze requires him to believe what is contradictory or impossible, as that two and two make five, or that the same body may be in a thousand different places, or that to be and not to be are precisely one and the same thing; in that case, if the Indian says he has faith he lies, and if he swears that he believes he commits perjury. He says, therefore, to the bonze: "My reverend father, I cannot declare that I believe in these absurdities, even though they should be worth to you an income of ten thousand rupees instead of five hundred."

"My son," the bonze answers, "give me twenty rupees and God will give you grace to believe all that you now do not believe."

"But how can you expect or desire," rejoins the Indian, "that God should do that by me which He cannot do even by Himself? It is impossible that God should either perform or believe contradictions. I am very willing to say, in order to give you satisfaction, that I believe what is obscure, but I cannot say that I believe what is impossible. It is the will of God that we should be virtuous, and not that we should be absurd. I have already given you ten rupees; here are twenty more; believe in thirty rupees; be an honest man if you can and do not trouble me any more."

It is not thus with Christians. The faith which they have for things which they do not understand is founded upon that which they do understand; they have grounds of credibility. Jesus Christ performed miracles in Galilee; we ought, therefore, to believe all that He said. In order to know what He said we must consult the Church. The Church has declared the books which announce Jesus Christ to us to be authentic. We ought, therefore, to believe those books. Those books inform us that he who will not listen to the Church shall be considered as a tax-gatherer or a Pagan; we ought, therefore, to listen to the Church that we may not be disgraced and hated like the farmers-general. We ought to submit our reason to it, not with infantile and blind credulity, but with a docile faith, such as reason itself would authorize. Such is Christian faith, particularly the Roman faith, which is "*the* faith" par excellence. The Lutheran, Calvinistic, or Anglican faith is a wicked faith.

SECTION II.

Divine faith, about which so much has been written, is evidently nothing more than incredulity brought under subjection, for we certainly have no other faculty than the understanding by which we can believe; and the objects of faith are not those of the understanding. We can believe only what appears to be true; and nothing can appear true but in one of the three following ways: by intuition or feeling, as I exist, I see the sun; by an accumulation of probability amounting to certainty, as there is a city called Constantinople; or by positive demonstration, as triangles of the same base and height are equal.

Faith, therefore, being nothing at all of this description, can no more be a belief, a persuasion, than it can be yellow or red. It can be nothing but the annihilation of reason, a silence of adoration at the contemplation of things absolutely incomprehensible. Thus, speaking philosophically, no person believes the Trinity; no person believes that the same body can be in a thousand places at once; and he who says, I believe these mysteries, will see, beyond the possibility of a doubt, if he reflects for a moment on what passes in his mind, that these words mean no more than, I respect these mysteries; I submit myself to those who announce them. For they agree with me, that my reason, or their own reason, believe them not; but it is clear that if my *reason* is not persuaded, *I* am not persuaded. I and my reason cannot possibly be two different beings. It is an absolute contradiction that I should receive that as true which my understanding rejects as false. Faith, therefore, is nothing but submissive or deferential incredulity.

But why should this submission be exercised when my understanding invincibly recoils? The reason, we well know, is, that my understanding has been persuaded that the mysteries of my faith are laid down by God Himself. All, then, that I can do, as a reasonable being, is to be silent and adore. This is what divines call external faith; and this faith neither is, nor can be, anything more than respect for things incomprehensible, in consequence of the reliance I place on those who teach them.

If God Himself were to say to me, "Thought is of an olive color"; "the square of a certain number is bitter"; I should certainly understand nothing at all from these words. I could not adopt them either as true or false. But I will repeat them, if He commands me to do it; and I will make others repeat them at the risk of my life. This is not faith; it is nothing more than obedience.

In order to obtain a foundation then for this obedience, it is merely necessary to examine the books which require it. Our understanding, therefore, should investigate the books of the Old and New Testament, just as it would Plutarch or Livy; and if it finds in them incontestable and decisive evidences— evidences obvious to all minds, and such as would be admitted by men of all nations—that God Himself is their author, then it is our incumbent duty to subject our understanding to the yoke of faith.

SECTION III.

We have long hesitated whether or not to publish the following article, "Faith," which we met with in an old book. Our respect for the chair of St. Peter restrained us. But some pious men having satisfied us that Alexander VI. and St. Peter had nothing in common, we have at last determined to publish this curious little production, and do it without the slightest scruple.

Prince Pico della Mirandola once met Pope Alexander VI. at the house of the courtesan Emilia, while Lucretia, the holy father's daughter, was confined in childbirth, and the people of Rome were discussing whether the child of which she was delivered belonged to the pope, to his son the Duke de Valentinois, or to Lucretia's husband, Alphonso of Aragon, who was considered by many as impotent. The conversation immediately became animated and gay. Cardinal Bembo relates a portion of it. "My little Pico," says the pope, "whom do you think the father of my grandson?" "I think your son-in-law," replied Pico. "What! how can you possibly believe such nonsense?" "I believe it by faith." "But surely you know that an impotent man cannot be a father." "Faith," replied Pico, "consists in believing things because they are impossible; and, besides, the honor of your house demands that Lucretia's son should not be reputed the offspring of incest. You require me to believe more incomprehensible mysteries. Am I not bound to believe that a serpent spoke; that from that time all mankind were damned; that the ass of Balaam also spoke with great eloquence; and that the walls of Jericho fell down at the sound of trumpets?" Pico thus proceeded with a long train of all the prodigious things in which he believed. Alexander absolutely fell back upon his sofa with laughing. "I believe all that as well as you," says he, "for I well know that I can be saved only by faith, as I can certainly never be so by works." "Ah, holy father!"

says Pico, "you need neither works nor faith; they are well enough for such poor, profane creatures as we are; but you, who are absolutely a vice-god—you may believe and do just whatever you please.

"You have the keys of heaven; and St. Peter will certainly never shut the door in your face. But with respect to myself, who am nothing but a poor prince, I freely confess that I should have found some very powerful protection necessary, if I had lain with my own daughter, or had employed the stiletto and nightshade as often as your holiness." Alexander VI. understood raillery. "Let us speak seriously," says he to the prince. "Tell me what merit there can be in a man's saying to God that he is persuaded of things of which, in fact, he cannot be persuaded? What pleasure can this afford to God? Between ourselves, a man who says that he believes what is impossible to be believed, is—a liar."

Pico della Mirandola at this crossed himself in great agitation. "My God!" says he, "I beg your holiness' pardon; but you are not a Christian." "I am not," says the pope, "upon my faith." "I suspected so," said Pico della Mirandola.

FALSITY.

Falsity, properly speaking, is the contrary to truth; not intentional lying.

It is said that there were a hundred thousand men destroyed by the great earthquake at Lisbon; this is not a lie—it is a falsity. Falsity is much more common than error; falsity falls more on facts, and error on opinions. It is an error to believe that the sun turns round the earth; but it is a falsity to advance that Louis XIV. dictated the will of Charles II.

The falsity of a deed is a much greater crime than a simple lie; it is a legal imposture—a fraud committed with the pen.

A man has a false mind when he always takes things in a wrong sense, when, not considering the whole, he attributes to one side of an object that which belongs to the other, and when this defect of judgment has become habitual.

Falseheartedness is, when a person is accustomed to flatter, and to utter sentiments which he does not possess; this is worse than dissimulation, and is that which the Latins call *simulatio*.

There is much falsity in historians; error among philosophers. Falsities abound in all polemical writings, and still more in satirical ones. False minds are insufferable, and false hearts are horrible.

FALSITY OF HUMAN VIRTUES.

When the Duke de la Rochefoucauld wrote his "Thoughts on Self-Love," and discovered this great spring of human action, one M. Esprit of the Oratory, wrote a book entitled "Of the Falsity of Human Virtues." This author says that there is no virtue but by grace; and he terminates each chapter by referring to Christian charity. So that, according to M. Esprit, neither Cato, Aristides, Marcus Aurelius, nor Epictetus were good men, who can be found only among the Christians. Among the Christians, again, there is no virtue except among the Catholics; and even among the Catholics, the Jesuits must be excepted as the enemies of the Oratory; ergo, virtue is scarcely to be found anywhere except among the enemies of the Jesuits.

This M. Esprit commences by asserting that prudence is not a virtue; and his reason is that it is often deceived. It is as if he had said that Cæsar was not a great captain because he was conquered at Dyrrachium.

If M. Esprit had been a philosopher, he would not have examined prudence as a virtue, but as a talent— as a useful and happy quality; for a great rascal may be very prudent, and I have known many such. Oh the age of pretending that "*Nul n'aura de vertu que nous et nos amis*!"—None are virtuous but ourself and friends!

What is virtue, my friend? It is to do good; let us then do it, and that will suffice. But we give you credit for the motive. What, then! according to you, there is no difference between the President de Thou and Ravaillac? between Cicero and that Popilius whose life he saved, and who afterwards cut off his head for money; and thou wilt pronounce Epictetus and Porphyrius rogues because they did not follow our dogmas? Such insolence is disgusting; but I will say no more, for I am getting angry.